BACKWOODS ETHICS

Environmental Concerns
for Hikers and Campers

Distributed by

THE STEPHEN GREENE PRESS, INC.

Box 1000
Brattleboro, Vt. 05301

BACKWOODS ETHICS

ENVIRONMENTAL CONCERNS FOR HIKERS AND CAMPERS

LAURA AND GUY WATERMAN

STONE WALL PRESS

*5 Byron Street
Boston, Mass. 02108*

Drawings by Neilan F. Jenks.

Much of the material in this book first appeared in *New England Outdoors* magazine and has been updated, revised, and expanded. Parts of chapter 9 appeared in *Backpacker* magazine, Winter 1974, and have been adapted with permission. Chapter 10 is reprinted, with minor revisions, with permission of *Backpacker* magazine, where it appeared in August 1977. Chapter 11 first appeared in *Appalachia,* June 1977–© 1977 by Appalachian Mountain Club; it has been revised, and is reprinted with permission.

LIBRARY OF CONGRESS CATALOGING IN PUBLICATION DATA

Waterman, Laura.
  Backwoods ethics.

  Includes index.
  1. Hiking–Environmental aspects–New England–Case studies. 2. Back-packing–Environmental aspects–New England–Case studies. 3. Camping–Environmental aspects–New England–Case studies. 4. Nature conservation–New England. I. Waterman, Guy, joint author. II. Title.
GV199.42.N38W37   917.4   79-16684
ISBN 0-913276-28-6

Dedication

For Chuck
. . . and, of course, for Ralph
two of the best companions in the mountains

Contents

FOREWORD

Toward a Wilderness Ethic

by William A. Turnage

ALDO LEOPOLD wrote that, "Conservation is a state of harmony between man and land." How simple, how eloquent, how true. But how do we best achieve this state of harmony called conservation?

The marvelous, exciting growth in the use of wild places—particularly by people on foot—is one important reconfirmation of our essential need for wilderness. On the one hand, it places upon us a heavy burden to love and protect the land we seek to experience. On the other, it clearly signals the need for preserving much more wilderness—so our children will have wild places to love, and a chance for challenge, solitude and high-country dreaming.

We are learning gradually, and from experience, that it is vital to go lightly in high places. The heavy use, even overuse, of prime wilderness areas requires that each of us learn to minimize our impact on the land. We must develop a personal ethic which respects the resource because to do so is *right,* and not simply because the rules tell us so. To go in harmony with the land is not onerous once it becomes instinctual. If we *think* about our behavior on a backpack trip and if we read to assimilate the experience of others, we will soon find that ecological living is easy, and that it actually enhances the experience we are seeking.

Once home, though, we have another responsibility: to fight for more wilderness. Because we use wild lands, we are obligated to protect them on all levels. Because we know what overuse does to the resource, and what overcrowding does to the experience, we know better than anyone how crucial it is to preserve as much wilderness as possible. *You* can play an important role by working with local and national wilderness preservation organizations, and by writing and visiting your elected representatives in Congress. It is your chance to repay the land for the pleasure it gives you—and to balance the impact of that ever-so-gentle footprint!

Washington, D.C.
May 1979

Acknowledgments

FOR FACTUAL information throughout this book, we are much indebted to many knowledgeable people who always patiently answered our questions: to Ned Therrien and others in the U.S. Forest Service; to George Hamilton, Buzz Caverly, and other state park officials; to Steve Golden and others in the National Park Service; and to numerous staff people in the hiking and conservation organizations of our region—the Appalachian Mountain Club and the Green Mountain Club.

For very specific help on the ideas and facts in particular chapters, we especially thank, for "The Alpine Aster Caper," Ruth Smiley; for chapters 6 and 8, David Langlois; for chapter 13, Joel White and Joe Brigham; and for chapter 2 and the following case study, Ed Ketchledge and Wally Herrod of the Adirondack Forty Sixers, Dick Stevens of the Four Thousand Footer Committee, and Father Ray Donahue of the Catskill 3500 Club.

For consistently supporting us to write what we think, for always publishing what we write, and for encouraging us to put it all together in the form of this book, we are most warmly grateful to that colorful group of people at *New England Outdoors* magazine—Mike Pogodzinski, Mike Ricciuto, Jim Barry, and the man who got us started, Lyle Richardson.

For kind permission to include particular articles of ours from other publications, we thank Bill Kemsley of *Backpacker* and Arlyn Powell of *Appalachia*. George E. Zink generously allowed us to list his six arguments for wilderness at the end of chapter 12.

For actually getting the book together and steering it through to publication, we are most thankful for the editorial skill and publishing competence of Henry Wheelwright of Stone Wall Press.

The most difficult acknowledgments are for those who influenced and guided our thinking about some of the complex problems confronting the backwoods environment. Going way back, there are early family influences, most of all Alan Waterman. Many, many people have exchanged ideas with us, challenged our theories, illuminated new possibilities, sometimes explained how wrong we were, and often stimulated and sharpened our perceptions. Of those who have contributed most to the development of our ideas, though we don't always agree on particulars, we feel especially appreciative of Lou Cornell, Bill Kemsley, Will Merritt, Ed Nester, Dan Smiley, Keith Smiley, Bill Thomas, La Verne Thompson, and most of all the friend who has for ten years discussed and debated back and forth practically every idea (and some of the grammar) in this book, Brad Snyder.

Our sources of facts and ideas are many, but the final responsibility for how they all came out, with whatever errors or misconceptions may have crept in, is exclusively that of the authors.

Grateful acknowledgment is also extended to the following individuals and publishers for permission to use the following excerpts: CHAPTER 2. Quotation of Benton MacKaye, p. 20: Reprinted by permission from *Backpacker* magazine, April 1976. © 1976 by Backpacker, Inc./Quotation of Dick Stevens, p. 20: Reprinted by permission from letter dated April 3, 1977. CASE STUDY: The Forty-Sixers. Quotations of Glenn Fish, pp. 23–24: Reprinted with permission of Glenn Fish. CHAPTER 3. Quotation from *Movin' On* by Harry Roberts, p. 28: Reprinted by permission from *Movin' On* by Harry Roberts. Boston, Stone Wall Press, 1977. © 1977 by Stone Wall Press, Inc. CHAPTER 7. Quotation of William Harlow, p. 59: Reprinted by permission from *Backpacker* magazine, August 1977. © 1977 by Backpacker, Inc./Quotation of David Langlois, p. 59: Reprinted with permission of David Langlois./Quotation of Nancy Rent, p. 60: Reprinted with permission of Nancy Rent. CHAPTER 9. Quotation from *Movin' Out* by Harry Roberts, p. 76: Reprinted by permission from *Movin' Out* by Harry Roberts. Boston, Stone Wall Press, 1975. © 1975 by Stone Wall Press, Inc. CHAPTER 10. Quotation of Zane Smith, p. 81: Reprinted with permission of the United States Dept. of Agriculture—Forest Service. CASE STUDY: Rock Climbers and Their Environment. Quotation from *Basic Rockcraft* by Royal Robbins, p. 85: Reprinted by permission from *Basic Rockcraft* by Royal Robbins. Glendale (CA), La Siesta Press, 1971. © 1971 by La Siesta Press. CHAPTER 11. Quotation of Philip D. Levin, p. 98: Reprinted by permission from *Appalachia*, June 1978. © 1978 by Appalachian Mountain Club./ Quotation from *Backcountry Management Report*, p. 102: Reprinted by permission from *Appalachia*. © 1978 by Appalachian Mountain Club. CASE STUDY: The Appalachian Trail. Quotation of Steve Golden, p. 111: Reprinted with permission of Steve Golden. CHAPTER 12. Quotation of Allen G. Gibbs, p. 112: Reprinted by permission from *Pacific Search*, September 1976. © 1976 by Pacific Search Press (Seattle)./Quotation from *The Living Wilderness*, p. 117: Reprinted by permission from *The Living Wilderness*, Oct.–Dec. 1977. © 1977 by The Wilderness Society./Quotation of John Cole, p. 120: Reprinted by permission from *Yankee* magazine, December 1978. © 1978 by Yankee, Inc. CASE STUDY: The Great Gulf Wilderness. Quotation of George Hamilton, p. 127: Reprinted by permission from a letter to John Lowe, April 1975. CHAPTER 13. Quotation from *The Screwtape Letters* by C. S. Lewis, p. 130: Reprinted by permission from *The Screwtape Letters* by C. S. Lewis. New York, Macmillan Publishing Co., 1942. © 1942 by C. S. Lewis./Quotation of Alan A. Smith, p. 130: Reprinted with permission of Alan A. Smith./Quotation from *The Lives of a Cell* by Lewis Thomas, p. 131: Reprinted by permission from *The Lives of a Cell* by Lewis Thomas. New York, The Viking Press, Inc. 1974. © 1974 by Lewis Thomas./Quotation from William O. Douglas, p. 134: Reprinted by permission from *National Geographic Magazine*, August 1961. © 1961 by *National Geographic Magazine*./Quotation of Ned Therrien, p. 137: Reprinted with permission of Ned Therrien. CHAPTER 14. Quotation from *The Spirit of St. Louis* by Charles Lindbergh, p. 138: Reprinted by permission from *The Spirit of St. Louis* by Charles Lindbergh. New York, Charles Scribner's Sons,

1953. © 1953 by Charles Scribner's Sons./Quotation from Robert Proudman, p. 139: Reprinted by permission from *Appalachia*, December 1975. © 1975 by Appalachian Mountain Club./Quotation from letter-to-the-editor, p, 139: Reprinted by permission from *Appalachia*, December 1975. © 1975 by Appalachian Mountain Club./Quotation of J. William Peppard, p. 141: Reprinted by permission from letter dated June 6, 1977./Quotation of Rodney A. Barber, p. 141: Reprinted by permission from letter dated June 14, 1977. CASE STUDY: Winter Above Treeline. Quotation from *Alone* by Admiral Byrd, p. 147: Reprinted by permission from *Alone* by Admiral Byrd. New York, G. P. Putnam's Sons, 1938. © 1938 by G. P. Putnam's Sons. PART IV. Quotation from *Backcountry Management Report*, p. 156: Reprinted by permission from *Appalachia*. © 1978 by Appalachian Mountain Club./Quotation from *So Human An Animal* by Rene Dubos, p. 156: Reprinted by permission of Charles Scribner's Sons from *So Human An Animal* by Rene Dubos. New York, Charles Scribner's Sons, 1968. © 1968 by Rene Dubos./Quotation of Frederick Harrison in *High Conquest* by James Ramsey Ullman, p. 157: Reprinted by permission from *High Conquest* by James Ramsey Ullman. New York, J. B. Lippincott Co., 1941. © 1941 by James Ramsey Ullman. CHAPTER 16. Quotation from *Backcountry Management Report*, p. 166: Reprinted by permission from *Appalachia*. © 1978 by Appalachian Mountain Club./Quotation of Philip Levin, p. 169: Reprinted by permission from *Appalachia*, December 1976. © 1976 by Appalachian Mountain Club./Quotation of Bradley Snyder, p. 170: Reprinted with permission of Bradley Snyder./Quotation from *Snowshoeing* by Gene Prater, p. 170: Reprinted by permission from *Snowshoeing* by Gene Prater. Seattle, The Mountaineers, 1974. © 1974 by The Mountaineers.

INTRODUCTION

The Preservation of Wildness

IN APRIL 1976, we began contributing a monthly column on camping and hiking to *New England Outdoors* magazine. The idea for this book grew out of the accumulated anecdotes, observations, reflections, cries of outrage, melancholy mutterings, and confused chuckles which flowed into those columns.

Our hiking experience and the focus of the magazine are largely regional, but the problems which confront the backwoods of New England have come to the Smokies and the Everglades, the Badlands and the Rockies, the deserts and the High Sierra, and even the arctic vastness of Alaska. The issues that stir the consciences of hikers and campers are found nationwide.

This book expresses strong views sometimes, and many may question or disagree. That's fine. While we may sometimes sound cocksure or arrogant, we are fundamentally perplexed and humbled by the difficulty of some of the questions confronting backwoods hikers and those who have the complex and thankless responsibility of managing the wild lands of this country. The aim of this book is not to provide answers so much as to provoke questions in the minds of all those who are concerned about the future of the backcountry environment.

A few words on terminology: As if backcountry issues weren't complex enough in substance, they are vastly compounded by semantic confusion.

To begin with, we say "New England" when we often mean the northeastern corner of the United States, including New York State's Adirondacks, Catskills, and Shawangunks, and the Hudson Highlands.

We use "backwoods" and "backcountry" almost interchangeably, since most of our region's backcountry is wooded. Elsewhere, great expanses of above-treeline or desert zones would make "backcountry" the preferred general term.

Like "coke,"^{TM} "xerox,"^{TM} and the hunter's "blaze orange," the word *"Vibram"*^{TM} is widely used by people who don't realize that it's actually a specific trade name used by one company. We'd like to make clear here and now that when we use the term *Vibram* in this book, we're using it in the broad popular sense, as people use "coke" and "xerox." We do not intend any special criticism of the Quabaug Rubber Company, American manufacturers of the *Vibram* sole. On the contrary, we have a high regard for the public spiritedness of this company, which offers plenty of less destructive non-lug soles for sale but finds that hikers seem to demand the high-lug sole instead. The

company has even put out an excellent little booklet on the need for environmental awareness in using the outdoors. The Quabaug people are sensitive to the
problem caused by high-lug soles, and we regret the grief which indiscriminate
use of their word *Vibram* may cause them, although they must be used to it
by now. To blame them for trail erosion would be, in George Stigler's felicitous
phrase (coined in a different context), like blaming waiters for obesity.

The words "wild," "wildness," and "wilderness" have created more confusion
than clarity over the past decade. The term "wilderness" now has a specific legal
meaning in the Wilderness Act of 1964; therefore it seems helpful to limit use of
that term most of the time to legally defined wilderness areas. On the other hand,
when referring to wild lands in general, regardless of legal status, we prefer the
terms "wildness" and "wild" because to us they conjure up the spirit which is a
fundamental appeal of backcountry: the sense of being away from civilization's
softening influences, of being in predominantly natural surroundings (woods,
mountains, waters), and of relying on one's own resources in a natural world
where man's powers and accomplishments seem puny in comparison with nature's.

When we speak of the "spirit of wildness," we do not refer just to a quanti-
fiable number of people per square mile or identifiable evidence of man's passing,
although these may be part of the picture. We refer more to an untamed grandeur in the landscape, a power in the elements, an excitement in the adventure
of being there.

People say, for example, that one can't expect to find wilderness on the
Franconia Ridge in New Hampshire's White Mountains. What they mean is that
a whole lot of people can be found there on a good summer's weekend, and the
evidence of man's passing is abundant in trampled trails, eroding soils, and the
ruins of the old summit house on the top of Lafayette. But we invite you to
venture onto that ridge on a stormswept mid-week October day, when the wind
nearly blows you off your feet and the mist swirls among the pinnacles and
boulders, coating them with ice. Those who cannot feel the spirit of wildness
on the Franconia Ridge at such a time are poor in spirit indeed.

All of us who hike in this area had to admit long ago that New England's
mountains aren't spectacular. They're rounded domes, not jagged spires. Most
of the tops are wooded. Even the towns around them are rather prosaic. Instead
of romantic names like Chamonix, or Talkeetna, or Thangboché, Vermont's best
mountains have Jonesville and Johnson at their base.

For New Englanders, as for Ben Jonson,

> . . in small proportions we just beauties see,
> And in short measure life may perfect be.

Nevertheless, adventure is there. The woods are deep enough and the mountains are rugged enough and the weather is treacherous enough to supply plenty
of wildness to those who seek it with a discerning eye.

Preserving the opportunities to experience such wildness is partly what this book is about. It's also about quieter times in deeper woods. It's about hilarious times when the fundamental absurdity of hiking and camping is all we can see. It's also about the growing concern of hikers and campers to walk more softly over the land. These issues transcend New England and challenge the consciences of outdoorspeople in Colorado, in Alaska, in Tennessee, in every place where there are hills to climb, valleys to explore, trees to walk under, birds to hear, moss to touch.

The reader will note that there are two motifs to our concern for preserving the backcountry environment. When we speak of this concern, we refer to both:

(1) The purely *physical* environment of plants, soils, water, mountains; and
(2) The *experiential* environment, to use the jargon of modern backcountry management.

By the latter, we mean the psychological feeling which the hiker experiences in getting out in the backcountry. As we see it, the two motifs are closely inter-related much of the time. Nevertheless, it might be possible to miss the point, for example, by zealously safeguarding the physical setting through imposing tight restrictions on what hikers might do or where they might go. The material environment could thus be saved, but the experience would be degraded.

The thoughtful outdoorsperson of today is anxious to help preserve not only the physical landscape of the backcountry, but also the spirit of wildness that makes it such a wonderful place to be. Sometimes these twin goals seemingly conflict and trade-offs must be weighed. Sometimes the choices may be very difficult, and reasonable people may disagree.

Implicit in these environmental concerns is another underlying theme of this book, that of the unshirkable responsibility for all of us to maintain a sense of *stewardship for the land*.

Safeguarding this heritage of wild country is a responsibility for everyone. If we want our children's children to have the same opportunities to enjoy the backwoods, we have to do the right things—as hikers and climbers, as back-packers and campers, as voters and concerned citizens.

The question of how to exercise this stewardship may lead to disagreements as well. For example, we have heard it said that one prime weapon in defending the backwoods is a loud voice with which to accost anyone you meet who violates the new backwoods ethics—e.g., anyone who discards a piece of litter, sets up a tent on a fragile stream bank, walks off-trail on alpine vegetation, etc. Well, maybe a stern word spoken to other hikers now and then may be appropriate and timely, but we have to confess that as a general procedure it just isn't our style. We wonder whether the good word is always accepted when presented in such a package. If we find someone about to tent right on a delicate stream bank or cut a bough bed, we try to fall into a friendly conversation first and gently work it around to a question about the offending practice. Once we found a couple just finishing setting up their tent right on a trail where it was illegal to do so, as the last light was fading and a violent thunderstorm was obviously about to break. We did *not* tell them they had to move. Some people may be able to come on with the more direct approach and still make it palatable. We know a ranger for a private land-owning agency who can tell anybody to do or not do anything and still come out on friendly terms—a rare quality (especially among park rangers). But unless you have that golden touch, you have to weigh, as we do, zeal for land stewardship with good manners. You could harm the good cause by creating a backlash reaction; moreover, the backwoods is not, in our opinion, a good place for arguments and unpleasantness, but a place for serenity and good will.

Nevertheless, we remain fundamentally committed to the concept of steward-ship, and we earnestly hope that the messages of this book will help preserve wild lands and the wild spirit that goes with them—and that an adequate level of tact has been maintained in presenting these messages, even when our strong feelings may have made us a bit enthusiastic in preaching the good gospel and smiting the heathen.

Thoreau's oft-quoted injunction—"In wildness is the preservation of the world"—is apt enough. If it remains as true today as when Thoreau wrote it, the question that this generation must concern itself with is *the preservation of wildness*. The spirit of wildness can be threatened from many sources—"develop-ment" speculators, unrestrained economic exploitation, tourist mania, overuse by thoughtless hikers, needless restrictions by wilderness managers, and others. Recreation itself can be just another form of exploitation—or it can be under-taken in a spirit of stewardship of the land. The choice is ours.

New England's Emily Dickinson, who so loved the Holyoke Hills near the Amherst she never left, wrote:

> . . . But God be with the Clown
> Who Ponders this tremendous scene—
> This whole experiment in green,
> As if it were his own!

Laura and Guy Waterman
East Corinth, Vermont
January 1979

PART I

The Hiker: Idiosyncrasies, Eccentricities and Style

". . . A Fine Kind of Madness . . ."

HIKERS and backpackers are a breed apart. What they do provides ample reason to question their good sense, if not their sanity.

Many sensible Americans spend their weekends in rational, socially responsible pursuits like pushing (or riding) a lawn mower in concentric circles, staring at football on television, or getting plastered at neighborhood cocktail parties. Not so the hiker/backpacker of the neighborhood. His weekend is divided roughly into four parts:

(1) Grunting and puffing uphill, carrying a load on his back which can only be good news to the nation's back doctors;

(2) Plunging jerkily downhill, drumming up trade for the nation's knee doctors;

(3) Sitting on damp logs, slapping mosquitoes, eating (if not digesting) partially cooked dehydrated or freeze-dried inedibles, before sleeping on an uneven surface of roots and stones, only to arise at an ungodly hour when his rational neighbor remains fast asleep, secure in the knowledge that the first pro game won't start till noon; and

(4) Sitting behind a steering wheel, careening through Friday and Sunday night darkness, to get to and back from what his Puritan ancestors sagely called "that dismal wildernesse."

Who is this backpacker? Studies tell us that he (who is often but not usually a "she") is apt to be from the upper end of the income scale (but *not* the top end); to live in an urban setting during the week; and to have a string of diplomas that would make you think that somewhere along the line he might have learned enough to stay in out of the rain, which he didn't. Very often he is of college

5

age, though many backpackers are considerably older. This much is statistically ascertainable.

But *who* is he? What *kind* of person self-inflicts this strange weekend-and-vacation life of hardship and deliberate avoidance of the amenities with which Thomas Edison, Alexander Bell, and Sir Thomas Crapper went to so much thought and trouble to provide us all? Who is it that would give up technological blessings like televised football and premixed martinis for a life of blisters, downpours, and gorp?

Is the average backpacker an aspiring mountaineer? Does he dream about feats he knows he'll never pull off, of conquering Himalayan heights? Is he a latter-day Thoreau, seeking to contemplate the richness of the natural world? Or is he more related to his ancestral outdoor cousin, the hunter and fisherman, but has merely discarded rod and gun in the interests of doing more walking? Sherpa Tenzing, who climbed Everest with Hillary and spent a lifetime observing the passing parade of expeditionary mountaineers in the Himalayas, described them all as "odd people, idealists, eccentrics, men with curious obsessions." Does this description fit the American hiker and backpacker?

We raise these questions not because we can fully answer them, but because groping toward answers is essential if we are to come to grips with some of the issues we discuss in this book: the new backwoods ethics of concern for the environment, the *kind* of backwoods environment we want to preserve, the values that ought to shape management policies in the woods and hills where hikers go.

One thing seems clear: The backwoods tramper we're talking about is *not* seeking physical comfort. He is deliberately leaving the easy life to go where he'll get rained on, eaten by bugs, and exhausted by the physical effort of getting himself and his backpack there and back. Whatever the specifics of his motives, he's obviously a seeker of challenge and difficulty. If he weren't he'd stay in the cities or suburbs. With British explorer Sir Francis Younghusband, who walked across the deserts and ranges of central Asia, the weekend backpacker takes joy in "the pride in his prowess that is such a satisfaction to his soul."

It's not just sitting on a remote summit that matters. It's how hard it was to get there. It's the fact that you got there on your own power, testing your knowledge and experience of the woods trails, your judgment, your physical condition, and most of all your drive and desire to overcome the difficulties. "The summit's in the climb," writes mountain poet Borghoff.

Not that every weekend hiker is out there to set speed records or attain summits at all costs. Quite the contrary. Most of today's outdoorspeople seem deliberately contemptuous of the minority who push themselves hard in the backcountry. Peakbagging is definitely out of style these days. The backwoods majority set themselves modest trip goals and try to enjoy the scenery along the way. They try to be reasonably comfortable in their outdoors homes. Nevertheless, they wouldn't be there at all if comfort and ease were their goals. Whatever the grade of their hair-shirt, they're still out there to enjoy being tough.

Another quality that seems common to all of this breed is a "sense of place."

If exercise were the sole goal, they could walk around the block all weekend long—or even mow their lawns with old hand mowers. If suffering were the sole goal, the Marquis de Sade devised a number of tools and techniques that would suffice to hold attention. But our backpacker seeks exercise and hardship in a particular setting: a world of natural surroundings.

The deserts of Arizona, the mountain ridges of the Sierra, the wetlands of the Everglades, the trodden paths of the Catskills, the vast forests below the Brooks Range are greatly different worlds—but in underlying spirit they are similar.

The backpacker seeks wildness. He wants to look at mountains, streams, deep woods, jagged rock formations. He has visions of the caribou that once roamed the spectral barrens of Katahdin's high tableland, and still migrate in untold numbers across the vast Alaskan tundra. He wants to feel the thin, cold air, to hear the pure whistle of the white-throated sparrow, to see the delicate lacework of green moss on a boulder, to sense the solitude of remote places.

Whether he seeks *real* solitude is a question that's more difficult to answer. Backlands managers assume that he does and the Wilderness Act proclaims that goal. Yet the tendency of so many to head for so few choice wilderness meccas, to hike the same trails, climb the same summits, sleep in the same campgrounds, makes one wonder how much solitude they really want. A rough life in a natural setting, yes. Solitude? Doubtful.

. . . Which is fortunate. If the backpacker is seeking true solitude in the backwoods today, he's not generally finding it. The woods are overrun with solitude-seekers. But that's getting ahead of our story.

In this first section, we present a few thoughts that have occurred to us over years of watching that curious breed, the hikers and backpackers of this country, and their principal preoccupation. This can best be viewed as a fundamentally absurd madness—though, as Warren Harding said of that other ridiculous avocation, rock climbing, ". . . a fine kind of madness. . . ."

1

That Pack on the Back: Mae West vs. Twiggy

And seeing the snail, which everywhere doth roam
Carrying his own house still, still is at home,
Follow (for he is easy pac'd) this snail,
Be thine own palace, or the world's thy jail.

John Donne

WE MEET two distinct types of hikers in the woods: the kitchen-sink and the hair-shirt. Maybe you know them too. Maybe you're one or the other. Some people carry more than you can possibly use on a two or three day weekend; others less than you need to enjoy a reasonably good time.

The kitchen-sink believes in carrying it all, everything to make himself comfortable in the woods, plus every precaution against a wide range of possible emergencies from hypothermia to a hangnail. With his pack bulging and stuff sacks strapped on top or hanging below, he grunts along, sweat pouring from his overworked body. Maybe you can't take it with you, but this fellow will obviously try.

The hair-shirt subscribes to the go-light school, toothpick-and-a-match, survive on as little as possible. He drills holes in the handle of his toothbrush and bivouacs in a rain poncho.

These two traditions have deep roots. It's Atlas vs. Mercury. He who bears the weight of the world on his shoulders vs. he of the winged foot. It's Paul Bunyan vs. John Muir. Goliath vs. David. Late Gothic vs. Rococo. Mae West vs. Twiggy. (As we said, some people carry more than you can possibly use on a two or three day weekend; others less than you need to enjoy a reasonably good time.) The difference is more than a matter of pack weight; it's a contrast in approach to the outdoors, a divergence of personal style, almost a split in philosophy.

On his pioneering explorations of Yosemite Valley and the Sierra Nevada, John Muir carried incredibly little—sometimes just a couple of blankets plus a food box small enough to strap to his belt, containing only grain meal, sugar, and tea. Muir is not only one of America's greatest champions of conservation, he is also the patron saint of the go-light school.

Muir's modern-day successor as lord of the Sierra backcountry was Norman

Clyde, who spent 40 years exploring hidden valleys and making solo first ascents of difficult routes almost right up to his death at age 87 in 1972. But Clyde was the opposite of Muir as a backpacker. His typical 100-pound pack might include elaborate fishing gear, two pistols, camera equipment, extra pairs of boots and clothes, several large kettles, a wide assortment of dishes, bowls, and cups, canned food, and perhaps a few chunks of firewood if he were going above timberline; plus the famous Clyde library of books. "The pack that walked like a man," he was called. Surely Clyde was the patron saint of the kitchen-sink breed.

The New England inheritors of the Clyde legacy have traditionally been the hut men of the Appalachian Mountain Club's chain of huts in the White Mountains. These college-age lads used to stock all the food and equipment for huts that were as far as 6 miles from the road over mountain trails, with as much as 3600 feet of elevation to be gained. Their packs of well over 100 pounds humbled many a tired vacationer whom they steamed past on the trail. Back in the fifties, the hut boys at the 4900-foot Madison Springs Hut began packing all the parts of a Model T up to that remote and rocky windswept col, intending to assemble it amongst the boulders. Sober authorities intervened and a helicopter flew out the parts as part of a cleanup campaign in the sixties. These days AMC is deemphasizing the load-carrying legend of hut life; modern hut men are hired more for their hospitality or their ability to interpret the ecology around the hut, and there are even female "hut persons." Loads are still respectable, but packs over 100 pounds are frowned upon. An era has passed.

The modern backpacking ideal is to cut weight ruthlessly. The western outdoors painter, Roy Kerswill, says he gets along fine for five days on a 16½-pound pack, including camera, sketch pad, and brushes. He carries no cooking gear because he eats cold food only, and has worked it out so that he survives comfortably on a half pound of food per day.

Considering the obvious advantages of this approach, we wish we could report that our normal packs are models of how to go superlight. Not so. Part of our problem is that we do a good deal of winter camping, when some heavy gear is unavoidable. Somehow we can't bring ourselves to part with it in summer.

For example, for years we were accustomed to a roomy, storm-proof tent. It's very useful in winter, especially in exposed campsites or spots where you may have to sit out a storm for a full day or more. Being accustomed to this luxury in winter, we went on enjoying it year-round. We carried the Bauer Expedition model, with the front *and* back vestibules, snow flaps (in July?), and a weight of 12 pounds (grunt!).

It took the "new ethic" of clean camping to wean us away from our beloved Bauer for summer camping. Now we swing along the trail with somewhat lightened loads (and fewer backaches), since we made the switch to hammocks. We'll tell you more about that in chapter 8.

We like to have a top-notch camping stove, so we carry the Optimus 111B.

It's great for melting large amounts of snow (again . . . in July?), but virtually the heaviest of the thirty-odd models of backpacking stoves on the market.

For many years we were hung up on a model of headlamp that gives strong light while leaving both hands free; but it ran on four D batteries, while the handy Mallory miniature flashlight runs on two tiny AA batteries. Fortunately a couple of years ago we converted to a new headlamp that runs on two C batteries.

Last fall, we noticed in an obscure corner of our pack that we'd been carrying— all summer—a file for sharpening crampons on ice-climbing trips. . . .

An anthropologist (?) named Woody Allen claims that there are tribes in Borneo that do not have a word for "no" in their language and turn down requests by nodding and saying "I'll get back to you." Well, our ability to reject articles from backpacking trips sometimes seems about as effective. So, in go the extra batteries, the extra sweater, the extra fuel.

If you want to avoid getting into this bind, we can suggest a number of things that we've seen in the backcountry that you *don't* need:

(1) A folding fox-hole shovel, an old Boy Scout favorite; it might have been great in World War I, but who needs the weight in today's backwoods?

(2) A mallet for driving tent pegs; you'll need it to set up a circus tent, but not for the typical camping set-up.

(3) A tool kit, including a wrench, needle-nose pliers, screw drivers (regular and Phillips), and scissors; we find that a 4-ounce Swiss Army knife, plus a little parachute cord, will suffice for emergency repairs.

(4) Various camp stools and folding chairs—even folding toilets, as if these matters can't be taken care of without specialized equipment.

(5) Cosmetics for the ladies. One recent handbook for women in the woods advises that "Using a deodorant daily in the backwoods is a must." And we've seen recommended equipment lists that include a nail file and clippers (again, these are handy on a Swiss Army knife).

(6) Carbon monoxide detection kit. No kidding—one widely quoted authority on camping says that you should never use a portable cookstove inside a tent without a carbon monoxide detection kit. Who wants to lug a kit around when thoroughly ventilating your tent will solve the problem?

If you eliminate all such non-necessities, but you *still* find that your pack outweighs a Notre Dame linebacker, we could suggest a few tips on how to co-exist with the enemy. Alas, these ideas grow from long personal experience. If your pack is heavy:

(1) Keep the weight high; load the heavier items near the top of your pack.

(2) Keep it all close to your back; avoid bulky items strapped on the outside in such a way as to pull you over backwards.

(3) Get everything into or onto the pack; don't try to carry *anything* in your hands, unless you go in for a walking staff (or in winter, an ice ax or ski pole).

(4) Use a waist strap to transfer most of the load from your shoulders to your hips; on most modern packs this is standard.

(5) Once you put the pack on, plan to walk steadily for long periods and *not* to stop for "rests" very often; frequent rest stops, taking the pack off and wrestling it back on, will delay your progress interminably and use up more energy than the rests restore.

(6) Adopt a slow *sustainable* pace, with a steady rhythm of regular steps; if you can sort of roll your weight from one foot to the other you can get a momentum that eases the strain. A stop-and-go, herky-jerky motion continually makes the full presence of the pack felt.

(7) Think positive; like so many activities that seem purely physical, packing a heavy load is 75 percent mental. If you can pick up a pack, you can walk all day with it—*if* your frame of mind is right.

We know a marvellous fellow, Win Thratchett, with whom we've been on several winter camping trips in the Adirondacks. Thratchett's the kitchen-sink type, *par excellence*. He carries an enormous pack, but he's ready for anything. In fact, he's never so happy as when some unusual emergency requires some obscure item that only a pack of his size could possibly provide. When a trip goes smoothly, Thratchett's unhappy—all that extra weight for nothing.

On one trip, a young friend broke a snowshoe, and was bemoaning the inadequacy of his planned patch job with a stick of wood, rawhide, and tape. Along came Thratchett and asked (somewhat eagerly, we thought) if he could help. Our young friend allowed as how what he really needed was a pair of wood screws just the right size.

Thratchett looked delighted. "What size?" he asked as he swung off his enormous pack and started into it.

The other man felt this was just too much and remarked somewhat acidly: "Five-eighths inch, and only flat-heads will do."

Thratchett looked momentarily nonplused, but buried deeper into the dark recesses of the pack. When he came up, triumphantly clutching his tool kit, you could sense his immense satisfaction as he said:

"Brass or steel?"

2

Peakbagging

He's got 'em on the list—he's got 'em on the list,
And they'll none of 'em be missed—they'll none of
'em be missed.

W. S. Gilbert

PEAKBAGGING is a cross between outdoor recreation, competitive athletics, and a religion. Originally climbing mountains was primarily a recreational experience, and for many people it still is. Its overtones of aesthetic appeal and communion with nature make a formal listing of peaks "bagged" seem harshly inappropriate. However, when a mountain range has, let us say, 46 summits over a given height—and for some reason a disconcerting number of the world's ranges do have precisely 46 such peaks—it is only human nature to want to climb them all. Thus is born the sport—eventually the religion—of peakbagging.

NORTHEASTERN PEAKBAGGING

The first known peakbaggers in our northeastern mountains were the Marshall brothers, Bob and George. Bob Marshall was to become one of the most influential figures in national forestry circles, a founder of The Wilderness Society, arctic explorer, and widely read author. But he got his start tramping the backwoods of upper New York State.

It all started innocently enough. Bob and brother George climbed Whiteface Mountain on the first of August, 1918. To the south and west of their summit perch stretched peaks and ridges filling the horizon: the high peaks of the Adirondacks. The brothers were captivated. They then embarked on a series of summer trips, in company with a crusty woodsman named Herbert Clark, who made his living as a guide in the Adirondack backcountry.

By June 10, 1925, when the three men stood atop the wooded summit of Mount Emmons, they had climbed all 46 of the Adirondacks' peaks over 4000 feet in elevation. It had taken them eight summers to do so.

Eight years passed before the feat was repeated by a fourth person. In the eight years after *that*, however, 21 more stalwart Adirondack trampers had reached all 46 summits. In the *next* eight years, there were 43 more successful peakbaggers, and the race was on. Today the number is well over 1000 and they have their own club, the "Adirondack Forty-Sixers," complete with officers, dues, and an official magazine.

By coincidence, the White Mountains over in New Hampshire also turned out to have 46 peaks over 4000 feet in height. By the 1950's ardent lovers of the Whites were keeping their lists of peaks climbed too. Ultimately a group within the Appalachian Mountain Club organized the "Four Thousand Footer Committee" and began handing out scrolls and patches and decals for those who had been to the tops of the New Hampshire "46."

Peakbaggers zealously pursuing membership in either the Adirondacks or White Mountains group climb mountains with a religious dedication like that of monks resolutely repeating their rounds of prayers or good works.

Over the years the map-makers of the U.S. Geological Survey have not treated the sacred number "46" with proper veneration and respect. Relatively early in the game, the impious triangulations of the U.S.G.S. uncovered the heretical revelation that the holy roll of 46 summits originally climbed by the Marshall brothers included four peaks whose elevations were several embarrassing feet short of 4000. One (Couchsachraga) was only about 3800 feet. Not only that, but another mountain which the Founding Fathers had completely overlooked (McNaughton) was in fact *over* 4000 feet high.

Like all uninvited scientific discoveries, the impact of this revelation on the organizational hierarchy of the revealed religion—in this case, the peakbagging Forty-Sixers—was traumatic. Like many ecclesiastical orders before and since, the High Priests decided that the best way to deal with this new fact was to ignore it. To this day the anti-Darwinian Forty-Sixers gallantly carry on with the original tablet of 46 peaks handed down by the Marshalls. Aspiring Forty-Sixers must still climb those three 3900-footers and little scrubby 3800-foot Couchsachraga, while the offending McNaughton may be omitted.

For many years the rival High Priests over in New Hampshire smirked behind their vestments about this humiliating inaccuracy of the Adirondack "46." Then, just a couple of years ago, the anti-clerical forces of the U.S.G.S. slipped into the temple of the White Mountains and smashed another icon. The Four Thousand Footer Committee had overlooked, it seemed, a 4000-foot eminence called Galehead. Sorry, reported the cynical scientists, you have 47, not 46.

Consternation and dissension struck the upper priesthood of the Four Thousand Footer Committee, to the undisguised amusement of the Adirondack Forty-Sixers' fathers. One might have thought the state of Meldrim Thomson safe from the machinations of modern science. An editorial in the Appalachian Mountain Club's official publication called for leaving Galehead off the formal list, whatever the spurious findings of the surveyors. Dark suggestions were whispered about omitting the apostate mountain from AMC maps. Meetings and correspondence flew back and forth. Finally the duly authorized Four Thousand Footer Committee met in close recess and secret conclave and, sending up the white smoke, announced that henceforth there were indeed 47, not 46, 4000-foot summits which aspiring peakbaggers must climb.

Thus the two groups are now in somewhat the position of baseball's major leagues relative to the designated hitter's rule. One accepts the findings of science and requires initiates to climb the 47 (sic) measured 4000-footers; the other clings to tradition and the memory of the Marshalls, and hews to its beloved 46 summits, despite the cold water thrown by the surveyors.

Meanwhile, down in the Catskills, the devotions of peakbagging were slower in coming. There are only two 4000-foot summits in the land of Rip Van Winkle, but the impulse to form a club overcame nature's oversight by dropping the cutoff point 500 feet. For the "Catskill 3500 Club" you must bag the 34 Catskill peaks over 3500 feet in elevation . . . *and* climb four of them in winter. The Catskill group never has taken its orders quite as seriously as the more prestigious Adirondack and White Mountain faiths. "After all," wrote Catskill tramper Henry Yong last year, "when you are grabbing peaks that are only 3500 feet high, you have to have a sense of humor. . . ."

The mania for peakbagging in the northeast has spread beyond the mystical limits of 46. Maine, it appears, has a dozen 4000-footers. Vermont has five more. This gives the New Englander a total of 63 peaks to shoot for, and many do, to become members of the Four Thousand Footer Club of New England.

Put these 63 together with the Adirondacks' 46 and the Catskills' two, and you have the Northeast 111.

About ten years ago, not satisfied with reclimbing their 4000-footers (like the Adirondacks' Jim Goodwin, who has climbed his 46 thirteen times each), a New England group drew up a list of the "Hundred Highest" in New England. Currently it is estimated that about a dozen hardy trampers a year attain membership in this select group.

Vermont, with only five 4000-foot mountains, has set up a somewhat different goal of its own. The Green Mountains' gentler contours are traversed north-south by the celebrated Long Trail, stretching 262 miles from Massachusetts to the Canadian border. First cut all the way through in 1931, the Long Trail now has over 1000 End-to-Enders.

The end-to-end mania is more widely associated with the world-famous Appalachian Trail. This 2000-mile feat now has become so much of a status symbol that trail traffic presents serious erosion and overcrowding problems. Some 698 miles of the A.T. run through New England, from its northern terminus at Maine's Katahdin, over such celebrated summits as Mount Washington and Mount Greylock, and crossing the Bear Mountain Bridge into New York on its way south toward Georgia.

There are other north–south supertrails in the west, such as the Pacific Crest Trail and the Continental Divide. These are both over 2000 miles long. Some years back an aggressive walker named Eric Ryback pulled off the first grand slam, by hiking the A.T., the Pacific Crest, and the Continental Divide.

Back here in New England, a further challenge has been discovered: climbing the "46" in winter. With heavy snow, formidable temperatures, and the wind that sweeps New England's loftier summits, winter climbing is a considerably more challenging undertaking than summer trail walking. Miriam Underhill, considered by many to be America's greatest woman mountain climber, after a distinguished career in the Alps and other remote ranges, set herself the goal of doing all of New Hampshire's 46 between December 21 and March 21. During the 1950's, Miriam and her husband, Robert, a formidable climber himself during the 1920's, succeeded in pulling off this difficult achievement—the first two to do so. Their feat was made even more astonishing by the fact that the great lady was 62 years old and Robert over 70 when they finally stood atop 5715-foot Jefferson, having done all 46 on snowshoes, crampons, or skis. Even today, despite many aspirants, there are no more than 50 people who have achieved this remarkable goal.

Naturally, when New Hampshire's 46 had been climbed in winter, some hardy snow-lovers set their sights on the 63 of New England, including the Maine and Vermont summits. Interestingly enough, one of the first four to achieve this tough objective was also a woman—Penny Markley, a Maine apple grower's wife.

The Adirondacks' 46 have also been done in winter, and those who have climbed in both ranges in winter rate the Adirondacks as tougher. This is because many of the New York peaks are without formally maintained trails and must be climbed as genuine map-and-compass bushwhacks. In winter that can be super-rough. Nevertheless, a dozen or more hard-men have climbed the Marshalls' sacred 46 in winter—and one woman, Swiss-born Elsie Chrenko, a Scotia, New York housewife and mother.

Inevitably the toughest goal of all—the Northeast 111 in winter—has attracted the aspirations of the most confirmed of peakbaggers. On January 2, 1971, Jim Collins, the second man to do the Adirondacks 46 in winter, reached the summit of remote North Brother in Maine, to become the first conqueror of the 111 in winter. It is noteworthy that, despite the boom in winter climbing, it was not until 1977 that a second man, Guy Huse, achieved this goal.

There is no end to the imaginativeness of the dyed-in-the-wool certified peakbagger.

Fred Hunt, an Adirondacks hiker of prodigious ground-covering talents, has set himself the goal of climbing all 46 in each month of the year.

Ed Bean, the first hard-man to climb the Adirondacks' 46 in winter, then began going back with different parties of climbers, surreptitiously hoping to become the first man to kiss a different girl on the summit of each of the 46.

The resourceful and ingenious Bean also set himself a goal that once proved very helpful to these writers. It seems that Ed wanted to take a leak on the summit of each of the 46 in winter. One blustery March day, the two of us were snowshoeing up Santanoni's windswept ridge, having heard that Ed had been there the day before with another party. As we emerged on the summit ridge itself, we were surrounded by dense clouds and terrific winds. Visibility was reduced to a few feet. We groped our way along the ridge, buffeted by those cyclonic gusts, trying to figure out how we could be sure that we were on the true summit. Suddenly at out feet, we saw—yellow snow! Old Ed Bean had left his trademark the day before. We knew we were on the summit.

Another incurable peakbagger, the Reverend Henry Folsom, set out to do all of the New Hampshire peaks in one continuous walk, rather than driving to different trail heads. The resulting 244-mile trek took him 19 days. He dubbed his feat "the Four Thousand Footer Directissima."

In recent years, we heard of one girl who was out to climb the New Hampshire 46—oops, 47—in bare feet. We don't know whether she made it.

Several dogs have done each of the two 46. Our own dog, Ralph, had climbed all of the New Hampshire peaks at least three times (some much more often) before his death in 1976.

One of the great pranksters of the AMC's White Mountain hut system, the late Tony MacMillan, once organized what he called the Six Thousand Footer Club. Since there is only one true 6000-foot mountain in the northeast, Tony contented himself with locating three or four outcroppings of boulders somewhere near the top of Mount Washington. A devotee of high living as well as high mountains, Tony and his epicurean friends would gather annually to parade from bump to bump, fortified by champagne and lavish hors-d'oeuvres at each "summit." The hilarious venture in peakbagging would climax when the celebrants tottered back to the summit buildings to collapse in merriment among the bewildered tourists—perhaps a suitably iconoclastic approach to the often overbearing posture of peakbaggers.

NATIONAL AND INTERNATIONAL PEAKBAGGING

The mania for climbing many peaks in a short time or in unusual ways is not confined merely to New England's back hills.

Colorado has 54 mountains that are over 14,000 feet. Two hikers climbed these peaks in 21 days, which they figured made a cumulative climb of 147,000 vertical feet (an average of 7000 feet per day) and a total of 300 miles. Their main purpose was not to speed-run the "Fourteeners" (they *could* be done faster—although their time was very good), but to make an endurance test out of the stunt and document their medical histories. One of the climbers was a doctor.

Some hikers play the game of trying to reach the highest point in each of the 50 states. One can go from the lofty mountain bulwark of Mount McKinley in Alaska at 20,320 feet, to a record low of 345 feet in Florida. This "peak" is not even a mountain, just the highest sand hill in a flat state. Colorado has the distinction of having the highest lowest altitude: 3350 feet. In other words, wherever you are in Colorado, you can't be lower than the summit of New Hampshire's Mount Monadnock.

One zany couple set out to walk the entire perimeter of the contiguous United States—roughly 19,000 miles! They started in July 1975 and finished in late 1978.

By an almost unbelievable coincidence, the Alps have 46 peaks that are over 4000 meters. Except for the metric conversion, the good old White Mountains and Adirondacks have something in common with the snowy Alps of Europe, though not their glaciers and crevasses. As we all know, Mont Blanc is the highest at 15,771 feet. Many people have climbed all these 4000-meter peaks. The trick is to do them all in one season. We understand that Fritz Wiessner, a Vermonter born in Germany, and one of this century's greatest climbers, has done just that.

What happens if we move this game to the great mountains of Asia—the Himalayas? This is the home of Mount Everest, at 29,028 feet the highest point on the globe. Over 50 mountaineers have reached this apex of the world, but no one has yet climbed all 13 of the 8000-meter peaks. When mountains get this high—the lowest of the 13 is 26,287 feet—they get a lot harder to climb.

But there is a mountaineer, of world class, who has climbed more 8000-meter mountains than anyone else. Reinhold Messner has reached the summits of four of them, one twice.

What if someone, stuck on the number 46, wanted to climb the highest peaks in the Himalayas? That *would* be a feat. These would be, of course, the 46 highest in the world, and the elevation of the lowest would be a cloud-splitting 23,890 feet.

There is one more stunt for world-record makers. That is climbing to the highest point in each of the seven continents. Both Messner and a Japanese climber, Naomi Uemura, have reached six of these points—including Everest, McKinley, Mont Blanc, and Africa's Kilimanjaro. They so far have missed Antarctica's Mount Vinson at 16,860 feet. It's not so terribly high for fellows who have already climbed Everest, but it is very hard to get to.

Scotland has its own special game—or inanity. This mountainous country has 280 peaks over 3000 feet, which the Scots call "Monros," after the man who first listed them. In about 100 years only about 120 climbers have "bagged" all 280 Monros. This pastime may make no more sense than bagpipes, but some Scots go for it. One of these was a dog, who chaperoned his master on these climbs, and ascended as well the 3000-footers in England, Wales, and Ireland, a feat only about a dozen humans can claim.

SPEED RECORDS

The ephemeral quality of records is demonstrated by the astounding feats of hill-walking (actually running) that hikers employ on the "Fourteen Peaks" of

Wales. These summits are all over 3000 feet and the walk is 22 miles long, with 11,000 feet of cumulative ascent. Back in 1919 we have a record of this walk being completed in 20 hours. Welsh hill-walkers took up the gauntlet and the time was whittled progressively down to 7 hours and 25 minutes by 1946. This is fast—very fast—but still within the realm of human imagination for a 22-mile walk, even one taken over mountainous terrain. In 1954 a fellow named Bertie Robinson came in at 6 hours flat. Eleven years later Eric Beard struck off nearly another hour with a time of 5 hours and 13 minutes. Within recent memory, in 1973, Joss Naylor made the walk in what seems like a breakthrough to the impossible: 22 mountain miles in 4 hours and 46 minutes. When we think that many runners consider 3 hours a respectable time for a marathon (26 miles plus), Joss Naylor's time is truly astounding.

Speaking of speed, our northeastern hills have come in for their share of speed trials, also.

One of the most famous treks, coveted by New England walkers, is the 50-mile traverse of the eight Appalachian Mountain Club high huts that range through the very roughest trails of the White Mountains. These huts are built to be one hiking day apart for someone reasonably fit. It's considered quite a haul to go to two huts instead of one. But every once in a while someone comes along and tries for all eight in one day.

Back in 1958, a Harvard climber named Chris Goetze broke an earlier record for this hut-to-hut traverse, with a time of 16 hours 41 minutes. In 1977 two hut boys, who had prepared for the traverse by packing huge loads of supplies up to the huts in which they worked for the summer, zipped over the course in just under 16 hours. In 1978, a lone speedster reduced that time to 14½ hours.

Vermont's 262-mile Long Trail, which runs the length of the state from Massachusetts to Canada, has been traversed in nine days by an eager young athlete named Warren Doyle.

The 2000-mile long Appalachian Trail was recently loped by marathon runner John Avery in just under 66 days.

The Adirondacks have their challenges for speed-hikers, too. Here the stunt is to see how quickly one can climb all 46 peaks. About ten years ago a record was set at nine days. Not bad—that's averaging over five mountains a day. In the summer of 1972 two hikers came to grief trying to better this record. Their bold plan was to cut the time down to five days. Unfortunately, the timing of their venture couldn't have been worse. When they were about half way through the feat, and well on schedule, a hurricane struck the Adirondack peaks with stunning violence. The hikers, carried along by the momentum of their goal, persisted. Events ended in tragedy—one climber died of a massive heart attack on the very summit cone of the Adirondacks' highest peak, Mount Marcy, while pushing toward the top through the teeth of the gale. But memories fade, even bad ones, and in 1978 the record five-day run of all the Adirondacks' 46 peaks was achieved.

CRITICS OF PEAKBAGGING

When death struck a peakbagger the outcry against the mania for speed records was predictable. Nor was that the first such protest. Benton MacKaye, the man who is credited with having more to do with creating the Appalachian Trail than any other, years ago deplored those who tried to cover the 2000-mile trail in the fewest number of days. "What I hope is that it won't turn into a racetrack," grieved MacKaye in *Backpacker* magazine. "I for one would give the prize to the person who took the longest time."

Conservationist Edward Abbey is another who has spoken out against speedy traverses of trails and peaks. "Stop-watch hiking," Abbey calls it.

Even everyday hikers can sometimes take offense at trail speedsters who pass them at a breakneck clip. One hiker was heard to remark to a group of trail-runners: "Why do you people hate the woods so much?" He explained his question by acidly commenting that they seemed in such a hurry to get through the woods that they must not enjoy them very much.

A few years back, influential leaders of the Appalachian Mountain Club began calling for the abolition of the Four Thousand Footer Committee. (For example, see the article by Phil Levin in the AMC's journal, *Appalachia*, in June 1973.) The critics charged that peakbagging clubs tended to lure people out onto remoter summits that would otherwise remain less heavily trampled, causing trail erosion, damage to vegetation, and overcrowding problems. Critics also contended that peakbagging was a deplorable motive for going to the mountains. Last year, Four Thousand Footer Committee Chairman Dick Stevens told us, "Our present attitude is that we do not urge anyone to climb the 4000-footers; however, we are prepared to provide official recognition to anyone who completes the list and wants to apply."

Systematic peakbagging is "a numbers racket," according to one critic, and "seems sacrilegious" to another. The growth of peakbagging clubs introduces "an undesirable artificiality into the natural scenery of the mountains," according to the articulate former editor of *Appalachia*, Philip D. Levin. The gist of the attack on peakbaggers is the charge that they rush breathless from one mountain-top to the next without enjoying the view or contemplating the details and mystery of the mountain environment. "I often wonder if they ever appreciate any of the beauty that surrounds them," sighs one observer.

We'd like to rise to the defense of the peakbagger. Unquestionably there are those who grind through their list of 46 peaks with little of the spirit of appreciation which most of us think the mountains deserve. But we would guess that they are the minority. The ranks of overt peakbaggers include many people whose deep and lasting love of and commitment to the mountain environment is beyond dispute. Let's cite some examples:

(1) Robert Marshall—the man who started the whole game back in the 1920's with his brother and their guide-friend, Herbert Clark. Yes, Marshall was a

peakbagger, but he also devoted his all-too-short life to conservation and wilderness preservation. He climbed mountains because he loved them.

(2) Dr. Orra Phelps—a grand lady whose dedication to peakbagging was so strong that she was among the first to climb all the Adirondack 4000-footers. That was way back in 1947. Then she went on and "bagged" them all again. Peakbagger, yes—but Dr. Phelps is also a botanist of exceptional knowledge and insight. She has probably led more people to share her appreciation of mountain flora than anybody in the Adirondacks through her talks, slide shows, writings, personally led walks, and work as ranger–naturalist at the Adirondacks' Nature Museum and Nature Trail.

(3) Miriam Underhill—an inveterate peakbagger, the first to do the New Hampshire 46 in winter, and early conqueror of all 111 4000-foot peaks in the northeast. Her abiding affection for the mountains she climbed stands out on every page of her autobiography, *Give Me the Hills,* and in her work as both an editor of and photographer for *Mountain Flowers of New England*.

(4) Almost any of the great peakbaggers we know, whose love for the hills keeps taking them back to the high ridges to feel the thin, cold air and see the wild, uncompromising scenery and hear the clear call of the white-throated sparrow in a mist-clouded alpine landscape.

An odd psychology infects many people in the mountains when they see other hikers moving rapidly along a mountain trail. Some people resent the fast hiker with a depth of resentment that's difficult to understand. Most of these people are not so narrow minded as to insist that everyone should enjoy the mountains in precisely the same way as they do; yet they seem to want to exclude the hiker who gets enjoyment from maintaining a fast pace on a rugged trail.

We plead for tolerance—and caution the critic not to jump to conclusions when he sees someone move past him rapidly on a ridge. It's been our experience that most of the fast hill-walkers we know are people who deeply appreciate the mountain environment. They may be going fast, but they're taking it all in.

We've mentioned the young men who traversed all eight high huts of the Appalachian Mountain Club in a single day—an astonishing feat of strength and endurance. We know that at least two of these same young men are keenly interested in the alpine zone, deeply committed to efforts to preserve the fragile environment of the mountains, and often enjoy more leisurely strolls among the high ridges without regard to speed or summits.

Yet we've seen people become actually angry at the sight of a hiker moving fast. This "vague prejudice," as Mr. Levin calls it, even found its way into print in the Green Mountain Club's brochure on "Guidelines" for use of the Long Trail: One of its 15 instructions, along with such useful admonitions as carry out all trash and stay on the trail above treeline, is: "Take your time: The Long Trail is no place to break speed records."

We're sorry to see people with one approach to hiking try to impose their personal prejudices on people with another approach. The mountains are a place for people to enjoy themselves in their own way as long as that doesn't interfere with enjoyment by others. The fast hiker isn't making noise, or littering, or doing anything else to interfere with anyone else's enjoyment. We wish his critics would get off his back.

We find that we go to the mountains for many different reasons. Sometimes we poke along slowly to look at the wildflowers or gaze on an exceptional view. Sometimes we travel with one or a few friends and enjoy leisurely companionship in the mountain setting. Sometimes we push off-trail to explore valleys or ridges we've never been to before. However, sometimes—often, in fact—we like to push ourselves and take in a considerable amount of trail mileage and several summits in a single day. On some of our "biggest" days, when we've covered lots of miles and peaks, we've also treasured moments of spectacular scenery, or cloud effects, or unusual wildlife sightings, or hard-to-define moments of exaltation absorbing the majesty and mystery of the hills around us. Neither peakbagging nor fast hiking are inconsistent with complete appreciation of the mountain scene.

We are unreconstructed peakbaggers, no question. One of us is working on her fourth round of the New Hampshire 47; the other on his ninth. We've done them and the Adirondacks' 46 in winter too. Once we did all the New Hampshire peaks in a continuous two-week trip. This kind of thing may strike many people as silly. That's O.K. But we see no reason to dispute the spirit in which we or anyone else approaches the hills—as long as nothing is done to downgrade the experience of others.

A more sophisticated argument against peakbagging relates to the existence of official "clubs" that pass out badges or scrolls to people who climb all 46 or whatever number. The charge is made that such clubs lure more people to the already overcrowded mountains or encourage "artificial use patterns" and spread a lot of traffic onto peaks and trails that otherwise might remain relatively pristine.

This is a respectable argument that deserves to be thought about. Probably 4000-footer clubs do bring more people to some of the lesser-known high peaks. This is a problem that ought to concern the clubs. It seems unlikely, though, that such clubs increase total traffic in the mountains significantly. People who hear about a club and start trying to "bag" peaks are probably people who already had taken up hiking seriously.

We do deplore groups that attract more crowds to the mountains, because we think that many ranges are already reeling from the effects of too many people. But we don't believe the peakbagging clubs attract people who wouldn't otherwise be there anyway. Others are guilty of that.

At any rate, whether or not clubs and their attendant publicity are valid, there seems to be no defensible argument against the pursuit of peaks as an individual's objective. It's all part of that "fine kind of madness. . . ."

CASE STUDY

The Forty-Sixers

The objects of the organization shall be the fostering and protection of the natural resources within the Adirondack Forest Preserve of the State of New York. . . .

Articles of Organization and By-laws,
the Adirondack Forty-Sixers

ONE OF THE northeastern peakbagging clubs, the Adirondack Forty-Sixers, has taken a long hard look at its own role in the mountains, sensitive to the critics described in the foregoing chapter.

About seven years ago, the Forty-Sixers held a meeting at which they seriously considered disbanding. Just to hold such a meeting in itself was a serious violation of Parkinson's Law and sound bureaucratic tradition. However, the group decided instead to reorient its focus toward one of responsible action to help preserve the environment of the Adirondacks' High Peaks. In the years since the meeting, they have moved forward on at least four major programs that deserve attention and commendation. Critics of peakbagging should consider whether any other group can show such a record of responsible stewardship, as demonstrated in these four programs.

(1) An anti-litter campaign. The Forty-Sixer litter-bag program was the brain-child and personal cause célèbre of Glenn Fish, a large authority-figure of a man who served a term as President of the Forty-Sixers a few years ago. The objective of the program is to get hikers to carry out all of their own trash plus any other they may find in the Adirondacks.

After meditating long on the litter problem, Mr. Fish reasoned: "I have a deep conviction that many hikers are induced to 'litter' simply because they are unsophisticated enough to leave home without making any provision for carrying out their litter generated while they are in the woods." Hence, the solution: Give them each a bag and they'll lug it out.

The Glenn Fish system is based on a two-bag principle: The outer bag (to be reused) is made of plastic and displays the Forty-Sixers' emblem; the inner bag is biodegradable paper and is thrown away, with the accumulated litter, at home or in trash baskets at trail heads.

23

The energetic and exuberant Mr. Fish, who sometimes lurks at trail heads to see how his program is working, reports with pride that "I have witnessed hikers emptying litter from a Forty-Sixer bag into a trash can, and then carefully folding the outer bag and stuffing it in a pack for reuse." He then surfaces and approaches these surprised hikers to thank them "for joining with the Forty-Sixers in cleaning up our recreational areas."

Currently, the Forty-Sixers distribute 5000 litter bags annually at key points around the Adirondacks. And the club can proudly say that "not one single report was received relative to misuse of the plastic bags. They were not scattered in the woods, stuffed down privies, tucked in corners of lean-tos. . . ."

Because of programs like that the woods are getting cleaned up—and staying cleaned up.

In New Hampshire the White Mountain National Forest and the Appalachian Mountain Club have their own "Carry In–Carry Out" programs. They have been going on for many years now and White Mountain hikers are (we hope) all familiar with the Carry In–Carry Out poster tacked inside shelters, at trail heads, or displayed at the AMC huts. It must be working, for one doesn't see half as many freeze-dried food packets at campsites, or gum wrappers on the trail, as before.

We usually come out of the woods with a pocketful of litter—our own, as well as odds and ends that glint at you hoping to be picked up as you amble along the trail. The skilled litter-picker can bend and scoop up the offending object without even breaking stride.

Virtue has its own reward. You'd be surprised at what valuable things you find when your subconscious is continually trained on noticing and seizing shiny objects. We've come across two handsome woodsman's knives, and even, over the years, a handful of nickels and dimes (once a quarter!) that wink beguilingly at you just like aluminum foil. Reimbursement in the pursuit of a just cause?

We hope the Forty-Sixers and others will keep on the pressure. Newcomers are taking to the woods daily, and they need to become initiated litter-pickers too. It's a fine madness that can't have too many converts. To join the Litter-Pickers Society, all a hiker need do is bend down at least once on a woods walk to pick up a candy wrapper, a cigarette, a piece of tinfoil, perchance a dime.

(2) Trail maintenance.   The Forty-Sixers, being peakbaggers from way back, do a lot of walking on mountain trails that can't stand heavy foot traffic without showing wear and tear. This means erosion that turns trails into deep gullies, or pitiful widening around wet places that obliterates trailside vegetation.

Among the 46 peaks of the Adirondacks are several which are called "trailless." In the old days, this term meant a bushwhack through spruce, fir, and birch of impenetrable thickness and tenacity. Adirondack bushwhacks, in fact, were as legendary as their black flies, and just as mean. But now a "trailless peak" has come to imply only that there is no *officially maintained* trail: There are sometimes as many as three or four "herd paths" leading to the summit. The

Forty-Sixers, as stewards of the Adirondacks' High Peaks, and harboring a particular fondness for "these mountain orphans," realized that proliferating herd paths leading to the same point would never do. Too much damage was being done to the woods.

Now the Forty-Sixers, consulting along the way with New York's Department of Environmental Conservation, have blocked out with brush all but one herd path leading to each summit. They have *not,* however, put up trail markers, in an effort to maintain the *spirit* of off-trail walking. Above treeline, the Forty-Sixers have placed cairns showing where the preferred trail goes.

This past June the Club took another step in caring for their beloved mountains. They appointed an official "Trailmaster," who will not only make the state of the trailless peaks his business, but also organize volunteers to work on trail improvements all over the mountains. Jim Goodwin, the man who fills this newly created post, knows his Adirondacks: He's climbed all the 46 peaks 13 times. That's dedicated peakbagging!

(3) Summit reseedings. The impact of hiker traffic is nowhere so damaging as it is on those few summits of the northeast that are above the treeline. The alpine, tundra-like ground cover on these peaks is astonishingly well-equipped by nature to withstand the ferocity of arctic cold and hurricane winds—but when a large volume of hikers tramps over, it's in deep trouble. Almost ten years ago, under the direction of scientist-peakbagger Ed Ketchledge from Syracuse University, an experiment began to see if man could reintroduce vegetation in areas where boot traffic had seriously impacted both plant life and soils on above-treeline summits.

Starting on Mount Dix, a 4900-foot spiny ridge in the eastern Adirondacks, and Mount Colden, a dramatic peak near New York's highest (Marcy), Dr. Ketchledge and his associates began carting grass seed and special fertilizers up the long mountain trails. They achieved surprising and gratifying results in getting the impoverished and trampled soils to support life again. The grass would take only temporarily—that high, hostile environment is not its natural home—but with the grass started and the soils stabilized, native species then took a new lease on life. Mosses, lichens, liverwort, the hardy little mountain sandwort, and native grasses and sedges moved back in. Encouraged, the Forty-Sixers, with other volunteers cooperating, moved on to other above-treeline summits.

Having given the alpine vegetation a second chance, the Forty-Sixers and the state Department of Environmental Conservation then had to convince hikers to stay on trail and not wander all over the tiny plants. This they achieved with a happy absence of regulation or regimentation. Cairns were built over each of the summit areas, to encourage traffic to stay on one route. Small signs were placed at treeline, politely and positively asking (not ordering) hikers to "please stay on the marked trail to prevent trampling of the fragile summit vegetation." By every conceivable means of word-of-mouth, the message was spread—in talks and slide shows to hiking and camping groups, through the publications of clubs using the area, in the announcements and posters of the state agency, and most effectively in the personal presence of "ridge runners," young people who spent the summer ceaselessly roaming the high peaks, advising and counselling hikers.

The Adirondack Mountain Club has played a helpful role in this and many of the Forty-Sixers' efforts at high-peak stewardship. Fortunately there is good cooperation between these two concerned and responsible groups.

The results of this continuing summit reseeding program have been very promising. "I feel very optimistic," says Dr. Ketchledge. "Everyone has become a steward—become aware of their responsibility for the alpine environment."

(4) Wilderness Leadership Workshop. Recognizing that their own good deeds alone would never save the mountains in this era of the outdoor recreation boom, the Forty-Sixers have attempted to spread the message to other major groups of recreationists.

The Club decided to aim at children's camps, Scout troops, YMCA's, college outing clubs, and any other sources of large groups coming to the Adirondacks. Reach these people, they reasoned, and you get the message to perhaps the principal causes of impact on the mountain environment.

Since 1972, the Forty-Sixers have staged an annual Wilderness Leadership Workshop—an intensive 2½-day course covering all aspects of taking groups through the mountains. The workshops are well and attentively attended. In fact, the leaders turn away half again as many applicants as they can accept, to keep the seminars small enough to allow for full participation by everyone.

Much of the advice deals with just plain practical problems of how you steer a bunch of energetic and hungry kids through the backcountry without losing any. But in between the nuts and bolts, the Forty-Sixers weave the message of the new environmental ethic: Walk softly, don't cut bough beds, think about using campstoves instead of burning up every stick of firewood, carry out your litter, don't let the kids discard shredded plastic.

The entire "faculty" at these workshops is composed of peakbagging Forty-Sixers—people who have long worked with summer camps or school groups. They are brimming with practical tips on how to run a successful trip, and they are also sensitive to the need to soften the impact of recreation in the mountains.

The state DEC cooperates with the Club; in fact, in recent years the opening session has been conducted by Interior Ranger Pete Fish, whose presentation is a cornucopia of sensible and useful advice on all aspects of leading groups in the northeastern mountains, laced with the underlying message: "The responsibility for environmental quality rests with every single person every moment of his life."

We wish the critics of peakbaggers could attend one of these workshops and see the personal dedication of these people to making life better for the mountains they climb.

Dr. Ketchledge speaks for many of the Forty-Sixers when he expresses his own deep-felt sense of stewardship for the High Peak region that has given him and others so much enjoyment: "For 29 years I've climbed in this country," he told the 1978 workshop, in a talk delivered while standing on the very summit of Mount Jo, the panorama of the High Peaks circling around him and his listeners. "In a pantheistic sense, all of this," he said, sweeping his arm over the breathtaking landscape, "is part of me." It's that kind of sense of personal involvement and obligation that has sparked so much good work to help preserve the mountain environment.

Next time you hear someone criticize a peakbagger, think about these men and women in the Adirondacks, tirelessly passing out litterbags, tugging branches around to brush in an eroding trail, toting grass seed and fertilizer up a mountain, or giving up a splendid May weekend to help spread the message of stewardship to others.

These are the peakbaggers.

3

Winter Camping Idyll

If you're comfortable on a northeast winter hike, you'll survive—
yes even flourish—just about anywhere in the world.

Harry Roberts, *Movin' On*

GOING BACKPACKING in February? Sleeping out at 20 below? Covering ten miles over snow five feet deep?

Most New England hikers know better. They hang up their *Vibram* soles in November and leave them alone 'til April.

But then there are fishermen who *like* all-day downpours, skiers who *deliberately* pick those suicidal downhill runs, baseball players who *enjoy* batting against Nolan Ryan, book-lovers who *choose* to read *Paradise Lost,* and gourmets who *like* to add more curry to Indian dishes . . . and hikers who *enjoy* winter camping and climbing. Count us among this fraternity of nuts.

Most of our friends, when we mention plans for winter outings, look as dismayed as Mrs. Daniel must have looked when her husband announced before dinner that he was going into the den for awhile. (Before whose dinner?)

Unquestionably there is a strain of masochism in the winter backpacker. Unless you can decide that you *like* to be cold and to have a devil of a time to make one mile per hour if snow conditions are good, unless you want a challenge just to carry on life's normal operations of walking, cooking, sleeping, tying a shoelace, unzipping a fly, looking at your watch—all of which take excruciatingly longer on the third day out below zero—then you won't really enjoy the northeastern backcountry in February. In that case, take up chess, or yoga, or *Paradise Lost.*

"Many human beings say that they enjoy the winter, but what they really enjoy is feeling proof against it," wrote Richard Adams in *Watership Down.* That's a perceptive observation for a rabbit.

The early Icelandic saga-writers conceived of hell as a place of intense cold and ice. They were right. Even the orthodox Christian view of hell in the aforementioned *Paradise Lost* had room in it for a corner where . . .

Beyond this flood a frozen continent
Lies dark and wild, beat with perpetual storms
Of whirlwind and dire hail, which on firm land
Thaws not, but gathers heap, and ruin seems
Of ancient pile; all else deep snow and ice,

which may prove that John Milton's been on Mount Washington on a merely typical February day too.

Trying to explain the attractions of winter camping and climbing is about as unprofitable as trying to explain why you voted for Nixon in '72. (We didn't— but somebody must have.)

Just walking along the trail isn't the simple pleasure it was in summer. Now in our mountains it's covered with three or four feet of snow, five or six feet or more as you get up in elevation. This means the first problem is that your booted feet alone would flounder hopelessly.

So you wear cross-country skis or snowshoes. The former are becoming very popular and chic, and an expert skier can travel smoothly over very rough country. On a moderate downgrade, a glide on skis is ten times as fast as a waddle on snowshoes.

Still, for climbing the steeper trails or bushwhacking, as we like to do, skis eventually can't make it. It's unbelievable what you can get up, through, and over with snowshoes. Not the long Alaskan models, built for covering flat or rolling open country, but the short flat bear paws or modified beavertails that you can work with in steep, broken terrain and through dense trees and shrubs.

But now you begin to learn some of the "attractions" of winter travel.

In the first place, that trail was cut in summer, blazes marked about four feet off the ground, and branches clipped to a height of maybe seven feet. With five feet of snow, say, you do the arithmetic: Few blazes are visible, and a loose weave of snow-laden branches obscures the trail at many points. Furthermore, the snow has covered all the thick undergrowth that told you where the trail *wasn't* in summer. So now all ways look equally open—or tangled.

In short, staying on trail is in itself a major challenge. We think you can tell an experienced winter traveler more by his ability to stay on trail, somehow sense the right way, than by almost any other indicator of winter experience.

To add to your troubles, your pack that's bulging with winter-required gear, much heavier than your normal summer load, is now up there in the branches getting tangled and shaking snow down your neck.

Next discover the pleasures of the Spruce Trap. This invention of an ill-humored Norse frost-god is based on the principle that falling snow doesn't pack in nearly as tightly around the branches of a small evergreen as it does elsewhere. Once a small tree is covered with loosely consolidated snow, the unwary snowshoer won't see it as he tromps along an otherwise fairly well consolidated surface. One enthusiastically slammed snowshoe in the vicinity of those covered branches and the whole fragile structure of unconsolidated snow gives way in a whoosh.

Oh, the fiendish fate of a Spruce Trap victim! At upper elevations where snow is really deep, we've seen an entire adult with full pack disappear below the surrounding surface into a Spruce Trap. (At that elevation the true villain is likely to be a fir, not a spruce, but who wants to hear botanical niceties when you're floundering with a 50-pound pack five feet below where you'd like to place your foot next?)

Once you've plummeted down inside a Spruce Trap, malicious little Snow-Elves go to work far down there somewhere, weaving the tree's lowest branches around your snowshoes in lacework of intricate complexity that defies your most vigorous efforts to extract your feet, to the accompaniment of language you never knew you had in you. Then there's always the inconsiderate soul who wants to document your absurd contortionist acrobatics on film. "Great!" the would-be cinematographic artist cries, "Can you hold that position a second?" Curses!

Get out from down in there, dust off snow, stop whimpering, and carry on 'til the grade steepens. You've strapped mini-crampons on the bottom of your snowshoes. Without them you'd slip hopelessly back on steeper grades. But let the temperature warm up unseasonably and the snow takes on a wet, heavy consistency that introduces you to the experience of balling.

No, balling isn't what you think it is, and not nearly as much fun. It refers to the tendency of warm snow to gather in great lumps between the points of your snowshoe crampons. As some snow adheres to the metal, more snow adheres to *that* snow, and presently you pick up a "ball" of nearly a cubic foot of heavy, packed snow with every step. Keeping your balance becomes difficult, your equanimity impossible. It's a bit like trying to walk with a large and irregular basketball strapped to each foot.

But warm temperatures that produce balling are rare. More likely, you'll be lucky enough to have it colder . . . and colder . . . and colder. . . .

Step out of the car at trail head when it's 15 below, and in the many minutes it takes to get under way you're getting so cold that you put on all your warm clothing. Five minutes up the steep trail and you're suddenly aware that you're so warm with the exercise of breaking trail through soft snow with a heavy pack that you're starting to sweat. A danger sign: Sweating into your clothes is a basic no-no in winter, since wet clothes (from whatever source of moisture) lose much of their insulating value.

So you stop, off comes that 50-pound pack, off comes the parka or a couple of sweaters, on goes the pack (with no car to prop it against this time). But every time the trail turns downhill your exercise may be so much less that you start to get cold and need one of those sweaters. So again, the tussle with getting pack on and off.

Then the trail turns uphill, and you run into the inexorable operation of Fye's Law—that for every 500 feet of uphill the pack increases in perceived weight by

10 pounds—and you start to sweat again. Off comes the pack, off the sweater, on the pack. . . .

See what we mean about the "attractions" of winter on the backwoods trails? Us, we love every minute of it.

It's critically important to keep your body temperature just right in winter. Overheat and you sweat into your clothes—a potentially disastrous mistake. Lose too much body heat and it may be hard to get warm again. For this reason, most winter hikers use the Layer System in clothing. First developed by Lester L. Layer, an avid winter climber and manufacturer of sweaters, the Layer System consists of carrying several different shirts, sweaters, and a wind-proof nylon outer shell, rather than just one great big down parka. Then you can wear just what you need, not more. It's a prudent approach, but it sure means a lot of stops and starts sometimes. Plus a lot of taking that pack off and on.

That's not counting the times you have to take it off because an uncooperative snowshoe binding keeps sliding off your toe or heel.

If you head for the challenging above-treeline terrain of Katahdin, the White Mountains' Presidential Range, Franconia Ridge, Mount Mansfield, or the higher summits in the Adirondacks, not to mention the higher reaches of the western mountains, you'll encounter a special world. There's nothing like the raw bone-blasting power of the above-treeline tandem of low temperatures, hurricane-force winds, and no place to hide. Sometimes that alpine world is far more benign—just often enough to lull the novice into thinking it's not so tough up there after all. But the weather can deteriorate with terrible rapidity.

Don't test this world 'til you're thoroughly at home below treeline in winter. When your experience has progressed and your common sense has deteriorated far enough, you'll find the alpine zone an experience without parallel in the outdoors world.

But be ready. Here the price of foolishness runs high: frostbite, hypothermia, even death. But even when the weather spares you from its worst, travel will be slower than in summer, every simple operation maddeningly time consuming.

Fortunately, though, daylight hours are so much shorter in winter that you have to curtail your carefree stroll. The short days of January and February seem to end right after lunch and you've made only about half the distance you'd planned on, but no matter: Now you get to the "joys" of winter camping.

Mushing around on skis or snowshoes, you catch yourself gazing at that quiet glade surrounded by drooping hemlocks. What a lovely spot to camp! How still and peaceful the night! How comforting the rich mounds of snow all around your snug tent!

The reality of winter camping is indeed a special paradise—but it may not turn out to be quite the idyllic scene you pictured.

First, when you stop moving on those skis or snowshoes, and start standing around doing camping chores, you find that you're getting cold. Your body isn't the efficient furnace generating heat the way it was when you were exerting yourself on the trail. So you put on every stitch of clothing in the pack and end up as rotund as Santa Claus. Warm (maybe), but hardly as mobile as you'd like to be for bending over, reaching around, etc.

Now set up the tent. At zero degrees you have to keep your mittens or gloves on for this process. Recall how easily the tent went up in summer? Now cold changes all. Tent stakes won't hold in the soft snow. Drop one and it disappears in the bottomless fluffy whiteness. Tent poles won't obey mittened hands. Take off the mittens and the metal sticks to your skin. Your hands are soon numb, as metal conducts heat away even through mittens. Leave your snowshoes on and you can't maneuver; take them off and you plunge to the hips at every third step. Tent lines are ticklish to get around stakes or trees. Knots take forever to tie. In fact, every little process takes two or three times as long. Meanwhile light is fading fast, temperature's dropping, maybe the wind's picking up and changing direction from what you had in mind when you oriented the tent.

At last you're inside, safe from the elements. But what's happened to the tent? Great gremlins, it's shrunk! No, it's just all that winter gear—puffy, voluminous down sleeping bags, myriad articles of clothing, cooking gear, big winter boots, not to mention an enlarged *you* (you're not wearing just T-shirt and shorts, remember)—all taking up a lot of space in a not-so-spacious accommodation. But if you think it's crowded now, just wait until morning when a foot of fresh-fallen snow presses against sides and roof. No place for claustrophobics.

Now to get dinner! Somehow you have to spread out the cooking gear, stove, pots, food, light the stove, melt great quantities of snow for water, get some of it into your canteen, get a pot of it boiling, cook dinner and wash up—all without spilling a drop or burning down the tent. Obviously impossible.

Many winter campers frown on cooking in a tent. They claim that unsafe amounts of carbon monoxide from white-gas stoves are dangerous in a closed tent. Carbon monoxide? Out here in this frozen wasteland? Sad, but true. Well, you'll just risk it and make sure the tent is ventilated because at zero degrees and a strong breeze getting up you know you are not going to cook any place else. You're flying in the face of the conservative practitioners of the art, but you rationalize that there are times when you couldn't keep a stove going if you were cooking outside the tent—above treeline in a howling gale, for instance—so you feel that it's only right that you "practice" cooking in a tent (well ventilated, of course) now and then.

You want to be inside that sleeping bag, that beautiful buffer between you and the darkening winter world, with just your nose, eyes, and mouth showing, and two hands sticking out so you can get dinner.

Oh yes, dinner. You need food. The bag isn't really warming you and that's because you're cold—from the inside. You burned up those lunch calories long ago. Well, you've already filled the snow bag—a garbage bag-sized obstacle at your right elbow filled with snow to melt for water. It takes up a lot of room, of course. With faultless dexterity you've managed to light the stove, get the snow melted, even boiling, and now you're having a warming cup of bouillon while you stir the pot of Dinty Moore beef stew. Things are looking a little less desperate.

But, what's this? Good grief! It's snowing inside the tent! Impossible. This tent's in perfect condition. You're right, the tent's fine—and it *is* snowing. Condensation from the boiling water vapor has, at zero degrees, built a lovely layer of icy crystals on the inside of the tent—roof, walls and all. Now you know another reason why the conservative faction cooks outside. You open the tent door a crack and mutter incantations designed to direct the steam from the pot out the small hole in the tent door.

Whenever you brush against the tent wall a delicate shower descends, covering clothing, sleeping bag, and you in a white blanket that rapidly proceeds to melt. You're horrified: water permeating your down sleeping bag! Wet down loses its insulating value—you'll freeze. So, with infinite care you avoid touching tent sides and roof, brush every bit of snow or frost off the bag. Not easy. The tent has shrunk still further.

Still having a good time? Oddly enough some of us couldn't be happier. It has been said that winter camping doesn't build character, it reveals it. Sometimes, it may reveal that you're out of your mind.

Finally you're finished dinner. Even made a pass at washing up. Mixing last night's dinner with breakfast oatmeal never did appeal to you. How could it have taken two hours? In summer you eat in less than half that. All the melting of snow for every drop of water, and every tiny task takes twice as long with cold hands.

You sink luxuriantly into your sleeping bag, savoring the last bit of light from the two candle stubs which had lighted the process of getting dinner. You are full. You are warm. What a nice secure place to be! Let the elements rage outside! What was it Miriam Underhill, America's greatest woman mountaineer said: "I don't mind hardship, as long as I'm perfectly comfortable."

Oh dear. A tiny thought struggles within you. You try to ignore it. But there it is. From the depth of your sleeping bag you know that that stew and all that liquid you drank are not going to let you sleep through the night. What time is it? 7:30 P.M. Seems later. It's been dark for hours. You'll never make it until 7:00 the next morning. You resign yourself to the inevitable and struggle upward out of downy warmth. Boots go back on, then gaiters. Then sweaters. You search for your flashlight. Finally you're plunging through the snow into the trees, toilet paper in hand. Well, you think, you're just glad you're not camped above the treeline someplace with the wind howling down on you. You painfully recall such a time when, at the crucial moments, the toilet paper was whisked away in a blast that nearly flattened you.

You're back in your sleeping bag again, thoroughly chilled from being out. You feel slightly disgruntled as you wait for the bag to warm you. Let's see. Boots are in the bottom of the sleeping bag (wrapped in a stuff sack) so they won't freeze. Canteen is under your left knee, so you'll have water. (You *did* get that cap on tight, didn't you? Better check . . . a process inducing a gymnastic tour-de-force that Nadia Comaneci would envy.) The breakfast is sticking you in the side, but you don't dare leave it out for forest beasties to rob. A few bulky items like sweaters squeeze you on the other side. You have to keep clothing in your bag or the condensation might fall on it if a wind comes up during the night. You try to find a spot for your feet. You don't want them lying on your cold boots. No room. Oh well.

Morning. How difficult it is to stick a nose out of that womb-like bag. Oops. Ice crystals falling on your face. The top of your bag is covered with rime ice where you breathed out of it all night. You inch yourself toward the laborious task of preparing breakfast. At least you have daylight to work in now. A good two-and-a-half hours later you're trying to stuff an ice-coated tent into its stuff sack. You lay it out, brush off the ice and roll it up again. Tighter. It barely fits in a sack it floundered around in all summer.

Your fingers are freezing now. In fact you've got to get moving. All this inactivity of picking up camp has really cooled you down. Snowshoe bindings are stiff, awkward to get on. You hoist a heavy load—that water-soaked tent and sleeping bag have increased your weight—and mush on.

Idyllic winter camping? You bet it is. You can grow to love it. Wait till you try it above treeline . . . in freezing rain . . . two more nights to go and all your down gear wet . . . stove getting cranky about starting . . . ah, winter wonderland.

4

Backpackers' Favorite Lies

. . . they that are serious in ridiculous matters will be ridiculous in serious affairs.

Plutarch

"THERE WE WERE! Hadn't seen a sign of other people for six days. The temperature that morning was 20 below and the wind was gusting to 90 miles per hour, but we shouldered our 80-pound packs and. . . ."

If anyone tried to feed you that story, you'd wisely suspect half he said. Yet he'd only be slightly overplaying a game which most of us backwoods hikers play.

We're normally an honest enough crowd. You meet few outright car thieves or embezzling accountants in the backcountry, and we don't recall that backpacking was listed as the hobby of any of the Watergate conspirators. Still, there are certain subjects that a hiker simply can't discuss without Twainsian exaggeration at the least. If fishermen are more renowned for their estimates of the one that got away, it's only because we backpackers have not articulated our own stories adequately yet. But, God knows, some of us try.

For your guidance (and protection), we identify half a dozen favorite subjects for loquacious backpackers' tall-tale-telling.

Pack weight. This ploy has two versions.

The first version consists of grossly *overestimating* your pack's weight and thereby gaining points for superior strength and stamina. The figures usually given for this purpose range, for men, from 70 to 90 pounds; for women, 60 to 80 is the preferred range. Over 100 strains credibility and you lose points.

In the second version, instead of implying strength, you gain points by demonstrating your resourcefulness and toughness in surviving on practically nothing—which you indicate by *underestimating* your pack's weight. For instance, you went out for six days in the wilds and the pack weighed under 20 pounds.

We've seen many a relatively inexperienced backpacker come to ruin by playing the first version of this game in a crowd that turned out to have the experience and shrewdness to pull the second on him unexpectedly. Just when the poor duffer thinks his hearers are impressed with his tales of 80-pound packs lugged over Continental Divides, someone in the group remarks coolly that he used to carry weights like that but now he's got it down so that he can go five days on 13.5 pounds and have food left over. Others in the group then start in on how they cut handles off toothbrushes and remove the cardboard from inside the toilet paper, and pretty soon the air is dripping with scorn for the utter oafishness of anyone who'd carry 80 pounds even were he headed for Outer Mongolia from Singapore.

The old-time hard-men still can't resist the lure of the 90-pound pack. Once when we were in the Carter Range of New Hampshire's White Mountains, one of the hut boys of the Appalachian Mountain Club had just packed 135 pounds up to Carter Notch hut. That figure was authentic: They had scales right there. An hour or so later, he started down the trail to return to AMC's base camp at Pinkham Notch. Unbeknownst to him, one of us was sunning himself on top of a tall boulder next to the trail. As this young husky passed underneath alone, we heard him say quietly to himself: "How much did you take up to Carter today?" (Pause—then in casual tones:) "One hundred and thirty-five pounds." (Pause—then with hushed awe:) "Wow!" Evidently we were the unsuspected audience for a rehearsal of a conversation to which our young friend looked forward with all the relish of a true backpacker.

Distances hiked. Here is another ploy that can cut both ways: You'll hear some braggarts tell you about covering 25 miles of rough mountain terrain with full packs. But the more sophisticated gamesmen have learned how to lay waste the opposition by describing what a formidable bushwhacking trip they struggled through: "All day we fought through dense growth, only the compass to guide us, and in ten hours of monumental effort we'd covered less than two miles." The latter's listeners are cowed by the implication that only superhuman strength and resolution could keep a person going through such incredibly tangled jungle.

Days away from people. Most of us hikers yearn for the wilderness to be wilder than it really is in this day and age. Part of the true pleasure of hiking is the illusion of getting into a country where few people are or, better yet, ever have been. We speak wistfully of "mountain solitude."

Perhaps this is why some backpackers go in for the fantasy that "We didn't see a sign of other people for six days." It's still possible to go places where you can really escape all evidence of man, present or past. But few really get there. More likely you're bound to hear a plane overhead at some point, find a worn track that isn't just deer or moose, or worst of all kick up a Vienna sausage can on the edge of a clearing that you thought was your aboriginal discovery.

Stand on a remote New England mountaintop and look out over miles of rugged, heavily forested ridges, and you can be tempted to speculate that much of it is country where no one has ever been. As you sit staring at those ridges, you slowly realize that many of them show faintly discernible patterns of horizontal lines. These are the tracings of old lumber roads switchbacking up the ridges from the days when loggers criss-crossed the entire area. So, instead of your dream that no man has ever set foot on those ridges, comes the realization that 100 years ago they were crawling with logging teams.

So when someone tells you that they were out in country where no one had ever been before, control your envy. The nineteenth-century loggers, as well as hunters and trappers, combed over this grand country from east to west pretty thoroughly, and your pioneer friend was probably stalking the ghosts of several generations of outdoorsmen who never heard of Kelty packs or Mountain House freeze-dried food.

Wind speed. If you've ever been above the treeline when the wind was *really* hitting 60 miles per hour, you turn a benevolently skeptical ear to the tales of crossing rugged terrain with heavy packs in 90-mph winds. We don't know very many people who carry an anemometer with them. Those that do develop a conservatism in estimating wind speed that seems to elude the rest of us.

Once five of us were climbing on Maine's Katahdin in winter. It was one of those wild days above treeline. When we climbed out of our snow gully onto that remarkably flat "tableland" plateau of Katahdin's upper elevations, we were engulfed in clouds. Visibility was reduced to 50 feet at best, and there was no place to hide from the wind or cold. Before starting out on a compass course, we huddled together for a bite of lunch, numbed by the cold, and buffeted by the wind that seemed stronger than most of the party had experienced before. At this point one of our group produced an anemometer from his pack and invited our guesses on the wind speed. The other four of us guessed speeds ranging from 30 to 50 mph; no doubt, had there been no instrument around, the Monday morning office stories would have definitely fixed the speed at least at 50. (Usually speed increases in memory from the already exaggerated estimates of the actual moment.) Then our iconoclastic friend gave us his reading: 18 mph.

Once, when we were coming down from New Hampshire's Presidential Range, we met another party at trail head who asked how it was above treeline. "Windy!" we said. "How fast?" they asked. Clearly we were being invited to spout a figure, but out of what whole cloth are such figures supposed to be concocted? We didn't know and we suspect that few people have any real ability to judge wind speed. Our refusal to give a dramatic figure, though, seemed to disappoint the other hikers: We weren't playing the true backpackers' game.

Temperature. You might think that Doc Fahrenheit's handy invention might keep us all honest when reporting the temperature extremes in which we've camped or hiked. But the resourceful tale-teller has carefully sanded down the sharp edges of his memory so that he can leap gracefully from hard observed reading to speculations about what it "probably" was—and thus come up with some astonishing tales of extreme cold or heat.

We've been winter camping in northern New England for over a decade and yet we've seen the thermometer actually reach 20 below on nights that we've been camped out on only three or four occasions. Yet we've regularly heard novices who took up winter camping for a year or two during that period regale their friends with what it's like to camp at 20 below above treeline. Well, *maybe* they saw the red line sink to 20 below—but we're skeptical.

We've been told by our western friends that desert hikers become just as imaginative in exaggerating the *high* temperatures they've walked through. ("We had to walk 15 miles carrying 80-pound packs in 120-degree heat with no water.")

Bird species.   This is a highly specialized branch of the art. The very fact that backpackers who know anything about birds are as rare as Kirtland's warbl— oops, sorry, we mean they're very rare—gives lots of leeway to those who have little more than a nodding acquaintance with a Peterson Field Guide.

If you hear some far-off chirp, you'll rarely be caught off base if you say, "Hey, did you hear that? Black-throated green warbler." If your companions ask you to point it out, the bird can generally be stuck with the blame for not repeating the call, if it ever issued it in the first place. Of course, you risk having some unsuspected amateur Audubon turn up among your companions and challenge your identifications. If you've just confidently snapped "yellow-throated vireo" as a winged creature flitted momentarily in and out of view among some hemlocks, you may be aghast to have someone in the group venture an apparently better-informed view that it was in fact a robin. (Sometimes you can get out of this predicament by smilingly observing that the female immatures are not always readily distinguished.)

Variants of the "bird species ploy" may be explored in such areas as tree identification, ferns, rock types, and especially alpine flowers.

These are just a few of many areas in which the joys of the hiker's memory may transcend the confines of mere experience. Hiking speed, angle of slope climbed, and wild food foraged are some other possibilities.

We do not offer these suggestions in any critical sense, nor as definitive. Backpackers are still developing the state of the art, and we have much to learn from our fishing and hunting brothers. You might want to work up your own subjects and refine your own tips for successful playing of the game. After all, this activity will provide interesting employment for your mind while you're ticking off the miles on those 50-mile day hikes. . . .

5

The Greatest Walkers
of Them All

There were giants in the earth in those days.

Genesis, VI, 4

They were swifter than eagles, they were stronger than lions.

Samuel 2, I, 23

WE'VE ALWAYS been intrigued with those year-end "ten best" lists that you read in the papers—the ten best-dressed celebrities, ten best college football teams, etc.

NEW ENGLAND HIKERS

We'd like to salute the ten greatest hikers in New England history. Why not?
Some ground rules: To make the "ten greatest hikers" list, you have to be dead; that's so we won't make any enemies among living egos. And we include New York State's hiking country, the Adirondacks and the Catskills, as part of the over-all northeastern region.
O.K.? Here's our list:

(1) Chocorua: This name evokes a legend and a curse. Chocorua was an Indian, whom we list as representative of what must have been a great many outstanding Indian hikers of pre-European settler days. For Chocorua, New Hampshire's rock-turreted mountain now climbed by thousands each summer is named. Legend has it that the chief's beloved son was accidentally poisoned by a settler's family named Campbell. Chocorua took vengeance by slaying Campbell's wife and children. In his turn, Campbell tracked the Indian to the top of the rock-spired mountain and shot him down. The dying Chocorua pronounced a terrible curse upon the white man as he fell, the effects of which have plagued New England ever since—as evidenced by the hard, rocky infertility of her soil, the great storms that wrack her coast, and recently the results of the 1978 American League pennant race.

(2) Darby Field: Mount Washington's first conqueror in 1642. Field made the ascent with two Indians, and was the first European to tramp for pleasure and exploration in the White Mountains. Even in those days, Field experienced "typical" Mount Washington weather—cloud, wind, and rain. It's been like that ever since.

(3) Abel Crawford: Back in 1792, this gigantic figure strode into New Hampshire's most spectacular mountain "notch"—the one that today bears his name—and hacked out a homestead. For over 50 years he lived a robust mountain life there, becoming the first innkeeper to exploit tourist interest in New England's mountain scenery. A vigorous woodsman and climber himself, he and his son Ethan cut the very first hiking trail to the summit of Mount Washington. The "Crawford Path" is still heavily used by hikers today, and is the oldest continuously used footpath in North America. Crawford was the first and possibly the most impressive of the true mountain men of New England.

(4) Verplanck Colvin: The Adirondacks, slower to be explored than the White Mountains, produced some colorful and eccentric mountain guides, from Old Mountain Phelps and Bill Nye to Noah John Rondeau, the twentieth century hermit of Cold River. Nevertheless, the most significant figure in this area was probably the chief surveyor for the State of New York at the end of the last century. Colvin it was who organized and personally led the guides and surveyors all over the Adirondacks' High Peaks, identifying, measuring, and mapping the entire region, and making numerous first ascents in the process.

(5) Robert Marshall: The Adirondack tramper extraordinaire. He and his brother George, with guide Herbert Clark, first climbed all 46 Adirondack peaks over 4000 feet. He started this game, and all Adirondack peakbaggers who follow walk in his footsteps.

(6) Benton MacKaye: The father of the Appalachian Trail. A native of Massachusetts, in 1921 MacKaye, a professional forester and city planner, began work on the idea of a continuous footpath from Maine to Georgia. The trail cutters did not lay down their tools until 1937—15 years and 2000 miles later. The Appalachian Trail's 700 miles in New England are a landmark to MacKaye that has brought pleasure to untold thousands of hill-walkers. (See the Case Study on the Appalachian Trail in section III for more on MacKaye.)

(7) James P. Taylor: As MacKaye was to the A.T., so was Jim Taylor to Vermont's Long Trail. Associate Principal of Vermont Academy back at the turn of the century, Taylor took his boys on many hikes, but found the trails of the Green Mountains sparse and inadequate. So in March 1910, he called a meeting in Burlington which 23 people attended, and the Green Mountain Club was formed. From this grew that 262-mile "footpath in the wilderness," stretching the length of Vermont's Green Mountains from the Canadian to the Massachusetts borders—the vision of Jim Taylor.

(8) Roy Buchanan: A native Vermonter, Buchanan embodies the practical trail-workers who carried Taylor's concept of the Long Trail through to completion. Every visionary needs a doer. Where Taylor was the man with the dream,

Buchanan was the fellow with the indefatigable vitality, organizational skill, and dependable follow-through. He laid out and cut the final 10 miles through to Canada, built the waterbars and steps necessary to check erosion, and constructed camps where they were needed so that some shelter is available to the Long Trail hiker at intervals of never much more than 7 miles. A small man of enormous energy, strength, and humor, Roy is reported to have lived on strong black coffee and home-made donuts. The diet worked—he headed the Long Trail Patrol for 36 years and was still vigorous when he died at 95 in 1977.

(9) Percy Baxter: Maine's Katahdin is generally conceded to be New England's finest single mountain. It remains in isolated serenity, untouched by loggers or tourist development, largely due to the personal exertions of one wealthy, eccentric, and energetic man of vision, Percival Proctor Baxter. Baxter used his money and prestige (as a former Governor) to cajole the paper companies into selling him the whole blooming mountain and 200,000 acres around it, all of which he turned around and donated to the state as a park. There have been hikers of greater prowess associated with Katahdin, such as long-time park ranger Leroy Dudley, but if we seek to pay tribute to the man whose name is inseparably linked with New England's greatest mountain, that man just has to be Percy Baxter.

(10) Miriam Underhill: An alpinist of rare ability, she was the first person to claim title to three coveted New England mountaineering feats: (a) She climbed all 46 of New Hampshire's 4000-footers—in winter—many when she was over 60. (b) She went on to conquer New England's sixty-three 4000-footers. (c) She climbed the 100 Highest of New England. A knowledgeable enthusiast of alpine flowers, she was the organizer of the Appalachian Mountain Club's guidebook, *Mountain Flowers of New England,* for which she took the photographs.

These ten great walkers are the celebrities of the hiking fraternity. We concede that history has not recorded the walking feats of many unsung striders along New England's rocky footpaths. The early pioneers moving north and west into the hills; the logging scouts seeking the virgin White Pines of Maine's north woods; later, the Yankee peddlers and itinerant preachers roaming the rough paths between isolated settlements; still later, that hardy twentieth century breed, the Maine guide and his counterpart in the Adirondacks; still more recently, the tough hut men who stocked the high White Mountain huts, lugging 200-pound loads up steep mountain trails before the helicopter took over—all these must have been walkers of prodigious strength and energy.

We've also been forced to omit some giants of the past because, while their exploits are legendary, they are (blessedly) still alive and well and living in noble old age among the hills they loved and climbed—literally legends in their own time. Great walking seems conducive to health and longevity—witness Abel Crawford walking to Concord as a State Legislator at the age of 82, Roy

Buchanan living to 95, Benton MacKaye to 96. Some of the great ones live yet, such as:

Robert Underhill, Miriam's husband, who was arguably this country's greatest mountaineer back in the twenties and ranged widely over New England's crags, pioneering difficult ascents like the first climb of Cannon's 1000-foot high cliff (highest in the eastern U.S.)—still living at 90 in New Hampshire, with the Presidential Range in sight out his kitchen window.

Sherman Adams, known to most Americans as President Eisenhower's right-hand man in the White House, but who in his youth was a prodigious White Mountain tramper, whose typical hiking day covered about as many miles as the modern backpacker tries to cover in a week (he once walked 84 miles in a single day, over mountains too)—still active in the management of Loon Mountain ski complex.

Fritz Wiessner, an adopted Vermonter, whose illustrious mountaineering career carried him all over the world, from the Karakoram to the Alps, the Canadian Rockies to the northeastern U.S. crags, where he pioneered difficult routes all over the Adirondacks, New York's Shawangunks, Vermont's Smuggler's Notch, Connecticut's Ragged Mountain, and Cannon, to mention a trifling few—still vigorous and frequently climbing from his home in Vermont, though nearly 80.

It's heartening to reflect that some giants *still* walk the earth.

THE UNITED STATES

Let's expand our horizons from New England to the whole wide country—plenty of space to walk in. Here's our list of the ten greatest backcountry walkers this country's ever seen:

(1) Daniel Boone: Representative of those many prodigious walkers who pioneered the first footpaths off the eastern seaboard, Boone drew his pay as an advance agent for the Transylvania Company. He blazed the Wilderness Road, the first main artery used by settlers into the "southwest" (what is now eastern Tennessee), and on into Kentucky. Boone walked all over the previously unopened hills of that region, eventually reaching Missouri, suffering many hair-raising adventures along the way, which subsequent legends have doubtless greatly enlarged.

(2) Meriwether Lewis: Lewis and Clark have found their names as inextricably linked as Gilbert and Sullivan, Haldeman and Ehrlichman, and Sonny and Cher. We don't know who walked more and who rode the canoe more, but we pick Lewis to represent that first great western walk, the expedition from St. Louis to the Pacific—and back. Much of the trek was taken afloat on the Missouri River, but enough of it was on foot to make either Lewis or Clark qualify.

(3) Brigham Young: Quite possibly the greatest hike in the history of America was the incredible trek by the Mormons across the prairies and mountains of the uncivilized west in 1846–47. The man who led that excursion was Brigham Young, brilliant leader, stern moralist, and astonishing husband (he married 27 wives under the then-prevailing Mormon custom of polygamy).

(4) Johnny Appleseed: Most people seem to think this character was a myth created by Hans Christian Andersen or Walt Disney, or perhaps the public relations agency for the Apple Growers' Association. In fact, he really existed, as John Chapman, born in 1774, a pioneer who walked all over Pennsylvania, Ohio, and Indiana in the first half of the nineteenth century, earning his celebrated nickname by promoting apple orchards wherever he went.

(5) John Muir: the archetypal walker. Walks of 500 to 1000 miles were his delight. His quests took him from Niagara Falls to Florida, from Cuba and South America to California and Alaska. Always full of inquiry, he studied botany, geology, and glaciology ("the inventions of God," he called them) as he walked along, filling notebooks which were later to become such books as *Studies in the Sierra, Mountains of California, Travels in Alaska,* and many others. In 1892 he helped to found the Sierra Club, creating through his influence and writing a great sentiment for conservation at the turn of the century.

(6) Norman Clyde: Quoting Emerson, he shouldered his pack and walked into the mountains in 1928, saying: "Goodbye, proud world, I'm going home." He spent the next 40 years *living* in the High Sierras, climbing countless peaks, many previously unclimbed, and many by new routes of surprising difficulty for a man climbing alone. His strength was incredible, and so were the enormous packs he carried. His load often weighed over 100 pounds, because Clyde took everything an unusual man might need: iron frying pan, several large kettles, cameras, rope, ice ax, several pistols, fishing rod, cups and dishes, cans of food, and a library of books in Latin, French, German, and Italian.

(7) John Burroughs: perhaps this country's best known and best-loved naturalist. Patriarchal with his long, white, flowing beard, with a head that Hamlin Garland noted "had the rugged quality of a granite crag," he tramped the Catskill Mountains. Burroughs wrote 25 books, all on some aspect of nature, many while in residence at "Slabsides," his simple, country log hut. In later years his stature was legendary. The public imagination responded to his trip to Yellowstone with Roosevelt, his mountain walks with John Muir, his camping trips with Edison, Ford, and Harvey Firestone. Burroughs was not a ground-coverer like Muir. He saw walking as a state of mind. He wrote: "You are eligible to any good fortune when you are in the condition to enjoy a walk."

(8) Robert Marshall: We've named Marshall on our earlier list because of his Adirondacks exploits. But his long walks over Alaskan wilderness and in many areas of the Rockies, not to mention his leadership in conservation as an Assistant Secretary of the Interior and co-founder (with Benton MacKaye) of The Wilderness Society, rank him as a national figure in hiking circles too.

(9) Colin Fletcher: The men we've listed so far were mostly hiking with an

explicit goal in mind—usually one of exploration. Muir, Burroughs, and Clyde sought inspiration in the mountains, but they were also seeking to find new places or reach hitherto unattained goals. We list Colin Fletcher as the man whose name is perhaps most associated with that post–World War II development, pure recreational, noncompetitive backpacking. Both as walker and writer, Fletcher has touched a responsive chord in a generation of for-pleasure-only backcountry walkers. (Please note that we have not applied our dead-men-only criterion to this list: Mr. Fletcher is still alive and well—and still walking.)

(10) Grandma Gatewood: Three-time end-to-ender on the Appalachian Trail, she started hiking at the age of 65. An Ohio farm woman, Grandma raised 11 children and *then* took up long-distance hiking. She broke all the rules, wearing sneakers and carrying her duffle slung over one shoulder. Not content with her A.T. notoriety, she walked, alone and in her seventies, across most of the U.S. along the route of the pioneers, the Oregon Trail.

WORLD–WIDE WALKERS

Not to stop at our national borders and a paltry few hundred years of recorded history, who are the ten greatest walkers of all time? May we have the next envelope, please. Here are our nominations:

(1) Moses: Trip-leader for that hike from Egypt to the Promised Land, and only person to lead a hike through the bottom of the Red Sea, others having been unable to work out the arrangements. The Exodus was undoubtedly one of history's most significant walks.

(2) Po-Chu-I: Chinese poet of the ninth century who makes our list because he was the first person who recorded climbing mountains purely for recreational reasons. Some of his climbs sound technically difficult:

> Grasping the creepers, I clung to dangerous rocks;
> My hands and feet—weary with groping for holds.

Even Po-Chu-I, however, faced those Monday morning blues when, like most of us, he had to return from a great weekend in the mountains to go back to the office, as he wrote:

> Then with lowered head,
> Came back to the Ant's Nest.

(3) Marco Polo: Maybe history's most famous traveler, he went from Venice to Peiping and back in the thirteenth century. That sure beats the Long Trail.

(4) David Livingstone: Probably best known as a result of Henry Stanley's

presumption, this Scottish missionary crossed the breadth of Africa, including the Kalahari desert, discovered Victoria Falls and the Zambesi River, and made a prolonged search for the sources of the Nile. He probably did more to fill in European knowledge of African geography than any other single individual.

(5) *Sven Hedlin:* What Livingstone did in Africa, the Swedish explorer did on the grander scale of the world's largest continent. Hedlin crossed the great central regions of Asia, including the Takla Makan Desert and the Kunlun Mountains, eventually reaching Lhasa, the forbidden capital of Tibet. A fair hike from Stockholm.

(6) *Hernando De Soto:* As Livingstone in Africa and Hedlin in Asia, so De Soto in what is now the southern United States. Landing in Tampa Bay in 1539, the doughty Spaniard proceeded to walk across Florida, Georgia, Alabama, Mississippi, and Louisiana, touching base in Tennessee—all of it wild, Indian-infested backcountry at the time. He was the first white man to cross the Mississippi River, whereupon he continued his hike as far as modern Oklahoma. All told his hike was almost as long as the modern Appalachian Trail—but with no shelters, no trail signs . . . no trail. With all that walking, it may seem ironic that the poor man wound up with a car named after him.

(7) *John Muir:* We mentioned him in the American list, but he ranks among the greatest of all time too, as the man who most walked over and celebrated the great American west.

(8) *Roald Amundsen:* Beyond a shadow of a doubt, the toughest hiking in the world is polar exploration. Week after week of way-below-zero temperature, howling blizzards, and brutal sled-hauling (those dogs need help), make this kind of walking in a class by itself. Several extraordinary men have walked across arctic and antarctic wastes to a place in history—giants like Scott, Shackleton, and Peary—but we give the nod here to the man who first reached the South Pole, the greatest post-Viking Norwegian explorer, Roald Amundsen. As Wilfred Noyce wrote of another of the great antarctic walkers: "He was tough, and he enjoyed being tough. . . ."

(9) *Tenzing Norgay:* In the annals of history's great walkers a place surely must be reserved for one of the two men who first walked to the top of the world, the summit of Mount Everest. Without wishing to limit credit due to that great New Zealander, Sir Edmund Hillary, we award this spot to his partner in the Everest climb, the redoubtable Sherpa, Tenzing. Nepal is a land of few motorized vehicles; people still walk wherever they go, even between cities a hundred miles apart, over ground which might fairly be described as hilly (the Himalayas). Tenzing is a worthy representative of the earth's greatest walking people, the Sherpas of Nepal.

(10) *Some nameless Buddhist pilgrim,* inch-worming his way from the plains of India over the mountain passes and across the Tibetan plateau to Lhasa. The approved system apparently involves a procedure as follows: (a) stand facing Lhasa, (b) utter a prayer (you'll see why in a moment), (c) throw yourself prostrate on your chest, (d) regain your feet, now one body-length nearer to Lhasa.

Now repeat this procedure as often as necessary to cover 1000 miles or so. As you cross the higher mountain passes, it becomes tricky to keep snow off your tie. In the lower valleys, check for cobras before step (c). You think the Appalachian Trail is tough!

We can't help but observe the strikingly cosmopolitan character of this list—almost as varied nationally as an "all-American" soccer team. It shows how worldwide is the impulse to walk . . . to explore . . . to discover . . . to find out what is on the other side of that mountain pass. Our list includes:

one Jew	one Spaniard
one Chinaman	one American
one Italian	one Norwegian
one Scot	one Nepalese
one Swede	one Indian

If any country deserves more credit for its walkers, it would be England. Besides those great antarctic heroes we mentioned, Scott and Shackleton, and their men, we could have included others like Sir Richard Burton, the disguised explorer of then-unknown Arabia (and translator of *The Arabian Nights*); Sir Francis Younghusband, who walked from Peiping to India over the Mustagh Pass in the Karakoram; or the late H. W. Tilman, the mountaineer and intrepid walker who once *bicycled* across Africa, despite few roads, broad rivers, and hostile beasts and tribes—to mention a few impediments not encountered daily by most ten-speed aficionados today.

Walkers one and all: from Chocorua to Miriam Underhill, from Moses to the out-of-shape weekend backpacker on Mount Chocorua today, they all heed the mandate of Isaiah:

"This is the way, walk ye in it!"

PART II

The New Ethic

The Coming of the Vibram *Army*

FOR THE FIRST half of the twentieth century, those who went off for adventure in the backwoods were a small band of uncommon people. After World War II a number of factors began to conspire to change all that: higher incomes, increased leisure, what we call "improved" transportation (by which we mean "faster"). When the sixties came along, bringing widespread alienation from urban and technological values, the backpacking boom began. In the seventies it reached staggering proportions. There are different views of the prospects for the eighties and beyond: Some say the boom will level off, some say it will still grow. But no one says there will be fewer people out there.

We have watched this boom hit our New England woods and hills and we've felt the changes it has wrought. The caribou are gone from the windswept heights of Katahdin, but the people have come—by the hundreds and thousands. The shelters on Vermont's 262-mile Long Trail are crowded, carved up, and occasionally burned by hordes of inexperienced hikers. For New Hampshire's Great Gulf Wilderness, "they" have installed a permit system to limit the crowds to 60 *per night,* in a place where not that many walked through in a whole summer just a few years back. The cathedral-like silence and majesty of the hemlocks in Dark Entry Ravine are now off limits to Connecticut hikers, because a landowner got fed up with the nuisance and vandalism of the inconsiderate few. The Appalachian Trail passes through an exquisite grove of spruce just below Massachusetts' highest point, Mount Greylock; but you have little chance to contemplate that spruce glade, because the trail has been beaten into a muddy quagmire up to 50 feet wide, stomped out by the passing of the *Vibram* army. On Slide Mountain, the Catskills' highest summit, near a rock where John Burroughs once bivouacked alone under the stars, the landscape is blighted, trampled, and scarred in an ever-widening ring of hacked stumps as up to 100 campers per weekend have sought that elusive summit solitude which Burroughs

enjoyed. Last time we were there, a dull-witted porcupine sat impassively in a fireplace, feeding on his accustomed fare, the trash of the previous weekend's campers.

These are some of the changes we've seen in our New England since World War II. Across the country, the scene is similar. The Rockies and the Sierra and the Cascades have a little more room, but the popular magnets—the Tetons, Whitney, Rainier—are under the same kind of pressure as Katahdin, Slide, and the Long Trail. In Wyoming's Wind River Range, where some of our friends used to go to avoid the Tetons crowd, the once-pristine waters of Lonesome Lake are now polluted and the still meadows are pocked with tent sites.

Even the Himalayas feel the crunch. Tenzing views the destruction of trees for tourists' firewood along the popular trek routes, and warns in his autobiography: "The tourists who come to Nepal to see the wilderness are actually destroying it as they go along."

The changes are not all measured in numbers of hikers and their impact. In response to the *Vibram* army, restrictions have descended on backcountry camping; once-rough trails have been tamed with bridges and steps; "facilities" have been provided where campers were once on their own; the entire experience has been softened, the rough edges smoothed, the challenge finessed.

In the last few years, though, a further change has been slowly spreading. Backpackers are beginning to recognize the consequences of their own actions. A conscience is awakening. Concerned about *both* the physical destruction of the natural environment *and* the degradation of the spirit of wildness which numbers, restrictions, and facilities imply, many hikers and campers have begun to feel their way toward a new backwoods ethic. Thoughtful managers of wild lands, who are daily involved with the problems of the backcountry, have helped guide opinion in constructive channels—wisely recognizing that regulations are but a small if sometimes essential part of the answer. The newer guidebooks and magazines like *Backpacker, Wilderness Camping,* and *New England Outdoors* have promoted more environmentally conscious practices in how we use the woods in which we hike. The large hiking clubs, like New England's Appalachian Mountain Club and Green Mountain Club, have embraced the new concerns. We have already described the admirable program of the Adirondack Forty-Sixers. Not surprisingly, the Sierra Club is at the forefront in this campaign, and has published the first how-to-do-it book which places emphasis squarely on environmental concerns: John Hart's *Walking Softly in the Wilderness.*

In this second section, we talk about this new backwoods ethic, as it implies changes in the habits and attitudes of *the individual hiker*. Later we'll get to the equally important question of how those who manage the wild lands in which we hike are modifying their approaches. But for now we speak of cookstoves and canines, of sneakers and hammocks, . . . and some ways of looking at the same old woods and hills with a new and awakened environmental concern.

6

"Clean Camping" Crusade

There is, nevertheless, a certain respect, and a general duty of humanity, that ties us, not only to beasts that have life and sense, but even to trees and plants.

Michel de Montaigne

WE THINK of the woods and hills as eternal, and most of the time from man's puny perspective, they are. And yet what a change is going on under those trees! Our camping fathers of pre–World War II would be astonished if they could come along on a modern backpack.

CHANGES IN CAMPING

On a recent three-day camping trip in New Hampshire's Pemigewasset Wilderness, we were struck with how different it all was from when we got started camping years ago. We were with a large group of campers in the "Pemi," a sizable chunk of rolling forest surrounded by peaks of the White Mountains. There were fourteen of us altogether. The seven two-person tents were the latest sleek nylon lightweight models, the brilliant colors ranging all over the rainbow (except purple). Each pair of campers reached into aluminum packframes and pulled out portable cookstoves fuelled with white gas. No one even suggested we build a crackling warm campfire. Had anyone started to cut himself a bough bed for extra comfort, he'd have been attacked with an ax—except that none of us even carried an ax or hatchet. Though we camped near the banks of Lincoln Brook one night—nearer than we should have—no one washed in the waters, and when "nature called" each person went well back into the woods away from stream and trail to answer.

Our group violated some canons of the new ethic. We were too many, to begin with. In the Adirondacks and the Wilderness areas of the White Mountains, responsible managers are trying to discourage groups of over ten. Those brightly colored tents are more of an intrusion on the woods scene than they need be ("like a light you can never turn off," says conservationist-author John Hart). And we should have gone farther from the banks of Lincoln Brook.

Still, if you went back to the places we camped on that trip, you'd find no sign of our having been there. Indeed, it might be hard to find the sites at all. Where the tents were, no tent has subsequently been, and the forest floor is well on its way back. You'd find no blackened fire ring, no stripped branches or bark, no cut boughs, no dug latrine, no litter or can pit unearthed by animals.

When we were on that trip, we couldn't help but think back with a smile to what it was like when we were learning how to live in the woods in the years just after the war, but before prewar camping technology and habits had changed.

Back in the thirties, Doc Waterman guided canoe parties down the Allagash every summer, and the camping way of life of the Maine north woods in those days was the pattern which his son Guy first learned. On Girl Scout trips just a few years later, Laura was schooled in the same equipment and techniques, which she practiced faithfully over Vermont and New Hampshire hills in the fifties.

Tents were larger and much heavier, with no sewn-in floors, and the color was invariably a kind of monotone noncolor somewhere between brown, green, and grey. Sleeping bags alone weighed about as much as an entire overnight pack docs today.

Camping without a campfire would have been unthinkable. We all carried an ax and/or hatchet (depending on the trip) and one of the first jobs on reaching camp was to scour the area for a judicious mixture of the right hard woods plus a little soft wood for kindling.

Thirsty? Drink out of any stream.

Dirty? Grab the soap, strip, and plunge into the nearest stream—yes, the same one you drank out of, but maybe downstream a little.

For a comfortable night's sleep, we learned to cut spruce branches and arrange them just right. In case of rain, we'd dig a small ditch around the uphill side of the tent.

In today's environmentally concerned world, we shudder to recall some of these camping habits. Yet for their time, there was nothing wrong with this way of living in the woods. In those days you could run the Allagash and the lakes around it for six weeks and see maybe two or three other parties, plus the lonely fire warden on Allagash Mountain who talked to himself unless you were there to talk to, and old Frank whose team toted your gear across the carry between Mud Pond and Umbazooksus on mud-rutted roads. Miles of true wilderness with no one else around—so it really was O.K. to take dead wood and even some live, wash in the streams, cut bough beds. It was sound woodsmanship. But in the wake of the backpacking boom of the sixties and seventies, it was a way of life that could not continue.

Consider an incident that we often recall when we think about the changing camping scene.

July 7, 1966. One of us (Guy) and two teenage sons were climbing Mount Moosilauke. This is a big slumbering giant of a mountain with a massive rounded top, not at all a picture-book summit like Chocorua or the Matterhorn. Though among the ten highest in New Hampshire's White Mountains, it stands way off by itself to the southwest, as if dropped there after all the other peaks were finished.

The three of us had been hiking for two weeks straight and were feeling in fine shape as we raced up the rough trail to the summit in late afternoon. On our way down, just below the summit, we passed two Boy Scouts. Exchanging the usual trailside courtesies, we asked where they were headed.

"Beaver Brook Shelter," said one of them.

Now this news was of passing interest, since we too planned to spend the night at that shelter, which lay at the foot of the trail, almost 3000 feet below.

Gingerly we asked: "How many in your party?"

"Fourteen."

Well, there's about room for six in that shelter, crowding it some, and it looked like rain. So we decided we'd better pour it on if we wanted a place under the roof. Being in the shape we were in, and large Scout groups travelling at the pace they do, we had no trouble passing them in bunches of twos and threes until, well before the end of the trail, we had counted fourteen, and could let up our pace a little.

When the first Scouts got down to Beaver Brook Shelter, they found our three sleeping bags rolled out. We were models of woods manners in offering them what was left of the shelter space. However, their leader cheerfully assured us: "That's O.K., we'll go camp a little way off toward the pond."

So we had a nice quiet evening alone in the shelter after all. But just before dark it began to rain and conscience began to prod us into wondering how the Scouts were making out. What we found is a scene that sticks in memory: a beehive of activity, centering around an enormous jerry-built lean-to, large enough to sleep fourteen underneath, with long fresh-cut poles (easily 6 inches in diameter) lashed together and covered over with a thick matting of fresh-cut evergreen branches. The Scouts had it almost completed when we got there, and had a roaring campfire stocked with plenty of wood. The entire area was trampled thoroughly with the milling and scuffling of thirteen eager Scouts. The crowning touch was that their leader was idly sitting by the fire whittling—a sure sign that the troop had performed this ritual many times before, thus requiring no direction.

Just multiply that troop of fourteen by several hundred other Scouting outfits, summer camps, outdoor clubs, and college outing societies—then multiply by twelve, for each of the years that has passed since 1966—and then try to imagine what would be left of the woods, had that pattern continued unchecked.

THIRTY TENETS OF CLEAN CAMPING

Nightmare speculation like that makes us welcome the "clean camping" crusade that has begun to inspire modern campers.

What is "clean camping"? It's perhaps too fancy a name. Certainly we don't wish to brand all other camping practices as "dirty." It's simply a convenient handle for referring to all those changes in attitudes and practices which reflect today's campers' concern for preserving the backwoods environment into which they migrate in great numbers these days. Here are some of the steps which we see the thoughtful camper of today trying to take:

(1) To camp at maintained and designated sites where local customs or regulations so require. Or, when in areas where camping sites are more a matter of individual choice, ...

(2) To camp 200 feet from water and trail. This helps distribute and therefore lessen impact on the forest.

(3) To be careful *where* you pitch your tent. The undergrowth is fragile. It's wise to try to disturb it as little as possible.

(4) To go back and forth to water source and trail as few times as possible and by different routes, so as not to tread out a discernible track.

(5) To fan out, whenever travelling off-trail, rather than tramping single file, thereby starting a herd path that could become a trail.

(6) To stay off trails during what we in New England call "mud season"—that time of early spring when the snows are finally melting and the trails are rivers of mud. That's when they're most vulnerable. The Green Mountain Club even officially discourages its members from hiking in Vermont then.

(7) To avoid camping in fragile areas, especially at timberline, or among the alpine flowers of the tundra. In western regions, mountain meadows are especially vulnerable, we're told.

(8) To stay on-trail when moving above treeline, or else to walk on rocks rather than on the vulnerable vegetation. Rock-hopping can be fun anyway. The key point is not to tramp heedlessly over delicate tundra.

(9) To limit group size. One of the primary findings of the 1977 report of the Adirondacks' High Peaks Wilderness Advisory Committee was that groups of more than ten hikers have "a greater pressure on the resource than would the same number of users as individual day hikers or backpackers." Both in federal Wilderness Areas and in the Adirondacks, official policy frowns on groups of over ten.

(10) To keep voices down near other parties, and especially to keep quiet after dark. As for radios ... ?!?!

(11) To carry out every scrap of litter. Even burying cans doesn't work, since animals dig them up.

(12) To refrain from picking flowers (especially where at all rare) or otherwise collecting irreplaceable natural objects.

(13) To leave birchbark on the trees.

(14) To use restraint in foraging for wild food. Some of it's self-renewing, some isn't.

(15) *Not* to wash in streams—oneself or dishes.

(16) *Not* to cut bough beds.

(17) *Not* to ditch around tents.

(18) To put on sneakers or moccasins after reaching the night's campsite. Cleated *Vibrams* tear up the groundcover something awful. More on this in chapter 7.

(19) Sometimes even to use as shelter a hammock and tarp. This gets you off the ground, so you won't have to worry about leaving a matted, crushed, and compacted tentsite. More on this in chapter 8.

(20) To purchase tents and packs of softer colors—green or brown—rather than the flaming reds and oranges that stand out so blatantly from far away, and trumpet your presence to every other passing hiker.

(21) To use a portable cookstove—not a fire. It's easier on the woods if fuel is scarce (and even if it isn't), lessens possibility of forest fires, won't damage forest floor, and is convenient—no smoke-blackened pots for one thing. More on this in chapter 9.

(22) To take special pains, if you *do* insist on a fire, to keep it safe and small, and to destroy all evidence of its having been there when you leave.

(23) To carry a gallon plastic water container so that you won't beat a path to the stream by repeated trips.

(24) To cover human waste with a layer of soil. It's biodegradable and will be gone in a week. The old-fashioned camp latrine, a giant hole in the forest floor, simply isn't necessary, and doesn't disappear as soon.

(25) To choose a different campsite every time. Most important: Never camp where someone else has. It's repeated use of the same site that causes the damage.

(26) To limit use of any one site to two or at most three nights. (Some would say just one night.) It's rather difficult to stay longer in one place and not have it look—and *be*—well-worn.

(27) To have consideration for the local regulations when pack animals are used. Nothing tears up mountain meadows and trails or pollutes watersheds quite so much as a string of horses, mules, or burros.

(28) To cooperate with the sometimes onerous restrictions which Wilderness managers install to cope with the impact of people.

(29) To contribute constructive thinking to the problem. Those in charge are looking for ideas, and "public involvement" is a by-word in the lexicon of modern backcountry management.

(30) To remember, every time you're walking up a trail, that the *mountain environment is fragile.*

The gospel of "clean camping" is being propagated by many organizations as well as by concerned individuals. The Appalachian Mountain Club has held workshops and published brochures on the subject. We described earlier what the Adirondack Forty-Sixers have been doing. We'll presently (see chapter 8) be describing one of several progressive summer camp programs. On a nationwide basis, the Sierra Club is preaching the doctrine of walking softly in the wilderness. The U.S. Forest Service is promoting more responsible backwoods practices on the part of visitors to National Forests. Progressive equipment sellers, like Gerry of Colorado and the Quabaug Rubber Company, have published and distributed to customers pamphlets detailing the need to change camping practices: Gerry's is titled "How To Camp and Leave No Trace," and it's a classic essay on what it will take to preserve the wilderness for future generations.

OBSTACLES TO CLEAN CAMPING

All these efforts to reform camping habits are up against an array of formidable and diverse obstacles, including the frontier tradition, democratic ideals, modern education theories, ideas of personal freedom, motherhood, the sociability of clubs, the mystique of the old campfire, the *Vibram* sole, and the black fly. That's an opposing lineup powerful enough to awe the most dedicated reformer.

(1) The frontier tradition. Too many hikers still have an image of going out to "conquer" the wilderness rather than live with it or as a part of it. David Langlois, a Vermont camp director whom we'll be talking more about later, cautions: "We try to remember that we're spending a night, not founding a settlement...."

(2) Democratic ideals. A lot of people think that if the woods are good for some of us, then everyone should have an opportunity to experience this blessing. You can be labelled an elitist if you see anything wrong with getting everybody in the entire city of Boston to tramp through the most beautiful sections of New England's woods. What would be left of the beauty when this had come to pass?

(3) Modern educational theories. Spearheaded by the highly successful Outward Bound program, many camps and school courses now see it as their mission to get every kid in the region to experience "survival" and "challenge" (the latest fad words) in the remote backcountry.

(4) Ideas of personal freedom. We are strongly in favor of as much freedom in the hills as can possibly be maintained in this day and age. But we sense that many hikers use personal freedom as a license for irresponsible habits in the backcountry. Of what value is the freedom to take a bath (with soap) in any mountain cascade you come to, if the result is a polluted water supply for the party that's camping downstream?

(5) Motherhood. How's that again? We're simply referring to the underlying fact of the population growth. That is, after all, what got us into this mess to begin with. Fundamentally it's a problem of simply too many people.

(6) The sociability of clubs. Nothing destroys the illusion of wilderness faster than running into a party of 20 or 30 people travelling together. Camp groups are among the worst offenders. Most clean camping advocates urge limiting group size, and many clubs have at last put an end to group discounts on club facilities. Yet club traditions die hard, and many hiking groups still schedule mass ventures, with large mobs of sociable hikers blasting along the trail making a mockery of everyone's hopes for a feeling of wilderness solitude.

(7) The mystique of the old campfire. One of the most deeply entrenched camping notions is that you're just not doing it right unless you build a blazing fire. This emotional subject deserves separate discussion (see chapter 9). Suffice it to raise here the question which the Appalachian Mountain Club has posed in a poster: "What if we *all* built fires?"

(8) The Vibram *sole.* Actually one of the biggest impacts of the backpacking boom is in the scuffing up of groundcover by that obsolescent status symbol, the *Vibram* sole. That's why many clean camping advocates urge everyone to take a pair of moccasins or sneakers to change into after reaching campsite.

(9) The black fly. Even this pesky insect has its impact. How's that? Because camping in hammocks does far less damage to the woods than tenting—but if you try to sleep in a hammock during black fly season, you come to realize that your dedication to clean camping has its price. When is someone going to come up with an effective and simple mosquito netting for a hammock, like the old World War II jungle hammocks that you don't see any more?

All of these obstacles to camping reform will make it difficult. But if we all go on abusing the wilds, we're going to run into restrictions and rules that will spoil it for everyone.

We don't greet these new attitudes and practices as unmixed blessings. Sometimes we're sad to see the change from those old days. Often we yearn for the yesterday when you could hike all day and never see another person. Our personal tastes run to the drab old canvas wall tents, rather than the sleek nylon International Orange light-weights. We love to wield an ax—and do so plenty, but at home in our own woodlot, not on overrun hiking country. Who is there that does not respond to the warm conviviality of the campfire? Sometimes we truly feel we were born too late—the golden age of camping lies buried in the good old days.

Sometimes we're more optimistic and feel good about the new era—to see that man is capable of adapting his exploitative ways, of trying to soften the weight of his impact, of conserving a natural world that renews and enriches the human spirit.

They say that an optimist thinks that this is the best of all possible worlds, and a pessimist fears that's the case. This dichotomy applies to attitudes about the changing camping scene. Pessimist or optimist, we have to acknowledge that it is changing.

In the 1840's and 1850's, Henry David Thoreau visited the Maine woods. As we read his narratives, we recognize many of the spots he visited. He too walked the carry from Umbazooksus to Mud Pond, and it was just as mud-rutted then as it was when we were there in 1946. The interesting point is that in many ways there was *less* change in Maine's north woods during the entire century from Thoreau's first trip in 1846 to ours in 1946, than there was in the 30 years from 1946 to 1976. The opening of the Allagash Waterway to vacationers, the new roads, the seaplanes, the big camp groups—all have completely altered the scene. Well, not completely. Some things don't change. The loon still sounds his enigmatic laugh. You can still experience today what Thoreau wrote about:

> It is a country full of evergreen trees, of mossy silver birches and watery maples, the ground dotted with insipid small red berries, and strewn with damp and moss-grown rocks—a forest resounding at rare intervals with the note of the chickadee, the blue jay, and the woodpecker, the scream of the fish-hawk and the eagle, the laugh of the loon, and the whistle of ducks along the solitary streams. . . .

Years ago, when the onslaught of the tourists began hitting the Alps and the English hills, the great Scottish climber Norman Collie wrote:

> Civilization has stretched out its hand and changed it all, and though those who knew the old days are somewhat sad that the old order has changed, yielding place to new, yet the new order is good, and the land of the great woods, lakes, mountains, and rushing rivers is still mysterious enough to please anyone who has eyes to see, and can understand.

7

Of Boots, Sneakers, and Grandmothers

Even in the land of Goshen
Hard lug soles cause erosion.

Winslow Thratchett

THE TALISMAN of today's hiker–backpacker is his boots. The hiker without his boots is like the hunter without his gun, the fisherman without his rod, Heifetz without his violin, Babe Ruth without his bat, Evil Kneivel without his motorcycle. And yet the image of the traditional hiking boot is changing, partly as a result of the new way we look at our hiking surroundings.

Throughout most of our hiking years until recently, virtually every experienced hiker we've met on the trail has been shod in a heavy, stiff-soled boot. The things make a terrific racket tiptoeing across a mountain cabin floor, and they track in dirt and mud every time they step inside. But no self-respecting backpacker dares be seen without his (or her) mammoth boots. We've got ours— it's been a badge of the tribe.

In fact, during the past decade's boom in outdoor recreation, the heavy, lug-soled hiking boot has become a kind of status symbol. Everyone who covets an outdoorsy reputation has to clomp around on big, stiff waffle-stompers. College co-eds, newly signed up for the outing club, stomp from class to class in their hiking boots with 3/8-inch raised cleats of *Vibram*.

ARGUMENTS AGAINST LUG SOLES

Lately the first signs of a revolution are peeping over the horizon. Two points are occurring to lots of outdoors walkers. The first is an environmental consciousness. The second is the question of whether the heavy boots are really necessary.

The environmentalist conscience has beset backwoods hikers in a big way in the past five or six years. Many backpackers now advocate environment-saving measures such as those we described in the last chapter.

When this environmental conscience took a look at the mud tracked in on the cabin floor, it began to ask some embarrassing questions. Questions like: Where did all that mud come from? Lug-soled boots were picking up a little bit of every trail they passed over and were carrying it out to shelters, cars, and homes. The impact of heavy, cleated boots on trail erosion began to be noticed.

A hiker named William Harlow determined experimentally that those little raised-earth footprints left by a cleated sole tend to wash away in rainstorms. Harlow found that the amount of earth left so exposed by one cleated sole weighs close to an ounce. Figuring a 2½-foot stride, he computed that one hiker travelling one mile leaves 120 pounds of raised earth in his footprints, ready to be eroded down the trail at the first rain.

Carry that logic out and you'll find that a party of four lug-soled hikers walking up a 5-mile trail just before a rain just might be responsible for a *ton* of earth washing down. That's a lot of backcountry being washed down into frontcountry.

Harlow wrote up his results for *Backpacker* magazine, arguing strenuously for hikers to use smooth-soled boots or light-weight footgear for any kind of travel except the most demanding mountaineering. "... Millions of backpackers," proclaimed Harlow, "wear lug soles in country where such footing contributes little to hikers' safety, yet claws at trails and smashes vegetation in cross-country rambles."

One environmentally concerned camp director in Vermont outfits all his campers in both boots and some sort of lighter shoe like moccasins or sneakers. "In campsite: Take off your *Vibram* soled shoes as soon as you can," he tells his people. "Sneakers, moccasins, or even bare feet, have far less impact on the ground cover."

There's no question that lug soles are tough on a wet trail. As we mentioned, Vermont's Green Mountain Club has officially urged its members not to hike during the early spring mud season because of the damage hiking boots can do when trails are wet.

So far we see little evidence on hiking trails that many hikers are giving up their beloved lug soles. But the environmentalist anti-*Vibram* reaction is strong enough to have engaged the attention of the Quabaug Rubber Company of Massachusetts, American manufacturers of the *Vibram* soles, which are by far the most widely used lug sole. This company has issued a public-spirited booklet on how to minimize hiker impact on the backcountry and has produced a variety of alternative soles that would cause less damage to trails.

"But I don't think they would sell," laments Quabaug's President Herbert M. Varnum. "They don't have the 'climbing look' that is in such demand."

If it were just an environmental conscience that argued against lug-soled heavy boots, the move to other footgear probably wouldn't get very far.

However, while relatively few hikers seriously ask "What are we doing to the environment?" quite a few are now starting to ask: "What are we doing to ourselves?" A lot of walkers we know are wondering whether it's really necessary to carry all that weight around at the end of each leg. Might it not be a lot more practical to wear something lighter and more comfortable? Are heavy hiking boots really necessary for safety or other reasons?

Grandma Gatewood, the fabulous woman who hiked the entire 2000-mile Appalachian Trail three times—the *first* time at age 67—wore sneakers. Perhaps she was the original Little Old Lady in Tennis Shoes. If Grandma Gatewood could hike 2000 miles in sneakers, does Joe Athlete really need heavy boots with lug soles?

Another grandmother, the Adirondacks' super-hill-walker, Trudy Healy—who climbed all 46 of the 4000-foot mountains in the Adirondacks at least six times and wrote the first guide to rock climbing in that region—originally climbed those 46 peaks in sneakers. So did her six children.

In the past few summers we've noticed that some of the young people who work in the high mountain huts of the Appalachian Mountain Club have discarded their big black hiking boots—formerly so much a symbol of their hiking prowess that many hut guests wondered whether the boots were surgically appended to their feet. Now we occasionally see hut people clad in sneakers or Adidas running shoes.

As mentioned in chapter 2, in the summer of 1977 two of these hut boys traversed all eight high huts in a single 16-hour day—racing up and down 49 miles of rough mountain trail with elevation changes of over 1000 feet at many points along the way. The two chose to wear Adidas rather than hiking or mountaineering boots for the incredible jaunt. Their achievement struck a body blow to the conventional wisdom that rugged hiking requires big heavy boots.

One American friend who now lives and hikes in Switzerland is a devotee of Adidas. "From the store shelf to an 8-hour walk and never a hint of a blister," she writes. "Dear me, when I think of all those bandaids and moleskin consumed! To say nothing of the weight. . . ."

Another friend recently travelled to the Andes to climb several high peaks, one over 20,000 feet. For the upper snowfields, he took mountaineering boots, but as high as 16,000 feet, he wore simple running shoes.

The idea is that hiking boots are simply a whole lot heavier than they need to be. Undeniably they give more ankle support than sneakers, but they also take their toll in having to be picked up and set down at every step.

One friend of ours, embarking on a long hike involving major ascents and descents through the mountains, carried both hiking boots and sneakers. On the uphills he wore the sneakers and carried the hiking boots, feeling much lighter afoot that way. Then on each summit he'd switch to the hiking boots and carry the sneakers for the jarring descents on those rocky trails.

Those super-walkers, the Sherpas of Nepal, have not traditionally enjoyed the questionable benefits of big heavy boots. Many walk their rugged trails barefoot, even crossing snow passes unshod. These days, we're told, the Sherpas that escort visiting hill-walkers on treks through Nepal's hill country wear a colorful variety of sandals, sneakers, work boots—whatever westerners' largesse may have brought them—and still occasional bare feet.

TYPES OF FOOTGEAR

In our rambles through New England's woods and mountains, we've noticed a wide assortment of footgear. Some of it seems to work quite well. Some seems distinctly out of place. Here are some of the things we notice on people's feet:

(1) Hiking boots with *Vibram* soles. There are a wide variety available, most of them made in Europe. They tend to come part way up the ankle to provide support, but they are not really a high boot. The lug soles vary in thickness from something not much thicker than the soles of street shoes, to great heavy pads that must add close to an inch of height to the wearer—not to mention pounds of weight.

(2) Woodsman's or hunting boots after the style pioneered by L. L. Bean. The original Bean boot is an authentic piece of Americana, much loved and *much* worn by its devotees. A number of similar boots have cropped up. Cowhide above and tough rubber below, they're durable, waterproof, and comfortable. The ankle support is not quite as solid, but the softer rubber tread is a lot easier on the woods' paths than lug soles.

(3) Sneakers, or the various contemporary equivalents much in vogue with runners. In the old days, "real" hikers disdained sneakers as the mark of a know-nothing novice, but as we've described, this traditional view has been badly shaken in recent years. Be it heresy, we see no reason why beginners can't do a lot of walking in sneakers before they decide to take the plunge and buy something more ambitious.

(4) Mountaineering boots. Climbers who do the big mountains out west or in Europe—or in New England in winter—sometimes get a pair of enormous mountaineering boots so well broken in that they're comfortable even on modest hikes in summertime New England. From the number of big mountaineering boots we see on the trails, we wonder if the status symbol value of such boots doesn't also contribute to their popularity.

(5) Work boots. The plain ordinary work boot is built to be rugged. If it's comfortable on the job or around the house, it may be perfectly feasible for moderate hiking. We've seen plenty of contented hikers in work boots. They don't win points for fashion, but they feel good on the feet, and their soft rubber tread is a lot easier on woods and meadows.

(6) Combat boots. Those high, close-laced monstrosities left over from the service seem to suit some hikers fine. They don't *look* that comfortable to us, but we have no experience with them.

(7) A diversity of sandals, raised-heel women's shoes, cowboy boots, and

various indescribable curiosities. We'd put these in the class of *not* recommended. You'll give your feet quite a workout over ten miles of mountain trail—or even two miles. What may feel nice and look great indoors or around a couple of city blocks of level surface just won't make it over rocky terrain. We'd put most moccasins in this category, even if the Indians may have done a good deal of walking in them. But moccasins or sandals are perfect around camp, as they are very easy on the undergrowth.

(8) Bare feet. Not our bag. Actually for all its appeal on grassy lawns, going barefoot isn't very practical either in the woods or on rocky trails.

A knowledgeable New England hiker, Nicholas Howe, himself a convert to the lightweight running shoe, tells a revealing story about the British army in the African campaign of World War II. The high command was concerned that their footsoldiers, scuffing across the desert wastes, were increasing the weight of their footgear by the sand sifting into their shoes. One day when they weren't being chased by Rommel, they did some calculations and figured that to offset the energy needed to pick up this extra weight, each man needed to be fed 250 pounds more rations every six months. The word came down: Every soldier was to empty the sand from his shoes—often.

Try it yourself—not the sand-emptying part, but the calculations. Weigh your hiking boots: 3½ pounds each? Weigh your sneakers: 0.75 pounds each? Howe figures that you take roughly 2000 steps a mile. Would you rather lift 3½ tons with every mile, or "only" 1500 pounds?

We think Howe has a point. (His article, "Boots/Roots," from the October/November 1978 issue of *Backpacker* magazine is a gem, highly recommended.) We confess we haven't made the switch ourselves—that's because we're devotees of that greatest of all hiking boots, the Stradivarius of shoes, the Limmer boot. These plain black boots, with all the stylishness of a baked potato, are custom-made by the family of an old Bavarian bootmaker, Peter Limmer, and one of our pairs is in its fourteenth year and fifth set of soles. But if our beloved old Limmers ever wear out, we'll probably wise up and join the ranks of the little old ladies in tennis shoes. In time the whole *Vibram* army may make the switch, and the woods will be a lot better off.

Ah now, if we could only get old Peter Limmer's grandson to design a sneaker. . . .

CASE STUDY

The Alpine Aster Caper

I will be the gladdest thing under the sun!
I will touch a hundred flowers and not pick one.

Edna St. Vincent Millay

TALK ABOUT mystery thrillers, whodunits, C.I.A. plots, Watergate cover-ups. We've not been involved in international spy rings, but one recent summer we went through a spine-tingling game of intrigue and conspiracy right in our New England back hills.

It all concerned a tiny flower no bigger than the eraser on your pencil. It grows in little clusters, each group about the size of a quarter, in rocky terrain high up in the mountains.

What brings mystery and intrigue to this minuscule plant is one simple fact: There is only one small colony of the species known to exist *in the entire western hemisphere*. Talk about an endangered species!

This rarest of rare flowers also happens to be about as fragile as any little plant can be. One careless or ignorant pair of boots walking through its alpine home, and a major share of its population would be destroyed—roughly the equivalent of dropping hydrogen bombs simultaneously on New York, Los Angeles, Chicago, and Plains, Georgia.

Given the extreme fragility of this precious alpine flower, you can imagine the zeal with which its location is guarded by botanists and mountain-lovers. The principal defense, in a world regrettably full of wanton vandals, is to keep quiet about where the rare colony makes its home. Old-timers may remember those World War II posters: Button your lip, loose talk costs lives, somebody talked (the last accompanied by a morbid scene of a troop ship sinking beneath the waves). That's the spirit in which the guardians of this plant react to any inquiries from outsiders. We came to agree with the policy of secrecy as a way of protecting this beautiful plant, and so we have invented a name for the flower and the mountain on which it is located. Call it the alpine aster. Say it's on Giant Mountain, near a high shelter for backpackers called Grandview Shelter.

One rainy June—all Junes are rainy in our mountains—we went to see this plant. We soon found ourselves involved in a cat-and-mouse game that any Hollywood script-writer would have loved. You know the kind of plot—probably would have starred Bogart and Bacall, and certainly Peter Lorre and Sydney Greenstreet in supporting roles. Maybe Hitchcock directing. Only instead of the flea-bitten bazaars of Bagdad or dark seedy bars in Dakar, this scenario played on the unlikely set of a wind-swept New England mountainside.

There are a whole lot of alpine flowers to see, study, and photograph in the above-treeline zone on Giant Mountain, and many of them come into bloom about the same time. For that reason, Grandview Shelter is crammed full every night during late June with botanists and other scientists, amateur and professional photographers, as well as the usual traffic of climbers and hikers.

In fact, the region's hiking club stations a full-time naturalist at Grandview Shelter for several weeks at the height of the flower-blooming season. This naturalist has several duties: to lead walks, to tell people about the flowers, to urge all hikers to stay on the trails or rocks so as not to disturb the delicate plants—and, it turns out, to guard the precious secret of the location of the alpine aster.

When we first arrived at Grandview Shelter, we elbowed our way through a diverse crowd of botanists and ecologists, photographers and artists. Many had cameras dangling from their necks, and nearly all clutched field guides. One or two had binoculars for bird-watching, but the chief preoccupation of most was obviously the flowers. There were whole groups from the botanical gardens and flower clubs of the larger nearby cities. There were student groups, under the tutelage of lean, bearded professors or earnest young graduate students fresh with their degrees in Ecology or Conservation or other subjects that weren't in the curriculum when we last saw a college.

We were accompanying one of the country's leading nature photographers, a woman with an uncanny ability to capture on film the beauty of natural subjects. She had never visited this alpine zone, and many of the delicate flowers of the tundra were new to her. She came armed with multiple rolls of film, and an inspiring enthusiasm and knowledge. Our job—done for love, not pay— was to guide her and her husband safely up and down the mountain and take her to the most interesting plant colonies.

We had heard of the rare alpine aster and were anxious that our friend have an opportunity to see and photograph it. Therefore, soon after our arrival, we sought out the resident naturalist at Grandview Shelter. We approached him in a spirit of genial friendliness and innocently asked where he might recommend we go to see the best floral displays.

Our innocence was instantly disabused. The resident naturalist—cast Sydney Greenstreet here—was a large, loud man who immediately sensed that we were on the trail of the alpine aster. He turned hostile right there. Instead of any useful suggestions for our flower hunt, he brushed us off saying that there were flowers all over the place up here, and sternly warned us to stay on the trails. If we had ideas about flowers growing away from the trails, he warned, "Just take my word for it that they're there; you just keep to the trails." This advice is given to everyone up there, to try to keep people from walking all over the flowers—but it also keeps the curious from getting too close to the delicate alpine aster.

We were a bit taken aback. Up in the mountains, most people you meet are friendly and relaxed. Indeed, the hiking club who sponsors this resident natural-ist program makes a big point of employing only cordial and outgoing young people to represent them in meeting the hiking public in the mountains. Yet Greenstreet here came on surly, if not actually belligerent.

We went outside the shelter. Up on the mountainside, a group of enthusiastic youngsters were having loads of fun playing among some rocky crags. Along came a zealous young lady, field guide and camera in hand, trailed by a troupe of botanists from Philadelphia. Hearing the happy cries of the children, her face darkened and she screamed at them to get down off the rocks and back on the trail. We winced.

We spent a pleasant two days poking along the trails and hopping from rock to rock off-trail, while our friend snapped photo after photo and told us much about the fascinating little plants. The other botanists and photographers busily potted about, spouting Latin genus and species. Even Greenstreet opened up a bit and led an interesting nature walk after dinner one night.

But no word was spoken of the whereabouts of the alpine aster. Little whis-pered conversations would be held in dark corners of the shelter at night, or out among the tundra rocks when no one else was too close, as all the botanists who *didn't* know the secret location strove to identify those who *did*—while those who knew played dumb. Greenstreet wasn't talking.

Toward evening of the second day, a group of three stalwart hikers—not the field-guide-and-camera types at all—stopped at the shelter for the night and we happened to eat near the same spot. An unguarded word was spoken, furtive glances exchanged, mumbled pleas and promises of unspecified future favors passed. After dinner, we maneuvered one of them outside in the dusk, and there on the windswept mountain ridge, extracted a promise that after breakfast the next day, if we swore eternal silence and above all protected our source, we might. . . . As we glided back into the shelter, Greenstreet eyed us uneasily.

The next morning we were in luck. A dense fog bank had settled on the moun-tain, reducing visibility to less than 50 feet. Perfect weather for mystery and in-trigue. Our furtive band would be hidden in the mist from prying eyes. After breakfast, the seven of us—the three hikers and our party of four—slipped away from the shelter and groped through the thick cloud. After reaching the sup-posed site of the alpine aster, we fanned out to search the rocky ground mi-nutely. Knowing the delicacy of these tiny plants, we felt like we were walking around a mine field, carefully placing our clumsy *Vibram* soles on rocks only. In the dense fog, we made a strange and eerie phantasm: seven figures shrouded in rain gear, bent over, eyes fixed intently between the rocks below our feet, mov-ing in exaggerated slow motion through the mist. (Our photographer friend was too good a photographer to miss a picture of this weird scene.)

Finally, one of our hiker guides pronounced in sepulchral tones the awesome news that he was standing next to one of the plants. We went over to join him, treading as between hummingbird eggs, and soon spotted a half dozen more plants, eventually some 20 or 30. On hands and knees we made our obeisance to the tiny blossoms that it had taken us so long to track to their hidden lair. Periodically one of us would cast a wary glance about to be sure that we were still unobserved, that Peter Lorre was not sneaking up on us in the mist.

The little alpine asters were unbelievably small and defenseless. The risks that last surviving colony ran, so close to Grandview Shelter and its thundering herd of hikers, made the blood run chill.

After our delighted friend had taken a number of pictures, we thanked our three hikers, again pledged eternal secrecy, and each glided off into the cloud our separate ways.

There's a sequel to this tale, but it belongs more in the realm of Marx Brothers comedy than Alfred Hitchcock thriller.

We were attending a meeting of a search and rescue group on which we serve, when an employee of that previously mentioned hiking club described a rescue of an injured hiker from Grandview Shelter. "We just set the helicopter down on that flat area above Grandview and put the litter aboard and whisked her off."

We cringed. Visions of a dozen litter-carriers tramping over the entire colony of alpine aster crowded in on our minds, not to mention the effects of the flattening wind from the whirlybird's blades. At the first break in the meeting, we mumbled a question as to how often the helicopter landed on "that flat area" above Grandview Shelter. "Oh, every time we have any injured parties in that area, plus when we stock the shelter in the spring, then in the fall. . . ."

We crawled a little way back down off the ceiling. "Does . . . ," we whimpered, "does the helicopter pilot know where the . . . (dropping our voice to a barely audible whisper) the alpine aster is?"

Our genial friend from the hiking club looked momentarily nonplussed. "Gee, never thought of that. I'll check into it." We were later assured that the numerous landings in that area are careful to avoid the Sacred Presence.

Enough of the alpine aster. Aside from this rarest of the rare, which you shouldn't go see (notice that we're already talking like Greenstreet), the alpine zones of mountains in New England and the western states, and especially Alaska, abound in mountain flowers which you *should* go see. Yet when hikers walk through the tundra, they might not "see" any flowers at all.

How come?

Most people reaching that rugged terrain above treeline are first struck by the absence of vegetation, not its presence. Most of the plants are very, very low to the ground and many are minuscule in size. For the most part, the flowers themselves are tiny. Even though many are brightly colored—reddish pink, sky blue, sunny yellow, snowy white—they are not very obvious to the inexperienced eye. To appreciate truly these tiny wonders, one must get down to *their* level. That means stooping or crouching.

How these plants manage to survive is one of the great miracles of adaptation. They live above the land of trees, which means they are prey to the harshest elements: the full force of the wind, which can be formidable in their habitat, heavy rains, ice and snow, the temperatures of an arctic climate, as well as parching sun and a short growing season.

From the viewpoint of a plant, the desiccating effect of that relentless wind is one of the chief challenges. Over the eons, they have developed certain tricks that enable them to cope with the never-ending torments of Aeolus.

First, they grow close to the ground and stay there. (So there is a good reason why you develop a backache bending over to look at them.) Many, like the white-flowered *Diapensia,* grow in tight clumps or mats, to conserve moisture and heat as well as gain defense from the wind. Often you will see several species growing all together in such a tight-knit commune that it takes a trained eye to sort the bearberry willow from the black crowberry from the alpine azalea from the mountain heath.

Some, like the Labrador tea, have leaves that curve inward on themselves, forming a roll like a leaf of tobacco. This helps the plant to conserve moisture and prevents drying out. Often you will find a plant colony flourishing in the lee of a rock, while those beyond the rock's protection are not as healthy-looking. The rock affords some defense from the wind. The rock also absorbs heat and reflects it back on the plants, making a crude sort of natural greenhouse. Plants sheltered by a rock may blossom earlier. Of course, the growing season is very short and the plants must manage to bud, flower, and seed themselves all in the months of June, July, and August.

We speak of these flowers as being fragile and delicate. Indeed they are—a few misplaced boots can obliterate a colony or even a species. But when it comes to withstanding the demands of their cruel environment, they put *homo sapiens* to shame. We hikers and backpackers are merely visitors to their alpine zone. Those who have spent a blustery, rainy day above treeline are glad to get back down to the shelter of the trees. Those who have walked the open ridges in winter know just how wild and unforgiving the elements can be up there. Few people care to spend even one night, much less their entire lives, in the home of these "fragile" flowers. Conditions are just too tough for us.

Those closest to the mountain environment of New England—the leaders of such organizations as the Appalachian Mountain Club, Vermont's Green Mountain Club, and the Adirondack Mountain Club, plus the field men of the national forests and the state parks of the region—have developed a number of strategies for the defense of this beleaguered vegetation. It is heartwarming to see these men and women, most of them tough, rugged, and independent mountain spirits, working so hard for the welfare of such tiny flowers.

In the Green Mountains, ranger–naturalists hang around the above-treeline areas and counsel hikers (in a friendly spirit) about staying on trails and watching out not to step on the plants. Signs have been posted on the trails where they reach treeline to reinforce this message.

In both the Adirondacks and the White Mountains, ridge runners are employed to wander the high peaks, talking to hikers about camping regulations, safety concerns, and the need for care of the fragile ecosystem.

In the Adirondacks, under the leadership of a hiker and botanist named Ed Ketchledge, an experimental effort at reseeding eroded above-treeline summit areas has been under way for ten years now, and has succeeded in stabilizing plant colonies on previously eroded ground—as we described in discussing the work of the Forty-Sixers.

The Appalachian Mountain Club in the White Mountains has also started summit reseeding, as well as posting signs urging people to stay on trail.

To forestall some of the grosser damage caused unwittingly by the hiking public, several restrictions are now a matter either of law or of strong exhortation throughout northeastern uplands:

> No camping above treeline;
> No wood fires above treeline;
> No cutting of bough branches for bedding anywhere;
> No trenching of tents.

In the Adirondacks most shelters above 3500 feet have been removed, as attracting too many inconsiderate campers. In the White Mountains, many old shelters have been replaced by tent platforms, designed to contain the impact of larger numbers of campers than could fit in the old shelters.

In some places, zeal for the protection of the alpine vegetation has been carried to extremes, and little stone walls have been erected to channel foot traffic into a single path and leave the rest of the mountain to the plants. We'll have more to say on this subject later (see chapter 12), but for now suffice it to say that it is not easy to draw the delicate line between saving the flowers on the one hand, and regimenting hikers (or intimidating them). For our part, we think that hikers ought to put up with a good many restraints in the interest of preserving that exquisite alpine environment. Once alpine vegetation is destroyed, it is tough to get it back.

8

Low-Impact Camping:
Swinging in the Woods

That fellow's got to swing.

Oscar Wilde

EVERYONE knows that summer camps of inexperienced youths are the most destructive of campers, hacking up the woods, peeling birchbark, littering, and destroying others' solitude by their presence—right?

In one case at least—wrong! An outfit called Killington Adventure in Vermont has set out a program of low-impact camping that has far-reaching implications for today's overcrowded backwoods.

Killington's camp director, David Langlois, is an innovator who has thrown away the heavy groundcloth, tent, foam pad, and air mattress. He has gotten camping off the ground, where most of the impact occurs, and into the air. His campers, a couple of hundred scattered in two or three week sessions throughout the summer, swing from hammocks to get a good night's sleep. Furthermore, they get off-trail and away from shelters and streams to set up camp, so their presence doesn't bother others. Because of their airborne tactics, they can go into the most fragile fern bed or the most rock-strewn sloping mountainside and set up camp quite comfortably—and with minimum impact. Langlois claims that with his method he can camp a large group for several days in one spot and the next party through won't know that anyone has been there since the Indians left.

The implications for the problems of the crowded backwoods are tremendous. The impact of campers repeatedly tenting on the same sites is devastating: Soil compacts, groundcover dies, trees get hacked and peeled in the voracious search for firewood. Then come official restrictions on camping, caretakers telling you what you can't do, and the dead hand of "permits"—all taking away what was once the freedom of the hills.

Langlois seems to have charted the only pleasant way out of this vicious cycle that we have seen yet. His "clean camping" methods go far toward reducing the impact of even a large group's passing—as well as removing the justification for stifling restrictions.

HAMMOCKS

Symbol of the new trend in low-impact camping is the lowly hammock.

Centuries ago, Duke Alexander J. Hammock grew tired of sharing the four-poster with Lady Hammock, who snored violently. The duke came up with a marvellous invention. For years the hammock has been perceived as a place for a backyard siesta for the tired housewife or husband who just finished cutting the lawn. Now imaginative backwoodspeople are realizing that Duke Hammock's invention is a great way to spend the night in the woods. It sure beats air mattresses, foam pads, heavy ("light-weight") tents, roots or stones sticking into your back, rainwater running under the floor, condensation on the ceiling, and all the other disadvantages of being grounded. Go airborne and you enter a whole new world.

One thing which may have attracted the attention of backpackers was the hammock's utility in big-wall rock climbing. Out in Yosemite, where climbers may take several days to work their way up the sheer 3000-foot walls of El Capitan or Half Dome, the best and sometimes the only way to bivouac is to string a hammock between two pitons. Many hikers gaped in awe at heart-stopping photos of climbers snoozing contentedly with 2000 feet of empty air between them and the rock talus below. But eventually the image of these admired hard-men using hammocks began to sink in.

Some campers have used hammocks for years, even in such noninnovative establishments as the Army. Sailors used them to offset the roll and pitch of the sea. But their widespread adoption among backpackers is relatively new.

It's catching on fast. Langlois is not the first person to think of using a hammock for backwoods sleeping, but with his evangelical zeal to spread the word, he may yet do for the hammock what Ford did for the automobile, Segovia for the classical guitar, and Billy Jean for tennis. The move to the hammock is not confined to the east. In fact, western outdoors writer Russ Mohney reports that "the light-weight nylon hammock caught on strongly with western backpackers last season." Out in the Cascades, apparently, people use them not only for spending the night but also for an occasional trailside siesta in mid-afternoon.

There are risks, to be sure. Langlois reports that one night he strung his hammock with 16 inches of clearance off the ground, only to be awakened when a 17-inch high porcupine chose to pass under the bridge. In cold weather or winter conditions, hammocks may not be practical, and on a night when the bugs are out in full strength, you're in for trouble. Nevertheless, from our experience in making the switch from tent to hammock for summer backpacking, we pronounce it well worth the risks.

Duke Hammock's original model was built of hemp and flax, with brass fixtures, and most backyard hammocks for years were luxurious cloth and rope jobs, far too heavy and bulky to carry any distance. The modern backpacker's version is made of light-weight nylon mesh, incredibly light and so small you can stuff it into your pocket.

If you want to try this new approach to low-impact camping, here's all the equipment you need:

Hammock. Most equipment stores and mail order catalogs offer hammocks these days. Prices range from $3.50 to a little over $10 the last time we looked— a pretty minor investment when you compare it with purchasing a tent!

Tarp, 8 by 10 feet, either coated nylon (expensive) or 6 mil poly (cheap).

Nylon cord, about 20 feet.

Tent stakes, four.

To set up your hammock, choose two trees about 12 feet apart. Suspend your hammock 3 feet off the ground. Make sure it is tight as a bowstring—otherwise excessive sag will place you in a "jackknife" position.

Next, tie your nylon cord about 2 feet, or at nose level, over the hammock. Now you have two parallel lines, the hammock below, the cord above. Then throw your tarp over the cord and stake it out at the four corners. The tarp should be well away from the sides of the sleeping bag and, if properly staked, will act as a very effective waterproof cover in case you're cooking dinner in the rain.

Getting into your hammock can be a little tricky at first. If you're not careful, you can get dumped faster than a special prosecuter at a Saturday night massacre. Once mastered, though, you'll find the technique becomes routine. Here's one Rube Goldberg-approved version:

(1) Unstuff sleeping bag.

(2) Stand beside the hammock near the middle.

(3) Place stuff sack on the ground and stand on it (with boots off!).

(4) Step into sleeping bag and pull it up around you. Zip it about two-thirds shut. Pull top well around your shoulders and hold in place with chin or teeth.

(5) Find one edge of the hammock and pull it down past your thighs to just above the back of your knees. Sit down, being careful to position yourself in the center of the hammock. Keep the sleeping bag around your shoulders.

(6) Swing legs (and foot of sleeping bag, of course) into hammock.

(7) Adjust sleeping bag around back and head.

(8) Lie back and sleep!

If that sounds too intricate, here's a method that requires fewer acrobatics:

(1) Unstuff sleeping bag and spread it out in the hammock. That sounds easier than it is, but with patience and about five arms, you can eventually get it centered.

(2) Partially unzip bag.

(3) Sit down, carefully and precisely in the middle of the sleeping bag, legs dangling over the side. The consequences of not being precisely centered are probably too obvious to require mention. If you weren't right in the middle, pick yourself up, shake out the sleeping bag, and repeat step 1. Then try again.

(4) Raising one leg at a time, maneuver yourself into the bag. Again—carefully.

No, really ... with practice it's not all that difficult. The resulting sleep is beautiful. And there's never a root in the small of your back.

DISPERSED CAMPING

Switching from tent-and-groundcloth to hammock-and-tarp is one giant step toward leave-no-trace camping. An equally important step is to make a clean break from the old habit of heading for a shelter or known campsite. This is a good idea whether you're in hammock or tent.

Be sure to find out what the regulations are in your area. In New England, customs and requirements vary. Along the northern end of Vermont's Long Trail, for example, hikers are asked to stay only at the closed cabins ("camps" or "lodges" in local parlance) specifically provided for overnight camping; this is mostly private land, and the landowners are friendly to hikers largely on the assurance that indiscriminate camping along their land will not take place. In Maine's Baxter State Park, also, camping is limited to designated sites, on reservation. However, elsewhere in New England, for the most part, camping spots are virtually unlimited and perfectly "legal" as long as you stay 200 feet away from trail or stream. Pick a spot where water is not too far away, naturally—but do *not* camp on the stream bank, the way everyone used to, causing so many blighted "bootleg" sites.

Under a truly dispersed camping approach, no one will ever wind up in the same spot twice—and that's what will save the land from degradation. Part of your strategy should be to go back and forth to the trail by a different route each time you make the trip. Similarly, pick different paths to the water. That way you won't start a recognizable trail, one that might attract others to your site. (This precaution will have the added advantage of protecting you from theft if you leave your gear set up during the day when you are off hiking.)

Take your bearings carefully when you leave the trail, with a compass if necessary. If you don't find your way back to your gear, it could be a long cold night.

The advent of light-weight backpacking stoves also helps protect the environment. The age of indiscriminate campfires all over the woods is past.

When you break camp, make sure every scrap of litter is picked up. Brush in areas that look heavily trodden; this will help them to regenerate, as well as conceal your passing. If you do set up a tent, drag some dead branches over the ground you flattened.

Camp in your chosen spot only *once*. Repeated use will turn it into a "bootleg" campsite that will quickly be discovered by other backpackers, and progressive degeneration will set in.

ADVANTAGES OF LOW-IMPACT CAMPING

The advantages of the combined innovations of hammock plus dispersing into the woods are legion:

(1) Loads are lighter to carry, by several pounds;

(2) Camp is easier and quicker to set up;

(3) Camp can be set up anywhere (except above treeline, of course)—the weary search for level, smooth tent sites is over;

(4) No roots will stick into your back all night;

(5) No other people will be around (ah, solitude!), since it's so easy to set up off-trail, out of sight;

(6) There is no risk of theft when you're gone, since only you know where your "camp" is;

(7) No well-trained "wild" animals will be waiting to raid your pack at night, like those that inevitably take up residence at shelters (though you still have to guard food against passerby squirrels and other potential marauders);

(8) You won't have to deal with caretakers, restrictions, crowds, and other hassles;

(9) You will help reduce the pressure for more regulations, sure to come about if we all continue to squeeze into already overcrowded campsites.

Perhaps the most satisfying thing about practicing low-impact camping is the experience of opening your mind to trying a new approach. It's easy to fall into a rut of maintaining the same camping patterns—head for the same good old shelters, build that heart-warming campfire. But once these routines are thoroughly mastered, they can become dull, and you can become set in your ways. "Powerful indeed is the empire of habit," wrote the Roman Publius Cyrus. Trying new camping habits can be a satisfying and rewarding experience.

9

Low-Impact Cooking:
The Nightmare of Julia Child

A little fire is quickly out;
Which, being suffered, rivers cannot quench.

William Shakespeare

HEAVY RAINS continued to pour from the wild mountain clouds on our forlorn little tent all day. A little past noon we began to reach that elevated state of boredom that only those know who have been cooped up in a 5- by 7-foot space for 20 hours and have just about exhausted the eight basic ways of trying to sit or lie comfortably for long hours in a sleeping bag.

So we were delighted when the monotonous sound of descending water on the tent fly was suddenly—and most unexpectedly—supplemented by a barely discernible human voice crying to us from somewhere out there.

Now many backpackers love to hike in the rain. In New England's summers, you *have* to love hiking in the rain, because the good Lord of our hills sees to it that you get plenty of opportunity all summer long. The theory that the Almighty is practicing up for a new 40-day flood has its strongest empirical support in New England's weather trends. We hear it can be wet in the Cascades too, and on the coastline of Alaska and Washington State.

However, this was not summer. This was mid-March: temperatures in the mid-thirties, six hours' slog from the nearest road, every possibility that the chilling winter rain could be followed by temperatures plunging to zero or below—a situation, in short, where survival depends on keeping dry. Mad dogs and Englishmen may go out in India's noon-day sun, but they have sense enough to stay inside for New England's winter rain. Invitation to hypothermia! We were holing up in our tent, prepared to sit it out and be alive to enjoy some more climbing when good weather returned.

But what was that voice out there?

Two bedraggled backpackers stumbled up to our tent, obvious candidates for an emergency. Blue jeans and summer boots, all soaking wet, betrayed their inexperience at winter camping. When they discovered that the shelter that they had hoped to find had been torn down two years earlier, they managed to string up a sagging tent and crawl inside.

The last communication we had with them before settling down for a long wet night was when one of them asked us how we were cooking. It developed that they had counted on starting a fire—a patently impossible achievement in their situation—and that all they had for dinner was two enormous steaks, destined to remain as raw as the day the poor cow died.

Here is the point of our story: Those two hikers, who so badly needed nourishment, went hungry (except for what we cooked them on our portable gas stove) because they had not brought food suitable for a backpacking trip under adverse conditions.

The predicament of these two was extreme, but it illustrates the modern backpacker's paramount need for simple meals, light-weight and compact equipment, and complete self-sufficiency.

FIRE-BUILDING: PRO AND CON

First off, reliance on fire-building in the backwoods has become a highly questionable policy in light of the new environmental concerns. If we could be sure that everyone going into the backcountry would disperse to a different spot every night, knew how to construct a small fire and then leave no trace when they were through, maybe fires would be O.K. But the dead wood supply has long been used up at most commonly visited campsites and the devastation wrought by irresponsible hatchet-wielders is an ugly sore.

As long ago as 1893, the Appalachian Mountain Club was urging a halt to the cutting of firewood in the fragile area of the Presidential Range. Asking club members not to cut the scrub growth around newly constructed Madison Springs hut, AMC's Councillor of Improvements warned that "the growth is disappearing too rapidly." If it looked bad in 1893, that worthy councillor should see some popular campsites today!

More than any other piece of the clean camping mosaic, the discouragement of fires encounters a hard core of deep-felt resistance. The good old campfire dies hard; its emotional embers won't go out. It has a deep meaning to many woodsmen, evoking time-hallowed (almost primeval) associations of warmth, light, security, and good fellowship. Ernest Thompson Seton, one of the patron saints of woodcraft, argued: "What is a camp without the evening campfire? It's nothing but a place in the woods where some people have some things."

It must be conceded that a good woodsman knows how to have his fire and leave the site without a trace. But when hundreds of novices get out their hatchets, the result is scenes like what we saw at the White Mountains' Desolation Shelter when we were last there, 9 miles from the road, yet surrounded by a wasteland of hacked stumps. Even ten years ago, when you camped at Chimney Pond in Maine's Baxter Park, you had to walk about a half a mile to find any dead wood on the forest floor. Dead wood performs important ecological functions as it decays back into the soil, and when armies of campers burn it all as it falls, the forest is deprived. Also, many inexperienced fire-builders don't appreciate the risks of underground fires that smolder for days under the duff and may spring to conflagration long after the fire-builder has left, thinking he has put out all his embers.

Harry Roberts, editor of *Wilderness Camping,* has labelled campfires as "ethically indefensible in heavily used areas." In high dudgeon, Roberts cries (*Movin' Out*):

> . . . Look at the trees! They're scalped up to eight feet off the ground. And those saplings. My God, they're chewed off a foot above ground! The poor, spindly stumps catch your boots and send you sprawling. Every twenty feet there's the curdled, half-charred remnant of somebody's cooking fire, adorned with unburnt poly bags and unburnable aluminum foil. The place looks like the morning after Shiloh; all because a large number of jackasses didn't give a damn about the environment or what the next guy would find.

A subtle and sensitive argument against fires concerns their effect on the relationship between the camper and the night. Fires have a hypnotic effect—that's part of their attraction. They draw your eyes and you sit gazing into the flickering flame and glowing embers. Meanwhile, you lose contact with the woods around you, the stars above you, the wildlife (which gives your fire a wide berth), and the silence and sounds of nocturnal nature. The campfire is its own uniquely satisfying world—but it tends to isolate you from the larger natural world around you.

We'd like to see this anti-fire ethic spread more generally. For example, many state campgrounds around New England are doing the cause no good by making firewood available to the public. People should be encouraged to make the transition to gas cookstoves, not indulged in the phony fantasy of building obsolete fires from trucked-in wood, sometimes procured from local lumberyards.

The Green Mountain Club of Vermont has been gradually taking the wood stoves out of its shelters on the Long Trail, after a bitter history of fires burning down some of the fine old shelters, and after noting that widening circle of destruction to the surrounding trees. It is interesting to note that the club has encountered next to no resistance to or resentment of this policy. Most of today's backpackers understand.

EMERGENCY FIRES

Among those who concede the undesirability of campfires as a regular way of life, there are still those who believe that everyone should practice how to build a campfire in case of emergency. We demur even here. The emergency use of fire is highly questionable for a variety of reasons.

There are rare circumstances in which an emergency fire could save a life, no question about that. So it's probably desirable for backpackers to know how to build one. But practice isn't necessary. Building an emergency fire falls roughly into the same category as treating a snakebite or performing an emergency tracheotomy on the trail. Furthermore, like performing a tracheotomy with a penknife, it has been done but should be undertaken only as a last resort.

Why is fire-building of so little use in emergencies?

(1) If getting warm is essential, starting a fire will be little help. An outdoor fire is an extremely inefficient heat source, even for the one side of you that gets any warmth. Great quantities of fuel are required to produce a negligible amount of BTU's.

(2) The modern backpacker usually carries a good sleeping bag, and he's much better off inside that bag than out. Inside, the considerable heat his own body generates is retained.

(3) If the backpacker gets a fire going, he should then get into his bag anyway. Once inside, how can he tend a fire effectively?

(4) If hot food or drink is his greatest need, it is much more efficient to use his cookstove.

(5) If he is above treeline, fire-building is a useless art because there will be insufficient burnable material at hand.

(6) Most emergencies in which fire is alleged to be needed occur in winter. If you start a fire on a 6-foot snow cover, you'll soon have a pit several feet deep with the fire at the bottom, where it will furnish no heat but plenty of smoke. It's not easy to cook anything way down there either.

(7) If a backpacker has the energy, tools, and daylight to amass many large logs to construct a fire platform on the snow, he should probably use his time and energy instead to do something of more lasting benefit—like walking out.

If you should be caught in a wintertime emergency without tent, sleeping bag, or stove, you *might* want to get a fire going. But you would probably be better off using the natural protection of deep snow by digging a snow cave or trench, if conditions permit, or burrowing under a blowdown where natural caves can occur.

Often you hear people cite Jack London's marvellous short story, "To Build a Fire," recalling how a backwoodsman died because he couldn't keep a fire going, despite great effort. We like to point out that while the *man* wasted his time on futile fire-building efforts, the *dog* in the story very sensibly devoted his energies to walking out. The man died; the dog lived. Where's the moral there?

One of the authors was once caught in a somewhat desperate situation at 35 degrees below zero with winds strong enough to knock him over. When camp was finally established, there was a difficult struggle to keep a Svea stove going long enough to melt snow to supply badly needed hot liquids. The idea of getting out of his down bag long enough to start a fire would have been patently absurd.

So why burn down the woods practicing fires that aren't really needed, won't keep you warm, and are out of step with today's environmental concerns? Read up on how to build an emergency fire, because you just might need to, just as you might need to perform an emergency tracheotomy. But as for practicing—keep away from our throats with the penknife and leave the trees alone too.

In making the transition to the compact, portable gas stove, we've found we don't really miss that old campfire—in fact, we wouldn't want one now. We prefer to get along with no smoke in our eyes, no soot on our pots, no scouring the forest for dead wood, no set-up and break-down time, no nighttime beacon of blazing light that makes the stars hard to see and scares off animal life. It's a matter of what you grow accustomed to.

COOKING EQUIPMENT

The hiker who wants to get into remote places, whether he uses a stove or fire, must carry only a bare minimum of cooking apparatus. It's all going to get there in his pack, and he's already got plenty to carry. He can only look with envy at the stationary camper's chuck-box full of a cast-iron fry pan, dutch oven, set of carving knives, exotic herbs and seasonings, and all the weaponry required for a full-dress culinary campaign. When you have to tote it all on your back for mile on mile of rugged mountain trail, you just won't let all that gear into your pack.

Julia Child would have a nightmare in the backcountry when she saw what little she had to work with. Our entire meal-preparation kit consists of one large pot, inside of which fits a smaller pot, two small plastic bowls to eat out of, two 8-ounce plastic cups, and a box of matches; plus a small portable stove, a fuel container, two spoons, and a pot-grabber.

Ms. Child would certainly testify that no gourmet cooking gets done on this limited gear. It's designed to do just one thing: Keep our pack weight down so we can get far into the backcountry. Trying to create a French chef's seven-course delight on a tiny gas stove would be like trying to reproduce a full Beethoven symphony on a harmonica—it just wouldn't come out the same. We trade off epicurean cuisine for the privilege of eating in remote and beautiful locations where Duncan Hines will never dine.

Notwithstanding, we eat well up there in the hills. If you work at it, you can develop a consistent fare of appetizing meals and still travel very light. Anyway, the exercise of hiking is guaranteed to produce a gargantuan appetite that makes your simple menu seem absolutely mouth-watering.

What equipment do you need?

(1) Main pot—neither too large nor too small, capable of cooking a glop of about six cups;

(2) Smaller pot—useful but optional if you're really weight-conscious;

(3) Measuring cup (eight-ounce)—can double as one person's drinking cup;

(4) Small plastic bowl—some people take just one large cup and use it for both main course and drinks;

(5) Spoon—large soup-spoon size—forget the fork and knife;

(6) Pot-grabber—very useful, but also dispensable if you're a nut on weight and are willing to use a glove;

(7) Portable stove and fuel container. Modern backpacking stoves generally use one of three fuels: white gas, butane, or propane. It's a trade-off as to which is best for you. Butane is certainly the most convenient and lightest, but it won't work in freezing weather. Propane is also easy to use, and is fine in the cold, but is the heaviest due to the strong cylinders required to carry it safely. White gas is tricky to use at first, but once you master the technique, it's probably the most versatile. There are over 30 individual makes of stove on the market, ranging from the simple Boy Scout favorite, Sterno, to the mountaineer's highly sophisticated "MSR" or the Optimus 111B.

10
Man's Best Friend-
or Menace to Wilderness?

Love me, love my dog.

John Heywood
(1497–1580)

THINK OF your favorite wilderness camping spot: a sparkling lake set among rugged mountains or a wooded glade where you can pitch your tent on a quiet carpet of pine needles. Now introduce a dog into that idyllic picture. What's your reaction?

Some backpackers will conjure up an image of their favorite shaggy friend and recall with inestimable pleasure days of trail-side companionship. But other hikers will snort with disgust at such a thought. To them dogs mean harassment, noise, pollution, and disruption of wildlife—a domestic creature jarringly out of place in the backcountry. And they will condemn the dog's owners, too, for their lack of consideration and insensitivity to a wilderness experience.

Both sides are slightly myopic in their views (the other person's opinion is always out of focus), and with increasing numbers of people in the woods, confrontations between dogs, dog lovers, and dog opponents are growing more frequent—and more provoking. Backs are up (to coin a canine phrase), and land managers, who write and administer the laws controlling dogs in wilderness, react by instinct to the loudest voices. Some parks prohibit dogs or require leashes at all times; some limit dogs' freedom around crowded areas; others have no restrictions. An objective look at both arguments is needed to formulate rational rules of conduct and regulation of dogs—and for their owners and detractors.

Tradition honors the outdoorsman and his dog; shades of Buck in *Call of the Wild* or of King, Sergeant Preston of the Yukon's faithful dog. The ranks of those who have marched the Appalachian Trail from end to end include several dogs. One pooch has climbed Mount Robson, the difficult summit in the Canadian Rockies which has thwarted many people. Dogs often hike across Alaska's tundra. The authors' dog has climbed all of the White Mountains' summits over 4000 feet—not once but three times.

To owners of such splendid hiking companions, restrictions on dogs in the backcountry appear unnecessary and burdensome, in conflict with the freedom we all associate with backcountry experiences. We go to the woods and hills to get away from onerous restraints.

As Zane Smith of the U.S. Forest Service put it, "One of the greater values of a national forest recreation experience is the absence of regimentation.... Strict control measures are warranted only if other means fail to keep a situation within acceptable limits."

Responsible dog owners reject the notion that all dogs should be banned because a few dogs are a menace and may argue that some children are as disagreeable as dogs—noisy, intrusive, and harassing—but we don't restrict kids in the woods.

Writing in the *Trail Walker,* the New York-New Jersey Trail Conference's official organ, A. C. Van der Kas pleads: "I am a 70-year-old hiker, and my only companion on the trails is my dog, who loves hiking. Why should I be denied my companion and my dog his joy of hiking?"

To such hikers dogs can be the finest of outdoor companions, sharing the pleasures of the walk without arguing over which trail to take or how far to go. Fresh air, especially in cooler seasons, puts a dog in a superb frame of mind. It bounds along, tail high and wagging. At evening it sticks close to camp, enjoying the companionship of its tired master.

If you watch a dog on the trail closely, you will notice that it observes its surroundings very differently from the way a person does. In fact, were you able to ask a dog what it experienced on a 10-mile hike, you would get an entirely different account from its master's report. We see panoramic views, birds, and trees overhead, an immensely complex visual impression; we hear birds, rushing streams, and rustling leaves; we occasionally smell some strong scent such as moist earth under a stand of hemlock.

The dog, coming back from the same hike, would report different observations, perhaps more complex and extensive. Its visual impressions would have been more limited than its master's—no panoramic or overhead views. Its ears heard what ours did and a bit more. But what a rich and wonderful world of smells it experienced! Furthermore, while most of us notice only the present state of things, the dog's nose recorded recent history: when a deer or rabbit passed by, what it did, where it came from and where it was going. Dogs' observations have a dimension of time that ours largely lack.

Despite this idyllic picture of dogs and masters in the backcountry, many backpackers object strenuously to canines in the outdoors on several counts:

(1) Dogs harass wildlife. Many dogs chase squirrels and rabbits and large game. At its worst, this fault extends to free-running dogs in winter chasing down and slaughtering deer. And some hikers complain that even well-disciplined dogs scare off wildlife by their mere presence.

(2) Dogs harass other hikers. Many large, strong dogs, whose owners are proud of their rugged image, are aggressive if not dangerous when encountered unexpectedly. Even if they don't bite, large, aggressive dogs can make other hikers nervous. Families with young children can be especially irritated

when they meet a large or noisy dog that is not carefully controlled by its owner.

(3) Dogs are noisy. The peace and quiet of the woods can be rudely shattered by the yapping of a nervous pooch as by a loud hiking party, trailbike or snowmobile. The evening calm of a campsite can be ruined by a dog whose owner permits its barking to continue unchecked.

(4) Dogs steal food. It's not safe to leave your lunch or dinner unattended if there's a hungry dog around—and all hiking dogs are hungry. Again, children can easily be victimized by the uncontrolled dog that finds a sandwich held at nose level.

(5) Dogs foul the trail, and the campsite. They also water the corners of tents—and once one leaves its mark, it's obligatory for all other males to mark the same spot.

(6) Dogs fight other dogs. One of the rudest interruptions of the serenity of the outdoors occurs when male dog meets male dog on the trail. Anyone who has been in or near the center of a dogfight knows how unnerving it is to pull apart a pair (or more) of snarling, slashing champions of canine virility.

(7) Dogs harass horses. In many western backcountry areas, horseback riders are frequent trail users. Land managers report increasing complaints involving dogs scaring horses.

(8) Dogs can be mistreated in the backcountry. Some owners fail to realize how much a dog can suffer from heat exhaustion over long stretches of waterless trail. And park officials report that dogs have been injured or killed in matches with bears, deer, mountain lions, snakes, scorpions, and spiders.

One annoyed state park official summed up a common view of antidog wilderness users: "It is selfish on the part of the pet owner, inconsiderate to other people and unfair to the animal itself."

Such an indictment, perhaps too mildly expressed to suit the most ardent antidog backpacker, will strike the dog owner as grossly unfair. A well-behaved, responsibly controlled pet does none of these things, the pro-dog hiker insists. It's not right to condemn the entire species because of the faults of a few—or, more likely, the irresponsibility of their too-casual owners.

Some argue that dogs need not be regarded as a threat to wildlife for at least three reasons. First, a responsible owner will restrain a dog from bothering other creatures. Second, even when a dog tries to give chase, its domestic upbringing has left it incompetent to catch much more than a few ticks. And finally, the idea that a domestic dog will be the first predator to appear in the life of a wilderness creature is absurd—all nature abounds with predator-prey hierarchies, and an occasional dog adds little to the perils of everyday life for wild creatures, which are constantly eluding natural enemies.

True, most dogs are not a problem, but if all dogs run loose on the trails, how can the errant few be controlled?

Most national parks prohibit dogs on backcountry hiking trails. National Park Service regulations require that any pet in any park be leashed or physically restrained, and they give authority to individual park superintendents to prohibit pets in specific areas. For many parks this means that a leashed dog is acceptable in roadside campgrounds but may not be taken on backcountry trails. To find out whether your dog is allowed on trails in a particular park, write to the park's superintendent. You will find that most of the popular parks, such as the Tetons, Grand Canyon and Yosemite, prohibit dogs from the backcountry.

National forests are less restrictive. At developed recreational sites leashes are required. On backcountry trails no general restrictive policy applies, and backpackers with dogs have more opportunities than in national parks. Again, for any specific area, you should consult local regulations.

Regulations in state parks vary, but most allow dogs only if leashed. In general, parks subject to intense hiking pressure have invoked more stringent restrictions on pets. California state parks flatly prohibit dogs on backcountry trails. Many states in the crowded northeast and northwest—New Hampshire and Washington, for example—require a leash on dogs even on remote trails. On the other hand, in Colorado dogs are generally allowed to run loose if they are under voice control, and in Alaska there is usually no restriction. There, park officials recognize dogs as useful hiking companions for protection against bears and for pulling sleds in winter.

With national forests, many state parks and countless privately owned recreational lands still open to hiking with dogs, it is difficult to reconcile the conflicting interests of all parties involved: the rights of the harassed hiker, who feels his enjoyment of the woods is rudely jolted whenever a dog yaps in his presence; the privacy of wildlife, which see dogs as an ancestral predator; the convenience of park managers, for whom dog controversies are a headache; the rights of the dog owner who keeps pets well trained and well disciplined; the principle of minimum regimentation of wilderness activities; the rights, after all, of the dog, which loves the smells and sounds of the out-doors.

Short of prohibiting dogs from wild lands, what can be done to improve the experience of all concerned? The answer lies very much in the hands of dog owners, who must behave responsibly and observe a code of ethics for dogs in the backcountry.

Here are ten points:

(1) Never let your dog chase wildlife.

(2) Keep your dog close to you when other hikers approach. If they are nervous or if your dog is aggressive, grab your dog by the collar or attach a leash, even if you know it won't bite. The other hikers don't know that.

(3) Be especially watchful of your dog when small children are around.

(4) Keep your dog quiet. In the wilds most people regard barking as an unforgivable intrusion, and there's nothing more annoying than an owner who does nothing about a continually barking dog. If you can't keep your dog from barking, leave it at home.

(5) Keep your dog away from all food.

(6) Keep it out of all sources of potable water. When you're at a spring, make sure it drinks from the runoff and not from the spring itself.

(7) Don't let it foul the trail. If it does, flick the droppings off the trail with a stick or piece of bark. Watch its toilet habits around campsites. The animal has to go somewhere, but use common sense and be considerate.

(8) If another dog comes along, restrain your dog and ask the other owner to do the same.

(9) If horses come by, hold your dog.

(10) Use common sense and courtesy.

As we have mentioned, many people want to see dogs prohibited from trails; many parks already restrict them. Responsible behavior is the best insurance that you and your dog will enjoy future hikes together.

Now, for all you dog-haters—goodwill and consideration of others can go far to reduce unpleasant confrontations and increase everyone's pleasure of the great outdoors—everyone, including man's best friend.

Here is a code of ethics for dog-haters:

(1) Show friendliness toward the dog and its owner. Hostile behavior by dogs is often touched off by subtle displays of fear in people.

(2) Exert reasonable prudence in keeping food inside packs or out of reach of hungry canines.

(3) Be tolerant of a fellow creature's enjoyment of the outdoors.

(4) Restrain from complaining to authorities or asking for restrictions on dogs. Remember that increased regimentation of activities in the backcountry is a burden on everyone who enjoys the freedom of the wilds.

CASE STUDY

Rock Climbers
and Their Environment

There used to be so few climbers that it didn't matter where one drove a piton, there wasn't a worry about demolishing the rock. Now things are different. There are so many of us, and there will be more. A simple equation exists between freedom and numbers: The more people, the less freedom. If we are to retain the beauties of the sport, the fine edge, the challenge, we must consider our style of climbing; and if we are not to mutilate and destroy the routes, we must eliminate the heavy-handed use of pitons and bolts.

Royal Robbins, *Basic Rockcraft*

YOU MAY never want to go near the mad sport of rock climbing. That would be very sensible. There are easy ways up every mountain in the east but one (the south summit of Seneca Rock in West Virginia), so why bother with the technical difficulties, muscle strain, and abject terror that are involved in rock climbing? The story that follows is not intended to alter one iota your very rational decision. The reason we relate it is because we're talking here about the new backwoods ethic of concern for the environment. The history of the last ten years in rock climbing is a story of how one strange and unlikely collection of outdoor recreationists . . .

(a) perceived the impact they were having on the fragile environment around them,
(b) set about to change their ways so as to protect that environment, and
(c) very largely succeeded through group consensus, peer pressure, and pure voluntarism, with no regulations, restrictions, or government action of any kind.

ROCK CLIMBING

First, a word about what technical rock climbing involves, because an understanding of one or two points is essential to appreciating this story.

The rock climber, contrary to what a lot of people think, doesn't climb the rope. (Rock climbers climb rock, rope climbers climb rope.) He ascends his cliff by using whatever cracks, tiny ledges, nubbins, or other protrusions in the rock may afford him handholds or footholds. The fewer or less well-defined these protrusions, the more difficult the climb.

So what's the rope there for? One reason: in case the climber falls. The rope and all of that jangling collection of things that climbers carry over their shoulders or otherwise attached—variously referred to as "hardware," "gear," "the rack," etc.—are used solely to protect the climber in case of a fall, or at least most of the time these days that's their sole function.

How does this protection system work? The fundamental point is that only one climber moves at a time, and another climber holds the rope in such a way that he can catch and control a fall if it occurs.

For the second person on the rope it's all extremely simple. The leader is up there somewhere, anchored to a ledge (by means which we'll presently describe), and holding the rope. As the second climbs, the leader takes up slack. If the second falls, he is instantly caught by the leader.

The leader is considerably more exposed. To protect himself, the leader either picks a solid tree growing on a ledge, finds a chockstone wedged in a crack, drives in a piton, or places an artificial chockstone (from his "rack") in a crack, and attaches a snaplink (or carabiner) to this "protection," through which he runs the rope. From then on, should he fall, the second person can control the fall through that point of protection. "Leader falls" obviously are longer, more scary, and more risky, since the leader will fall twice the distance he has climbed above his last protection—from his high point down to the protection point and then an equal distance below that—before the rope comes tight.

We trouble you, gentle reader, with all this detail only to point out one fact: the critical importance to the rock climber of this "protection." Without protection the leader would be literally risking his life on every lead, and would be strongly inclined to avoid any difficulty that he wasn't absolutely sure he could handle with complete confidence. But with good protection, new worlds open up of difficult and spectacular routes up incredibly steep and exposed cliffs. If a fall occurs it should have no serious consequences.

Now to the first point of our story: Up until ten years ago, rock climbers almost universally employed that well-known symbol of their sport: the piton. (Pronounced like "feet-on," not "bite-on.") Pitons were variously shaped pieces of metal that were hammered into cracks in the rock. At the outside end of the piton was a hole through which a carabiner could be attached for securing the rope. Pitons were in universal use by climbers as late as 1969. Every climber carried a hammer and a rack of assorted pitons, varying in size so as to fit the various cracks that the climber might encounter on the cliff.

Where the leader runs into a blank section of rock, or one in which there are no cracks or any other way of driving in a piton or fixing natural protection, he has a new problem. In most such situations, the leader either gulps and climbs carefully until he can get to some place higher where protection is possible; or, if it looks too difficult to risk that, he simply won't climb there—he "backs off," as they say. However, another possibility is to go up to some reasonable stance on that face and then stand there and laboriously drill a bolt hole right into the rock, using a kind of star drill, place a bolt with a hanger in it, and affix the carabiner and rope. Placing bolts was and is a very rare occurrence for most climbers, however. Many leaders climbed for years without ever placing a bolt. The piton was the standard protection used until 1969.

THE ADVENT OF NUTS

Slowly in the late sixties and especially the early seventies, an environmental conscience began to hit the rock-climbing community, as an outwash from the environmentalist awakening of these years.

The climbers looked around the areas in which they were climbing. They saw that the paths they trod to get to the base of popular climbs were becoming beaten down, and erosion was starting to take place. They saw that the places they camped were too often littered and unsightly. But most of all they saw that where they were repeatedly driving pitons into the rock and removing them, the cracks were becoming scarred and disfigured. On some popular routes, places that had once taken a ½-inch wide piton now required a ¾-inch or 1-inch piton, due to the widening of the crack as a result of repeated placements and removals.

The climbers also watched uneasily the growing popularity of their sport. They realized that all of these adverse impacts were made much worse by the increasing numbers of climbers at the better cliffs. They sensed that if the sport became a popular fad, the environmental destruction could become a tragedy.

Along about this time, a few climbers came back from England with some gadgets already in use over there, called artificial chockstones or simply "nuts." Instead of banging them into horizontal cracks, you quietly slotted them into vertical cracks. The ideal nut placement is in a crack of varying width (as most are)—you slide a nut in where the opening is large enough to take it in, then slide it down inside to a point where the opening is *not* large enough to let it out. If a fall is exerted on such a nut, it simply drives it farther into the narrow part of the crack, and it may (in the ideal case) be actually *more* secure than a hammered-in piton. Placing a secure nut, though, especially for those relatively new to the game, is often a bit more difficult than simply banging in a piton, and requires a careful eye to the possibilities.

It should not be supposed that the first climbers to use nuts were motivated primarily by environmental concerns. Not at all. The British climbers started to use them to save money, pure and simple: The first nuts were literally machine nuts pocketed by down-at-the-heels Britishers who couldn't afford to (or didn't choose to) buy pitons. Then they began to fabricate nuts especially for climbing.

The two men whom we first encountered using nuts in the northeast U.S., Willy Crowther and Chuck Loucks, did so primarily because they were intrigued with the more interesting art of placing nuts, the subtlety of the game as well as its novelty. The rest of us began to imitate them at first because Willy and Chuck were immensely popular climbers, whose style we admired and wished to emulate.

As we began to use nuts increasingly, we began to enjoy a new dimension to our climbing. Because some nut placements were tricky or tenuous, we found ourselves constantly on the lookout for possibilities. This brought us to a more continuous observation of the rock around us, a greater awareness of its qualities and configurations, a closer association with that vertical world of granite or conglomerate.

But in the climate of environmentalist concern that pervaded the years around 1970, it wasn't long before we noticed something else beside the economics and the engineering aesthetics of nuts. When you slotted a nut and your second removed it, the rock was undefiled. No ugly scar. No hammer damage. No obtrusive banging noise. In a very short time, a number of leading climbers perceived in nuts the key to ending the environmental havoc being wrought by pitons.

By 1971, a full-scale campaign was under way among the more environmentally concerned climbers, both in the popular northeastern climbing areas and throughout the country, to preach the nut ethic. "Clean climbing" was proclaimed as the new order. Pitons were condemned as virtually immoral. Influential climbers began ostentatiously leaving their hammers at the base of the cliff, committing themselves to either finding natural protection or using nuts. Great prestige was accorded to climbers who succeeded in climbing the classic routes "all-nuts"—i.e., without using a single piton, either of their own or of those left by preceding parties. If you can't find a way to protect a difficult move cleanly, said the new ethic, don't place a piton—back off and try again another day.

If pitons were frowned on, bolts became even more scorned. Drilling bolt holes was viewed as an offense several times more heinous than driving pitons.

Understand, now, that all of this was a matter of voluntary action, peer pressure, and education. There are no enforceable rules in climbing areas, no public regulations affecting the sport (except at a few highly resented parks). Climbers are as individualistic and unregimented a group as you'll find anywhere. They will *not* be told what to do by *anyone*.

And yet, within the space of roughly three years, 1969-1972, the nut revolution swept most climbing areas. In 1969 you could walk along the base of any northeastern cliff on a good weekend and hear the ring of hammers on pitons from one end to the other, on every route where there were climbers. By late 1972, the sound of hammered steel was so rare that it attracted considerable attention—and outrage. The British had a contemptuous expression: "A man who would drive a piton into British rock would shoot a fox!" Nuts reigned supreme.

The speed of this revolution, accomplished solely by moral suasion and consensus in a group that would not take orders from anyone, was and remains a miracle. It can only be explained by the intensity and sincerity of the feeling most climbers had for the environment in which they climbed.

In any reaching of consensus, there are bound to be individuals who take a more prominent role than others in articulating the impulse toward the new way of thinking. Within the eastern climbing community the leading force in getting the new ideas across was a most unusual climber named John Stannard. Well-known to every climber because of his extraordinary skill at the most difficult climbs, Stannard used his prestige to advance what he most earnestly believed in: the salvation of climbing areas by the transition to "clean climbing" and by climbers accepting the responsibility to be sensitive stewards of the land on which they enjoyed their climbing. Stannard ceaselessly evangelized for the abandonment of pitons, conducted and publicized tests to prove the safety of nuts, started a newsletter to spread the good word, made an effort to climb with as many climbers as possible to show them how it could be done and earn their good will, and otherwise set an example of dedication to environmental consciousness which others might sometimes think weird, but which they could not fail to respect—and ultimately to follow.

In the western climbing scene, another influential and astonishing figure was Yvon Chouinard. One of the earliest of the "big wall" climbers at Yosemite Valley, Chouinard started designing pitons back in the old days and built a business that dominated the market. Everyone used Chouinard pitons (as well as Chouinard carabiners, Chouinard hammers, etc.). Then, when the Great Nut Awakening came, Chouinard voluntarily took a leading position in scuttling his own piton business to get everyone to switch over to nuts. Chouinard makes nuts too, of course, but he has never achieved the ascendancy over the nut market that he enjoyed when everyone used pitons. Like Stannard, Chouinard put his money where his heart lay: in fighting for a better climbing environment.

Others were influential in advancing the new ethic, like Royal Robbins and Galen Rowell, but the main point is not to single out individuals. The main point is that the overwhelming majority of the heterogeneous and zealously individualistic climbing community embraced the nut revolution and made it work. In the particular climbing area that we were closest to at the time, the Shawangunks, we would think it fair to say that the transition from nuts to pitons would have happened in a remarkably short time anyway, but that without any question the driving pressure of John Stannard's enthusiasm and example was what made it happen in such a very short time.

OTHER CHANGES IN ROCK CLIMBING

There were several other ways in which the climbers' environmental concern showed up.

(1) Absence of litter. Rock-climbing areas came to contain less litter per number of people than any other outdoor recreation area. Climbers tend to pick

up not only their own trash, but that of thoughtless nonclimbers. Some climbers, Stannard among them, even prowl the edge of the highway near climbing areas on Sunday mornings, picking up every shred of litter from passing motorists.

(2) Erosion control. In the early seventies, climbers began to work out arrangements with owners and managers of the lands on which they climbed to provide for stabilizing the paths to and from the cliffs. Climbers volunteered their own labor to work on moving large rocks into eroded trail beds, digging waterbars, rerouting access trails where erosion seemed unstoppable, and brushing in the abandoned routes, to give vegetation a chance to grow in. On one weekend at the east's most crowded climbing center, a bunch of climbers decided to stabilize a path to an area known as the "Beginner's Slab." The volunteer crew included four of the country's top dozen climbers, men who could have no personal interest in a cliff as easy as the Beginner's Slab, but who gave up their own climbing for an afternoon in order to help preserve that particular area.

(3) Discouragement of publicity. With awakening concern about damage to the rock and to access slopes, climbers began to realize that the fundamental problem was their own growing numbers. There was an expression heard often those days: We don't want to have happen to climbing what happened to downhill skiing. (Once an adventurous sport for only the most hardy, the boom in popularity brought crowded slopes, lift line cues, great expense in both equipment and weekend costs, standardization of techniques and style, and an army of fashionable hangers-on, along with such abominable concepts as "après-ski" and the "ski bunny.") Rock climbers began actively to *dis*courage publicity. Reporters and photographers were treated to the unusual spectacle of people who did *not* thrill at the prospect of seeing their names and faces in print. The occasional climber who did a beer commercial for television was mildly ostracized by his climbing associates. Inevitably, some outsiders (and even some climbers) criticized this movement as elitist—climbers trying to keep their sport to themselves and shut off outsiders. This criticism sadly missed the point: Climbers deeply felt that the integrity of the sport and the beauty of climbing areas would be ruined *for everyone* if the scene were transformed into a popular fad.

(4) Rescues. Whatever the growing cost to the public of searches and rescues for lost or disabled hikers, the rock climbers try to take care of their own. If a climber does get hurt, as they occasionally do for perfectly obvious reasons, it is the climbers themselves who get him off the cliff, out to a road, and to a hospital. When an accident occurs in a popular climbing area, other climbers will stop the climb they're on and take on the difficult and delicate work of littering an injured person down off the cliff face and out over the rough terrain of the approach. Very often they don't even call for a public ambulance at that point. In any crowd of climbers, someone usually has a van (since climbers like to be able to sleep in their cars at trail heads) and will drive the injured to the nearest hospital. In recent years, this self-help effort has been formalized in the popular climbing areas of New Hampshire with the formation of the Mountain Rescue Service, an entirely volunteer group of climbers who are available for all kinds of

technical rescues, summer and winter. In many western climbing areas, similar rescue groups are on call. At other places the process may not be institutionalized, but it is still remarkably effective. Some climbing clubs schedule weekends devoted to practicing rescue techniques.

(5) Cooperation with related land objectives. Land managers began to find that where climbing impinged on other outdoor programs, climbers could be most cooperative. For example, on one popular climbing cliff, researchers decided that the habitat was perfect to attempt the restoration of the most marvellous of endangered bird species, the peregrine falcon. Discreet signs posted at the base of climbing routes that led up by the release site were all it took for climbers to cooperate. During the crucial period for the young birds, they stayed off those routes.

The climbers' record of environmental concern is far from perfect, despite all we've said so far. There are still a hard core of piton-drivers and a somewhat larger minority that hold it acceptable to drive a piton if no nut placement can be found. Some still drive bolts (horrors!): Recent new routes in Yosemite Valley involved as many as 21, 70, and 85 new bolts. (It must be conceded that these routes couldn't have been made without this aid, but Yosemite with its huge walls of sheer granite is not a typical situation.) The ethic is far better established at some places (e.g., the Shawangunks) than others (e.g., New Hampshire climbing areas). One serious flaw in the climbers' professed desire to leave the environment unmarked is the popularity of chalk as a medium for drying sweaty hands, which marks up the holds on the cliffs in a terrible way.

Nevertheless, the over-all picture remains a favorable one. In no other field of outdoor activity that we can think of has a group of recreationists so swiftly and so completely lived up to its responsibility to safeguard the environment from the adverse effects of its own actions.

In describing these trends, we have seriously erred if we've given you a picture of climbers as stuffy do-gooders, soberly and pompously standing up for law and order, motherhood, and the American Way. Good grief, no! Climbers are scruffy, bearded, sloppy, dirty, and foul-mouthed, and their devotion to most of society's laws falls somewhere between that of highway robbers and bank embezzlers.

Highly individualistic, they regard themselves as alienated from society's strictures, sometimes even conceiving of climbing as a way of achieving a freedom that is denied elsewhere to them. Some of them are tolerably well behaved, but others violate social mores at every turn. They change clothes on the highway, swear in public places, and wind up most Saturday nights drunk or stoned. Furthermore, they smell.

You wouldn't want them in your livingroom. But they'll take good care of the most fragile of mountain environments. You can't trust them with your daughter. But you can trust them with the outdoors, more than any other single group.

Why have we told you this story? Because this book is about the new backwoods ethic of concern for protecting the remaining wild places of this country.

We think hikers and backpackers have made a good beginning toward changing their attitudes and practices in the outdoors, so as to walk more softly over the fragile land. But the hiking trails and camping sites of the backwoods still reveal that we have a long, long way to go. Too much of the time it takes official regulations and rules to save a backwoods environment from destruction, and then we're all the losers anyway for having our freedoms curtailed and for having to confess that we couldn't exercise enough self-discipline to exist without regulations.

But look at what the climbers accomplished and gain hope. In three years— *just three years*—this band of unreconstructed individualists reached a consensus and changed their ways. Surely in a generation, we hikers and backpackers can do the same. The goal is worth the try. It is nothing less than the integrity of the backwoods environment which we all love so well.

PART III

What Backwoods Environment Do We Want?

"People Pollution"

IN THE preceding section, we wrote of the individual hiker, and how his changing attitudes and camping practices are helping to preserve the "wilderness experience."

In this section, we turn to matters largely beyond the control of the individual hiker. The "wilderness experience" is sharply affected by the attitudes and management practices of those responsible for managing the parks and forests, the hills and rivers and mountains that constitute America's remaining backcountry.

Watching over backcountry once was epitomized by the lonely fire warden, living in solitude in a cabin on the side of a mountain, tramping up to the fire tower every day, from which vantage point he could see over miles of uninhabited forest. Never a visitor for weeks on end.

Today's backcountry manager is a whole new breed, in a radically different setting.

For starters, loneliness is hardly the problem. Everyone's seeking "solitude"; everyone's fleeing the crush of the cities, getting away from the crowds. Now the crowds are in the mountains, at least on holiday weekends on the popular peaks. It's still grand scenery, and nature's wonderful yet. But solitude it ain't.

Look around the New England hills for illustrations:

(1) Mount Washington, New England's highest, on a good Fourth of July is a milling mob scene, as hundreds of hikers converge along with motorists who drive up the auto road and tourists who ride the famous Cog Railway to the top.

(2) Massachusetts' Mount Greylock, also stuck with the liability of a road and a lodge on the top, is overwhelmed with sightseers on any good weekend in season.

(3) Mount Monadnock, in southern New Hampshire, is a favorite pilgrimage

on Columbus Day. In 1977 over 5000 people elbowed their way up its hiking trails. Hundreds at a time sat on the broad rocky summit area.

(4) Maine's Katahdin, once a magnificent symbol of remote and forbidding wilderness, now has full campgrounds nearly all summer long, and a steady stream of hikers across its summit ridges on good days.

Not only the mountains suffer the onslaught of "wilderness"-seeking multitudes. The Appalachian Trail, that 2000-mile footpath from Maine to Georgia, has a continuous stream of walkers padding along its wooded ways. The Allagash River, once a test for the resourceful canoeist, is now an enormously popular vacation target, its designated campsites almost perpetually occupied, and the lonely solitude of mist-lined shores a thing of memory and sadness.

In New Hampshire's high country, the Appalachian Mountain Club's famed huts now require advance reservations and are often full to capacity. Solitude-seekers avoid the Lakes-of-the-Clouds hut, where one can rarely find less than several dozen fellow boarders, and nickname it "Lakes-of-the-Crowds."

Not far from that hut, in Tuckerman's Ravine, before camping restrictions were put in, you could count up to 800 people in tents on popular spring skiing weekends. Not that many people live in our entire town! Tuckerman's is the biggest off-road tourist Mecca: Estimates run as high as 60,000 visitors a year. If you're a small balsam fir near the trail, what chance do you and your roots have against 120,000 boots a year?

The boom in backcountry recreation, a product of leisure time, affluence, fast highways, and alienation from urban values, is not confined to New England, though our proximity to megalopolis intensifies the fate of our woods and hills. Colorado's Rocky Mountain National Park had a 730 percent increase in use between 1966 and 1976. In other words, if ten years ago you saw only ten other people on your three-day weekend in the park backcountry, today you would see 83 people. That's quite a difference in the flavor of your wilderness weekend.

"Overcrowding is the biggest problem facing the American wilderness," says Russ Mohney, author of *The Master Backpacker*. People pollution, some call it.

Oddly enough, many recreationists seem to like it this way. People will jam into popular camping areas cheek by jowl, rather than hike a couple of miles down the trail to find a secluded spot. Mount Washington swarms with legions of hikers breathing auto fumes and railroad smoke, while nearby peaks are enjoyed by a single party, or perhaps only by a solitary white-throated sparrow singing in the high cold air. People like people. Social rituals, such as that of comparing your latest backpacking equipment, seem to be more fascinating to many than the quiet contemplation of a moss-covered boulder.

A U.S. Forest Service researcher, John Hendee, has studies to show that "most wilderness visitors prefer to be in the wilderness with other people, usually intimates such as friends or family members."

So the backcountry manager of today rarely gets to watch over the endless forests and quiet loneliness of the fire warden's vista. Instead he sees gaily colored tents, bobbing backpacks along the trail, and people ... always people.

Many trails are badly eroded. In some places the walking surface is now a good 3 or 4 feet lower than it started, as clearly shown by the untrampled turf on either side. The Old Bridle Path, popular route up Mount Lafayette in New Hampshire's Franconia Notch, is gloomily dubbed the "Old Bridle Trench" by trail crews that try to check the erosion.

Many of the social problems of the cities have come with the crowds into the hills—crime and vandalism, water pollution, sewage disposal difficulties, noise, conflicts between people with different interests and values.

Perhaps the most insidious effect of having numerous people in the backcountry is the destruction of the elusive and precious spirit of wildness and adventure. The noise and bustle of all those people camped "next door" or bursting upon a remote summit kill that feeling of being "away from it all" which most people fled to the backcountry to seek.

"Of what avail are forty freedoms without a blank space on the map?" asked conservationist Aldo Leopold.

The manager's response has been to try to do something to save the backcountry environment which he is obligated to protect. Several results have followed:

(1) Regulations, designed to limit numbers of hikers and/or campers in an area, or to reduce their impact on the land;

(2) Information programs, trying to get across the importance of carrying out your litter, of using cookstoves instead of fires, of camping with minimum impact;

(3) "Tread-hardening": trail work aimed at checking erosion and providing a more stable surface for the *Vibram* army to tramp over;

(4) Backcountry facilities, to cope with camping hordes, provide for sewage treatment or disposal, and concentrate camping impact—or else disperse it over wider areas.

While the backcountry managers deserve support and cooperation in the difficult job they face, there do arise tough questions about just *how* the backwoods should be managed—questions embodied in the title we've put at the head of this section: *What backwoods environment do we want?*

In the following pages we explore questions like these:

(1) Should we save the physical environment at all costs, even if it means restricting hiking opportunities as well as camping?

(2) What exactly are we trying to save—just the physical environment? Or some more subtle and elusive spirit of wildness which includes both the physical (trees, soils, pure streams, alpine plants) *and* the feeling of being in a wild place, a feeling which is based partly on the physical landscape but also on intangibles

like solitude, remoteness, difficulty and challenge, freedom from overt controls and directions, an absence of things obviously manmade or man-modified, a sense of having attained a remote and difficult objective on the strength of one's own exertions and resourcefulness?

(3) What patterns of backcountry ownership and control will best preserve the kind of wilderness experience we want to preserve?

(4) Does the answer lie in designating more wild land as official "Wilderness," with the full and permanent protection of the Wilderness Act of 1964?

(5) How can we preserve opportunities for solitude (one of the explicit goals of the Wilderness Act)?

(6) What is the proper role of machines in the backwoods—like helicopters, for instance?

(7) What degree of safety should we try to preserve, and how should we go about it?

(8) Will we remove risk and challenge totally from the backcountry scene?

(9) In short . . . what backwoods environment do we want?

11

Values in Conflict
in the Backcountry

*Our managers are preoccupied with maximizing the availability
of the backcountry experience. But this has been done at the
expense of diminishing and cheapening the experience itself. I
think we should be involved in maximizing the experience
rather than the availability of that experience. And it is a curious quirk of the human intellect that a sense of unattainability
only increases the depth and quality of the experience which is
ultimately attained.*

Philip D. Levin

LET'S BEGIN by describing a few scenes in the White Mountains of New
Hampshire:

(1) Madison Springs hut, high up above treeline in the northern end of the
Presidential Range, maintained by the Appalachian Mountain Club for the benefit of the mountain traveller: Around the hut, the hiker is now presented with
stone walls that outline exactly where he is allowed to tread and which fence off
certain other areas. The objective is to permit alpine vegetation to regenerate on
its side of the fences.

(2) Imp shelter, in the Carter Range just across the valley from the Presidentials: At this heavily used camping site, wood railings have been erected to discourage hikers from cutting through the woods every which way. The objective
is to channel foot traffic in certain paths only, and allow forest vegetation to
regenerate.

(3) Carter-Moriah Trail, just south of Imp shelter, running along the ridgeline:
For long stretches, board plank walkways have been erected across wet areas.
These walkways are built of standardized lumber imported from the valley, in
contrast to the ruder hewn-log trail work done less systematically in many other
sections of the mountains. The objective is to provide hikers with dry passage
through mud patches and put an end to the trail-widening, vegetation-destroying
effect of hikers skirting around mud patches in wet weather.

(4) Mount Monroe, in the southern end of the Presidentials: On a popular
trail leading from AMC's Lakes-of-the-Clouds hut to the rocky summit of

Monroe, a prominent staircase of rock-work has been erected on the trail. The objective is to harden the tread, control erosion, contain all foot traffic on one route, and permit vegetation to regenerate elsewhere on the mountain slope.

In each of these cases, the paramount objective is protection of the vegetation. The objective commands broad support among hikers and all those who appreciate the mountains. No one can look at the damage which the *Vibram* army has wrought on soils and delicate alpine plants without wanting to see something done to save the purely physical environment.

At the same time, it must be conceded that in each of the cases cited, an element has been introduced into the hiker's experience that has a taint of regimentation about it and that does some violence to the hiker's sense of being in the wilderness. Most of us feel that the preservation of the resource is so vital in each of these four cases that a little spirit of the wild is worth sacrificing, and that hikers should be willing to tolerate some regimentation. But how much?

THE BASIC CONFLICT

The crux of the matter is that two values are in conflict here. How they are resolved depends on how much weight you assign these two values. They are:

(1) Protection of the resource; and
(2) Preservation of the spirit of wildness.

Protection of the resource is an objective that everyone can understand. Preservation of the spirit of wildness is a more complex and controversial value concept. It means different things to different people.

For one thing, note that we say "wildness," not "wilderness." That's so we won't stir up confusion with "Wilderness" in the narrow sense used in the Wilderness Act, where it has been given a precise legal definition. Anyone familiar with New England's history knows that the hand of man has come down heavily on the entire region. We all know it's not "real" wilderness, that it was all logged in the nineteenth century. Those who are bothered by this thought may prefer to refer to our second value here as preserving the "illusion" (rather than the "spirit") of wildness. But there is something there that hikers go to the hills to find. The cynic who would deny the validity of that quest on the grounds that what they find isn't "pure"—is a cynic indeed.

Granted that it is a valid objective that many hikers value highly, we must recognize that the "spirit of wildness" is perceived in very different ways. For example, some managers seem to define it largely in terms of numbers of other hikers seen. Thus, they propose to limit numbers by a permit system, so that the hiker will see fewer other people. Yet for many people the spirit of wildness also concerns the sense of freedom to wander where and when you will. For them, a permit system damages this spirit far more than the reduced numbers enhance it.

Probably most people would agree that the absence (or minimization) of man-made facilities is an attribute of the spirit of wildness. In fact, many would feel that the fewer overt indications of "management," the greater the spirit of wildness. This is not to say that artful management cannot be employed, as long as it is not blatantly evident: Tread-hardening by unobtrusively placed rocks, waterbars, brushing-in of switchback cut offs, can all be done in ways that won't be noticed by most hikers.

The paradox here is obvious: Without *some* management, "wildness" cannot survive the number of people who seek to enjoy it. Often the two values we've cited are *not* in conflict. That is, some steps must be taken *both* to protect the resource *and* to preserve the spirit of wildness. On the whole, we are favorably impressed with the sensitive balance worked out by the land managers in areas where we hike. The Forest Service, responsible for the national forests in New Hampshire and Vermont, seems cognizant of its dual responsibility—to safeguard the forest resource and to maintain opportunities for a pleasant and challenging backcountry experience. The large hiking clubs of the area—the Appalachian Mountain Club and Vermont's Green Mountain Club—are sympathetic with both needs too. That the two values *can* conflict, however, is the point which we are seeking to underline here.

IMPLICATIONS OF RESOURCE PROTECTION

Current emphasis in management of the White Mountains is somewhat on the side of protecting the resource. The policy implications of this emphasis are clearly evident: If you heavily value protecting the resource and place lighter value on the spirit of wildness, it leads you to:

• A preference for huts over tents or shelters. Huts of course totally obliterate the resource in their immediate area, but they do confine the physical impact of up to 70 or 100 overnight hikers. One often hears it expressed that huts "control" the impact—an apt choice of words. This is true. Nevertheless, it is also true that many people who place a high value on the spirit of wildness find that the huts do violence to that spirit: the presence of large buildings in the woods; the crowd of people; the clutter of steel drums and propane tanks in the backyards; radios playing; the anomaly of gourmet meals at motel-like prices, hot water, and bright lights in a wilderness where the backpacker is trying to preserve the illusion that "roughing it" is essential.

The partisans of the huts seem curiously defensive about them. They seem to want to deny that any trade-offs are involved, that huts are all gain and no loss.

We think that we will not begin to appreciate fully the very real values which huts may provide in the backcountry until we are candid about looking at both sides of the equation.

• Fencing off areas around huts, shelters, designated camping sites, and alpine zones. If protecting the resource is all important, then it doesn't much matter how much you regiment where hikers can and can't walk. If the spirit of wildness is of paramount importance, you might at least devote more effort to disguising the regimentation. Thus, artful brushing-in of areas where you don't want people to go, combined with positive educational efforts at explaining the value of staying on established trails can be very effective—but such a program takes a little more time and imagination than just slapping up a fence. If your value system places protecting the resource *way* ahead of preserving the spirit of wildness, then you're not likely to think it worth the trouble.

• Building "paved highways" on popular trails where erosion is a problem. When treadway-hardening first began to be applied in the White Mountains, great care was taken to have the rocks placed in a manner that looked reasonably natural. There are trails where erosion has been successfully controlled and the hiker may not even be aware that the rocks he's walking on weren't put there by nature. As time passed and the first creative bloom of trail maintenance wore off, more and more of the work seemed to set up a plainly discernible staircase look. The boardwalks in the Carter Range have all the charm of Fifth Avenue sidewalks. The resource is still being protected, but the spirit of wildness is evidently not deemed important.

• Using helicopters to supply huts and chain saws to speed up trail work. These two modern tools certainly assist in jobs deemed necessary to protect the resource, but their impact on the spirit of wildness is disastrous. Whether you favor their use or not depends on relative weights assigned to the two conflicting values. More on these machines in chapter 13.

In Carter Notch, much effort has gone into protecting the resource by prohibiting camping except at the hut, waterbarring, and step-building on trails. Yet on the nearby summit of Carter Dome, little effort has been directed to basic litter cleanup to remove the unsightly evidence of man's past abuses (twisted remains of a fire tower, painted rocks, long lengths of wire paralleling the Rainbow Trail down from the summit, etc.). The relative emphasis shows clearly.

FRANCONIA RIDGE

Controversy over conflicting values came to a boil in the summer of 1977 on the Franconia Ridge. This is one of the spectacular places in the east, a great spiny hogback that juts above treeline in a narrow 2-mile arete connecting the

jagged skyline between Little Haystack, Lincoln, Lafayette, and North Lafayette. Badly trampled over by hikers along the ridge, the alpine vegetation
had taken a beating and soil erosion was far advanced in some places. In 1977
the Forest Service and the Appalachian Mountain Club decided to get serious
about the problem. The AMC trail crew drew up lengthy scree walls on either
side of a treadway about a yard wide. The message to hikers was unmistakable:
Walk within this yard-wide "sidewalk" and let the soil and vegetation regenerate everywhere else. A great many hikers welcomed this work as vital to
halting the degradation of the plant and soil ecology. On the other hand, to
some who loved the wildness of this Franconia Ridge on mist-shrouded, wind-
blown days, these double "Berlin walls" were an inexcusable degradation of
the hiker's experience. What made the AMC's action hard for them to support
was that no intermediate efforts at hiker education were tried first—no signs
comparable to those on Adirondack summits, no ridge runners like those in
Vermont's alpine zones, no advice (to stay on-trail, be careful of the flowers)
dispersed at the roadside information booth or nearby hut, no explanatory
messages to hikers about the fragility of the tundra—just, suddenly, this mon-
strosity of a sidewalk on what had been a wild ridgeline. AMC's defenders
insisted that drastic action was essential, and that hiker education was too
slow and subtle a process (though, perhaps stung by its critics, AMC has be-
latedly instituted many of the measures previously neglected, like signs on
the ridge, a roving naturalist, and advice dispensed at the roadside booth).
When the shouting died down on both sides, the walls remained, but it seemed
unlikely that either the Forest Service or AMC would approach other areas
quite so crudely another time. Significantly, in 1978 the AMC's Council en-
dorsed a report from its Backcountry Management Task Force that warned
sternly:

> Large capital reconstruction projects are an undesirable ap-
> proach to a trails program. While trail hardening and other
> maintenance techniques can be widely used to protect or pre-
> vent damage to the resource, they must be used with restraint.
> Beyond a certain point they can assault and destroy the very
> experience they are intended to protect.

The flap over trail work is not the first time that the Franconia Ridge
has been the setting for a conflict in values. Several years earlier, some well-
intentioned researchers painted numbers and letters on many rocks on the
Ridge and drilled bolts into other rocks, all as part of an attempt to measure
and record trail erosion. The project was quietly dropped after protests over
this officially sanctioned graffiti. It takes a curiously weighted value system
to justify these numbers when we all flinch at initials carved in trees and
shelter logs.

OTHER CONFLICTING VALUES

Thus far we've been looking at just two values in conflict (see page 99). The backlands manager's job is vastly more complicated because there are still other values to be weighed. Three others, for example, are:

(3) The democratic ideal;
(4) Safety;
(5) Convenience or economics of wilderness management.

By the "democratic ideal," we mean the value of encouraging greater numbers of people to come into and experience the wilderness. This value currently receives considerable weight in backcountry management and articulate voices urge that it be given even greater emphasis. In pursuit of this ideal, there are burgeoning programs of bringing inner-city youths to the mountains, encouragement of large school groups, poster campaigns to "find yourself in the mountains," and marketing campaigns to promote attendance at huts and other backcountry facilities.

The pursuit of this value often conflicts with the first two we mentioned. For example, large groups of inexperienced hikers can be grievously destructive to the vegetative surroundings. Unquestionably measures which increase the number of people in the backwoods also have a detrimental effect on opportunities for solitude and the spirit of wildness. There is no way to enable thousands of people to experience some of the things which go with the spirit of wildness, because their very nature depends on a low level of use. The lovely, quiet needles-and-moss strewn trails of lesser-travelled peaks simply *cannot* be enjoyed by the multitude—by the time a small fraction of the *Vibram* army has passed by, the essence of the experience would be destroyed and the trail would be worn to roots and mud. "The good life," as Aristotle said, "depends upon intimacy and small numbers."

Giving more people an opportunity to see the backwoods may still be a valuable objective for a variety of reasons, ranging from the benefit to the individuals involved to the greater political support for wilderness legislation which may result. Whether you think these benefits are worth the cost depends on the relative weight you assign to these conflicting values in particular cases where choices must be made.

Safety conflicts with protection of the resource at times in motivating managers to mark trails more obtrusively or even to blast steps into steep, rocky places; and with preservation of the wilderness spirit by justifying facilities like bridges (even in Wilderness Areas!) and communications apparatus which reduce the sense of remoteness and isolation.

On Maine's Katahdin, park managers are so attuned to the value of hiker safety that they closely regulate when and where you can hike, and have splashed paint blazes so heavily along some trails that one must guess that they have little concern for preserving the physical environment if it should seem to conflict with hiker safety. The park managers at Katahdin have recently begun to listen to their critics and have made a few changes in the more extreme of their regulations, but that area remains the most tightly controlled hiking and climbing area in the east, if not the entire country. The reason is the disproportionate value placed on safety and the relative unconcern about how restrictions affect the freedom of the hills.

Management convenience and economics also conflict with resource protection and wilderness preservation in ways so numerous and obvious as to require no comment.

While our own relative value-weights are probably clear to most readers, this chapter has not been intended as an argument over which values *should* receive more or less emphasis. Rather, our purpose has been to make clear that managers *do* have these choices to make; and that all of us as voters and backcountry users should also weigh what relative emphases we believe are proper in maintaining the kind of backcountry environment we want. It is clear that values sometimes conflict. When we decide to pursue one objective, we should consciously realize that we may be doing harm to some other objective.

CASE STUDY

The Appalachian Trail

'Tis a long road knows no turning.

Sophocles

ONE FALL DAY on the top of Maine's Katahdin, we saw two young men
stride the last few steps to the summit rock cairn, exchange a warm handshake
and then produce a bottle of champagne.

We knew right away what the occasion was: Here were two hikers just at the
moment of completing a six-month, 2000-mile walk from Georgia to Maine—
the Appalachian Trail.

"The" Trail has become an immensely popular and prestigious testpiece, but
it's hurting as a result—hurting bad. According to a recent estimate, 4 million
people set foot on the Appalachian Trail in a year these days. That's about 8 million feet. The boot traffic is taking its toll in trampled vegetation, deep erosion
on steeper slopes, muddy quagmires in wetter areas, and depressingly overused
camping sites in what were once pristine, picturesque woods.

The volume of traffic has had other ill effects beside the purely physical
damage to the trail surface:

(1) Overuse has generated regulations on many public lands. On some parts of
the Trail, the hiker must obtain a permit just to pass through. Camping is se-
verely restricted in some areas.

(2) The boom in country real estate and second-home development has jeopardized much land through which the Trail passes. Sections that once rambled
through second-growth woods are now threatened with possible housing developments right along what is supposed to be a "wilderness footpath."

(3) Private landowners have grown hostile in some places. Some have even
kicked the Trail and its users off their land, requiring long detours on boring,
hard-surface roads.

(4) Trail crews, in a well-intentioned effort to check erosion, have taken
strong measures to "harden" the tread. Most of this work is done well, unobtrusively or inoffensively. But in places hikers are presented with stone walls
or jack-hammered steps that jar badly with the primitive and unconfined spirit
which attracted them to take up the challenge of walking the Trail.

(5) The federal government has moved into the scene, under legislation designed to protect the integrity of the Trail, resulting in some bitter squabbles with private landowners.

HISTORY OF THE TRAIL

With all of these problems, however, the Appalachian Trail remains a unique and wonderful institution. It passes over some of the east's finest wilderness scenery. It is splendidly democratic. You can meet anyone and everyone plodding along its trodden ways—not just hardened mountaineers or backwoodsmen, but families out for a picnic, city kids getting their first sweet taste of natural scenery, elderly strollers recalling bygone pedestrian days. We've seen dogs, cats, goats, and horses accompanying their owners along the Trail. We've also seen moose, bear, and hawks. And businessmen and governors and movie actors. Mostly just plain people. It's all things to all people.

In New England, the Appalachian Trail reveals the many faces of this region's backcountry. You experience at least four different outdoor worlds as the trail passes through five of the region's six states:

Maine: 277 miles. The northwoods. Here you get as big a sense of endless forest as anywhere on the trail. There's more A.T. mileage in Maine than in any other state save Virginia. It's not all idyllic woods-walking, as much of it is boggy and wet, while Maine's insect army is bigger and meaner than any. But that's all part of the true northwoods scene.

New Hampshire: 151 miles. Spectacular mountain scenery. The rugged, rocky ridges of the White Mountains afford views without parallel. It's a tough, uncompromising granite world up there.

Vermont: 138 miles. Deep green forest. This is the pure hiker's (as distinct from the mountaineer's) ideal state. Lush green vegetation enfolds the woodsy miles of Vermont, whose famed Long Trail (Canada to Massachusetts) coincides with the A.T. most of the way.

Massachusetts and Connecticut: 132 miles. Man-modified landscape. Instead of "wilderness," the characteristic views in these states are of alternating fields and woods, with many stone walls and old cellarholes, plus entrancing views over small villages.

In the course of this 698-mile odyssey, the trail passes over or near most of New England's outstanding scenic wonders—Maine's mighty Katahdin, the spiny ridge of the Bigelow Range, Mount Washington (highest point in New England), the spectacular Franconia Ridge, Vermont's celebrated ski meccas, Pico and Killington, Mount Greylock in Massachusetts, and the tri-state Taconic Range at the junction where Connecticut, Massachusetts, and New York come together.

Besides these big and famous attractions, there are many quieter vales and vistas that become personal favorite spots of hikers who grow to know them as old friends—places like Carter Notch tucked away in one of the White Mountains' more impressive cols between the Carter and Wildcat Ranges; Sage's Ravine, a deep hemlock glade in Connecticut's Hoosatonic Valley; Deer Leap, an overlook of massive rock buttresses in Vermont. Then there's "the most difficult mile"—a wild jumble of boulders strewn through the gorge of Maine's Mahoosuc Notch.

The trail doesn't hit everything there is to see in New England—it misses Vermont's best peaks, Mansfield and Camel's Hump, and it neglects New Hampshire's picture-book Chocorua and ever-popular Monadnock, just to cite a few examples. But it covers more than it misses.

This famous footpath from Maine to Georgia was the inspired brainchild of one man: New Englander Benton MacKaye, who died at the advanced age of 96 in 1975.

In 1921, MacKaye, who was a forester as well as a city planner by profession, conceived the idea of the Appalachian Trail, and wrote an article about it for the *Journal of the American Institute of Architects*.

His idea caught fire and the first work began at Bear Mountain Park in New York. MacKaye and those early trail-building pioneers tried to link up already existing trails to form the continuous footpath. But in all of the 14 states the Trail runs through there were only four of these systems, mainly in New England. From there on the trail-clearers were on their own, and work was not completed until 1937—15 years and 2000 miles later.

Along the way, the Trail acquired many friends, including the Appalachian Trail Conference founded in 1925, which greatly boosted construction by dividing up sections and parceling them out to local hiking organizations.

In 1968 the Trail, by now beleaguered by its own popularity, received another helping hand. It was designated a "National Scenic Trail," and all motorized vehicles were prohibited by law.

". . . The Appalachian Trail is accessible to 125 million Americans for weekend hikes" headlines an article in a national outdoors magazine. Some weekends it seems like all 125 million heed this invitation en masse.

The "Trail" has come to mean many things to many people. (When hikers speak of "the Trail" every other initiate knows of what they speak.)

Time was when just a handful had hiked the whole of it. (To make a continuous walk takes about six months.) But now, we run into "end-to-enders" regularly, several times a year. In 1978, 1500 aspiring trail hikers registered at its southern terminus, hoping to make it all the way to Maine.

Somehow it is not hard to spot a backpacker who has been on the Trail for several months. *None* of their equipment looks new, and their limbs seem to be outlined in a fine aura of trail dust. Boots are rather down at the heel. And they can pass the day hiker going uphill with their loaded backpack on.

Many have completed the trail, but not all do it in one six-month burst. Some take many, many years, hiking various sections on weekends and vacations. One family from Ohio did it in 85 trips, with 91,000 miles of driving to and from trail heads, over 2½ years. After completing it they commented, "Now that we have attained our goal, we are left with a lost feeling that is hard to describe."

The A.T. can offer an idyllic stroll through beautiful woods with soft autumn sunshine filtering through the golden hues of fall leaves. However, it just as often can disappoint the hiker who is not prepared to find vast stretches of water-logged, bug-infested bogs, on dismally damp rainy days where the air never seems to dry out even when it isn't actually raining. The idyll of the star-struck novice often ends in soggy disillusionment.

Many who have started brightly off from Georgia's Springer Mountain on a lovely April day have crumbled at the first prolonged rainstorm. But then, we met a couple recently on the White Mountain section who claimed that this was their first real hike. They'd come from Georgia and were going strong.

For many, probably most, who are desk-bound and city-tied, with just two weeks of precious vacation a year, the trail is a blessed retreat, a special haven near enough to go on weekends, taking the younger hikers in the family or just going by themselves. They hike the same familiar stretch of trail, loving every common stone and boot-scraped root, every mile of that worn footpath that gives them that last vestige of wildness so important to their daily lives.

TRAIL PROBLEMS

But, like Jimmy Carter, the Appalachian Trail has found that the legacy of popular success is—problems. Not very many of its 700 New England miles remain untouched by at least one (and sometimes several) of the following headaches:

(1) Physical damage. The *Vibram* army has left its mark. Where the Trail goes through boggy or wet areas, the continuous traffic has trampled the walkway into a muddy mess. As each muddy area becomes wet, hikers try to keep their feet dry by skirting to one side or the other, with the result that the Trail gradually widens into the woods on either side, until pools of mud 60 feet long and 30 feet wide are not uncommon.

One of the worst examples of this problem can be seen just south of Mount Greylock's summit in Massachusetts, in a stretch of spruce woods that might otherwise be one of the Trail's prettier spots.

On the steeper sections, the water doesn't sit in the Trail, but it does something worse. With each heavy rain and with spring's melting snows, water courses down the treadway, stripping the soil away. The resulting trenches have to be seen to be believed. In places you can stand in the Trail and place your hands on the original ground-level on either side, some 3 or 4 feet above the level to which the Trail has eroded.

Popular campsites along the Trail develop even greater problems. Live trees are hacked, birches stripped of bark, every conceivable tent site matted down to a hardpan on which no vegetation can grow.

We're painting a bleak picture of Trail conditions, and it's not all that bad. But it is a deep disappointment to many who hoped to find true "wilderness" on the Appalachian Trail.

(2) "Taming the Trail." The reaction of land managers—park superintendents, forest rangers, clubs like the Appalachian Mountain Club and the Green Mountain Club—has been to try to deal with the physical damage through vigorous trail maintenance steps.

Good trail work is a pleasure to see, because it can check the erosion and water damage described above while hardly being noticeable to the untrained eye. On steep South Twin mountain in New Hampshire, for example, the AMC's experienced trail crew spent weeks moving boulders into place and artfully slotting logs (known as "waterbars") in such a way as to divert water off the Trail at intervals. The result is so unobtrusively done and blends so well with the natural mountainside that we bet many hikers pass over that Trail section thinking that God put those rocks there that way.

In some other places, as mentioned in chapter 11, trail managers have been less artful. On sections of the White Mountains, some kind of jackhammer has bludgeoned away at steeper rock sections to create artificial steps, sometimes as many as 50 in a short uphill stretch. The boardwalks in the Carter Range and the Berlin walls on the Franconia Ridge are both part of the Appalachian Trail.

On some boggier sections of Trail, such as in the Mahoosuc Range on the Maine–New Hampshire border, trail crews have felt obliged to lay log bridges over the muddy tracts for mile after mile. Looking at some of these sections, one is tempted to speculate that the day may not be far off when the hiker seeking backwoods adventure may walk entire sections of the Appalachian Trail without even setting foot on real honest-to-goodness-put-there-by-God earth. An entire weekend may be walked on materials put in place by man, not nature. If this day comes, as it may soon, what has become of the hiker's dream of getting back to nature?

In some cases, most people would concede that trail crews had no choice. Given the volume of A.T. traffic, nothing better could have been done. In other cases, though, one can't help but wonder if the cure wasn't worse than the disease.

(3) Encroaching civilization. Not all of the threats to the Appalachian Trail are generated on its own ground. The boom in up-country real estate has posed a challenge. While much of the Trail passes through national forests and state parks, 31 percent of its 2035 miles is on privately owned land. In New England, the proportion is higher: In fact, over half of the trail sections there are on private property. Maine alone has 218 miles through private land, much of it held by paper companies. With second homes springing up in the backwoods, suburban

sprawl spreading farther and farther out, and recreational developments becoming good business, much of the Trail is in jeopardy.

New Hampshire's Senator John Durkin, in urging through the recent Appalachian Trail legislation, warned: "In many places, the Trail was in danger of becoming a path from a group of vacation homes to a roadside fast-food stand." Under the new federal legislation, the National Park Service has authority and funds to secure a "trail corridor" averaging 1000 feet in width, either by negotiating permanent easements with Trail landowners or by outright acquisition of the land—through condemnation and eminent domain if necessary.

A special problem exists in Maine: the threat of Indian claims. According to one source, two-thirds of the Maine A.T. is within the principal claim area of the Indians. This constitutes "a very serious cloud" on the Trail's horizon.

(4) Ownership squabbles. The new federal legislation seems like the kind of public-spirited step that all outdoors-lovers should applaud. Yet paradoxically the entry of the federal government is not universally welcomed by partisans of the Appalachian Trail. Indeed, there is evidence that the Trail has actually suffered as a result of the federal legislation. Here's an example:

A Vermont farmer who owns 110 acres, including a sugarbush, had for years enjoyed having the Trail run through his property. He welcomed the hikers he met and they never gave him trouble. Then came word of the federal law, and the prospect that the government would take away his land for its 1000-foot "corridor." You can imagine a Vermonter's reaction. He closed the Trail over his land rather than risk losing it.

That's not an isolated case. In the Cumberland Valley of Pennsylvania, some hikers and landowners organized a "Citizens Against the New Trail" to oppose land acquisition, protesting the "arrogant and demanding" attitude of government officials.

The paradoxical result is that legislation aimed at protecting the Trail has resulted, in several instances, in a poorer Trail. Hikers must now walk on roads, pounding pavement and breathing exhaust fumes, where they formerly walked through indulgent farmers' woodlots and pastures.

It's a real dilemma. The proponents of the legislation would protest that without federal protection even more land might one day be closed to the Trail. One government official involved (himself an avid hiker and A.T. end-to-ender) expresses confidence that "the over-all effect of the acquisition program will be a resounding improvement in the route of the Trail. Hundreds of miles of relocations away from roads and congested areas are being planned. No longer will the Trail need to follow the route of least resistance from landowners."

Our impression has been that the National Park Service group, which has responsibility for the new Appalachian Trail program, is sensitive to the traditional values of the Trail—its informality, the role of volunteers from hiking clubs in maintaining it, the wilderness values which hikers seek as they walk it, what MacKaye referred to as the "soul" of the Trail. One NPS spokesman, Steve

Golden, has argued: "I believe that we are making great progress in meeting the challenge of protecting the body of the Trail without sacrificing its soul."

Meanwhile, though, there's no question that in several particular locations, the immediate result has been bitterness on the part of some landowners. As the Green Mountain Club reported: "Was this their reward, grumbled landowners, that after more than 50 years of allowing hikers across their land, the government could just take their land from them?"*

Such are the problems and headaches that go with the Trail's popularity and prosperity.

But for many who walk the Appalachian Trail, the mud and erosion can be tolerated, the crowded and regulated campsites avoided, the government jargon ignored. "The" Trail is still the Trail. It's still basically what MacKaye conceived: a footpath through the woods, going ever on, a place to walk away your cares under the forest canopy and listen to the sounds of the earth around you. May it ever remain so.

*Preston Bristow, Jr., "GMC Has Effect On Final Form of AT Legislation," *The Long Trail News,* GMC, May, 1978.

12

Managing Wild Lands: The Green Mosaic

Too frequently we bureaucrats identify a problem and then write up a regulation to solve it. We would much prefer not to develop a lot of regulations to manage people's use of wilderness. Rather, through education we hope that the wilderness user will develop a sense of what constitutes an ethical use of wilderness.

Allan G. Gibbs
U.S. Forest Service

ALL OF US who love the outdoors were brought up to cherish the concept of wildness. From an early age we learned about how important it was for this country to set aside parks and forests—Yellowstone and Yosemite, the Tetons, the Great Smokies, the Adirondacks. Perhaps because of our frontier origins, Americans have felt a deep need to preserve these great tracts of wild natural scenery. As schoolchildren we learned about how these areas were set aside and shielded from the raw exploitation of natural resources which degraded too much of the land. We read of the battles to save the wilderness, and grew up to revere the patron saints of conservation—Teddy Roosevelt and Gifford Pinchot, Muir and Burroughs and Aldo Leopold.

Much of the history of winning the western parks comes through to us as a great crusade by the good guys (conservationists) defeating the bad guys (no shortage of these—railroads, mining interests, cattle grazers, lumber barons, the Army Corps of Engineers, to mention some of the blacker villains of the piece).

The western conservationist–recreationist is still very much inclined to see the "battle" in these terms. He may have good reason. The cattle and sheep herders are still shooting eagles and poisoning coyotes out there. The strip miners are still opening new mines, and the devastation of whole mountainsides is a thing not just of the past but of the present and the threatening future. The lumbermen still want to clearcut, and some of them itch to lay their saws on the incomparable redwoods. The dam builders always have their eyes on free-flowing rivers.

As one Montana conservation leader put it: "They say it's dangerous to get caught between a female grizzly and her cubs. But it's much more dangerous to be caught between *homo sapiens* and his nickel."*

*Quoted in *God's Dog* by Hope Ryden. New York: Coward, McCann and Geoghegan, Inc., 1975.

So the battle for wilderness goes on in the American west. It's still the good guys vs. the bad guys, Shane vs. Wilson, gunfight at O.K. Corral, showdown at high noon.

Many western hikers and conservationists have concluded that the only certain salvation lies in public ownership—probably federal government ownership—and most securely of all in formal designation of "Wilderness Areas" by an act of Congress, with all the protections of the Wilderness Act of 1964. This landmark legislation secured for the American people "the benefits of an enduring wilderness." Under its terms Congress set aside designated areas to be administered so as

to preserve "their wilderness character";
to keep "the imprint of man's work substantially unnoticed";
to provide "opportunities for solitude";
to provide places for "a primitive and unconfined type of recreation";
to allow "their use and enjoyment as wilderness"; but also
to "leave them unimpaired for future use and enjoyment as wilderness."

This act is the lodestar that guides the efforts of many western-oriented organizations like the Sierra Club and The Wilderness Society in their heroic efforts to save the great wild forests and mountains and rivers of the American west. Getting more land designated as "Wilderness" with a capital "W" is the name of the game.

EASTERN WILDERNESS: PATTERNS OF OWNERSHIP

A curious thing happens when people try to transfer this "battle" to eastern wild lands. The battle lines get fuzzy, the good guys and bad guys get all mixed up and muff their cues, and more than a few backwoods-lovers begin to wonder whether the campaign for "Wilderness" designation really fits here in New England.

The patterns of land ownership and recreational use are very different in the northeast as compared with the west. In the east there is a wide diversity of ownership and management of wild lands. In the 14 northeastern states only 10 percent of the land is in public ownership, compared to 50 percent for most western states. Those who think that public ownership is the only way or even the best way to guarantee wilderness values may be correct west of the Mississippi or even the Hudson. But they betray their ignorance of the history of New England's woods and hills.

Public use of private wild lands has a long tradition in this region. Hunters and fishermen have roamed the northeast with little regard to property lines for centuries. In modern times the hiker and other recreationists have enjoyed similar latitude:

(1) Hikers have long enjoyed the rugged terrain of the Mahoosuc Range on the Maine–New Hampshire border, on land mostly owned by a paper company.

(2) The northernmost 50 miles of the Long Trail, Vermont's "footpath in the wilderness" is all on private land, and it is peerless woods-walking country. Indeed, over half of the 263 miles of the Long Trail is on private land.

(3) Over half of the Appalachian Trail's Connecticut section is privately owned. In Maine, three-quarters of the A.T. is in private ownership—over 200 miles of woodland footpath.

(4) All during the twenties and thirties, the Allagash River afforded one of the east's magnificent wilderness experiences—virtually all of it on paper company land. It has been since the advent of public control and the formal designation of the Allagash Wilderness Waterway that opportunities for solitude and unconfined recreation have been lost, the crowds have come, the regulations have come, the experience has been degraded. Public ownership did not *cause* the backcountry boom that brought the crowds and the regulations, but it didn't solve the problem either, and the enticing publicity inherent in the designation as a public "Wilderness" waterway didn't help.

(5) Until very recently, some of the finest summits of the Adirondacks' High Peaks were owned by the posh Ausable Club. Hikers were permitted on the trails, but under rules which resulted in less degradation of the land than was occurring on adjacent publicly owned mountains.

(6) One of the most beautiful natural landscapes in the northeast, the Shawangunk Ridge in New York, has been privately owned through most of the past century. Much of it is still maintained by The Mohonk Trust, a private organization supported principally by voluntary contributions and modest land-use fees from the hikers, climbers, and other recreationists who enjoy the lands.

(7) Some of the finest walking in the east is on Audubon sanctuaries.

(8) The Nature Conservancy is very active in New England, with over 200 areas set aside as of the fall of 1978.

It's not just the availability of private lands for recreation that distinguishes the east. Many key recreational and scenic lands in the east are publicly owned. However, it's worth noting the rich diversity of ownership patterns even within the public sector.

Some of the very best hiking land in the northeast is in state parks, notably in the Adirondacks and in Maine's Baxter State Park, location of Katahdin. Two big national forests account for large blocs of prime hiking country in the White Mountains and Green Mountains respectively. These tracts were set aside as a result of 1911 legislation that stemmed from uncontrolled logging in northern New England, along with some spectacular forest fires that were blamed on poor logging practices. Within these national forests, logging is allowed, but it is closely supervised, and a heavy volume of hiking and other recreational use goes on alongside.

An elaborate "unit planning process" has evolved under which the Forest

Service solicits local views on use of the land and then sets up categories that emphasize different types of use—e.g., some areas on which logging is permitted, others where heavy recreational use of various kinds is expected, still others where only primitive recreation is allowed. If we refer to the "MA-IV" designation later in this chapter, it's not a robot cousin of "R2-D2," but a classification of national forest land under which the primitive and wild character of the woods is maintained to the exclusion of motorized equipment or civilized facilities. Designation of "Scenic Areas" also provides certain limitations on the amount of commercial exploitation or resource degradation that will be allowed.

Nor are the boundaries between public and private ownership rigidly held. One pattern common in the northeastern region is for private conservation groups to acquire open land and then turn around and transfer it to a public agency. The Hanover (N.H.) Conservation Council has preserved much greenspace for its town residents in this manner. The Nature Conservancy uses this approach on a broad scale throughout the region.

This complicated jigsaw puzzle of public and private ownership, along with widely varying use patterns, has given the northeast a very different history than the west. Another factor has been the different commercial significance of our wild lands. Mining is less of a factor here than out west and seems less of an intrusion on the landscape. Commercial grazing is limited to small farms and virtually never comes in conflict with recreational use of wild lands. Here we're concerned with paper companies and loggers whose forestry practices are sometimes challenged by conservationists, but who have also enjoyed generally good relationships with recreationists using the land.

Please note that the difference between east and west is not simply one of private vs. public ownership. It's much more subtle than that. What we have in New England is a green mosaic of private *and* public wild lands. Federal *and* state, individual *and* corporate ownership. Whether the hiker has the experience of deep unbroken woodlands or rugged mountain terrain, with true "wilderness" values, seems to depend little on any *one* pattern of ownership or control.

THE WILDERNESS ACT IN THE NORTHEAST

Against this background of the complexity of ownership and use, the "battle" for preserving wild lands in the northeast is hard to define. There are specific times and places where a distinct controversy comes sharply into focus. Local fights to save a pristine watershed, or stop an unwanted "second-home" development, save some lovely mountain from a proposed pump-storage system, or transfer some valuable forest plot to an owner that will preserve it—these do go on here. Then it's Shane vs. Wilson, just like in the west, for a few months, sometimes years, in a particular locale. No one who has waded through the battles over Dickey-Lincoln Dam, the Storm King pump storage project, or the

Franconia Notch highway can be complacent about the threats to eastern wild lands.

But when the move came along for designation of "Wilderness Areas" in the east, under the restrictive terms of the Wilderness Act of 1964, a funny thing happened on the way to the O.K. Corral. The principal hiking organizations of New England—the Appalachian Mountain Club and the Green Mountain Club— took a long hard look at the areas proposed for Wilderness designation, and said, "Well, wait a minute . . . let's think about this."

The Green Mountain Club pointed out that Wilderness designation was not needed to protect the wilderness experience enjoyed for years by Long Trail hikers. The Club expressed concern instead about potential "adverse and unknown" effects of wilderness designation. Specifically, GMC noted that the Wilderness Act as presently implemented would mandate removal of manmade shelters, and concluded:

> The experience of The Green Mountain Club has been that its shelters help to minimize the extent to which the earth and its community of life are trammeled by wilderness recreation. The probable impact of removing existing shelters will be to create a more widespread degradation of the landscape in the vicinity of the present shelters and to create some new degradation of the landscape at potential campsites hitherto unused.*

In short, "Wilderness" classification could do more harm than good to the woods! Furthermore, GMC noted that Wilderness designation usually has led to permit systems designed to limit the number of hikers (so as to provide those "opportunities for solitude" required by the Wilderness Act). Permit systems, felt the Vermonters, would be "an objectionable imposition on the hiking public." The club concluded that "sound land management with sensitivity to wilderness values" could better be achieved within the existing unit planning process.

Looking at lands proposed for New Hampshire "Wilderness Areas," the Appalachian Mountain Club came to somewhat similar conclusions, though AMC did endorse further study to work out the possibility of some areas receiving "Wilderness" classification. For the most part, AMC preferred to see New Hampshire's wild lands protected by less rigid mechanisms—Scenic Area designation, or that MA-IV category within the unit planning process. Many AMC members and other New Hampshire hikers registered dissatisfaction with how "Wilderness" classification had affected the hiking climate in areas in the Presidential Range. (More on this in the next chapter.)

One of the problems that has surfaced is that formal designation of a "Wilderness" seems to evoke a stampede among hikers and backpackers, all eager to see this wild new Wilderness, this primitive and unconfined place with all its opportunities for solitude. The result is a big increase in traffic—and, paradoxically,

*Position statement adopted by GMC Board of Directors, Oct. 28, 1978. From *The Long Trail News,* November, 1978.

less solitude. The increased use levels also tend to defeat the intended preservation of natural ecosystems. To prevent the crowds from completely destroying the land or the solitude, the land managers feel almost forced to limit entry by a permit system. The result is that the area in which Congress intended to preserve the possibility of "unconfined" experience becomes one in which the hiker is required to report to authorities where and when he will hike, and to wait his turn if the area is already "full."

In 1977, after running organized backcountry trips for 18 years under the title, "A Way to the Wilderness," The Wilderness Society discontinued the program, commenting: "The question has become, not how people can be drawn into wilderness in order to appreciate and enjoy it, but how the wilderness can survive without being overwhelmed by sheer numbers."*

In one of his darker moments, Aldo Leopold wrote, "All conservation of wildness is self-defeating, for to cherish we must see and fondle, and when enough have seen and fondled, there is no wilderness left to cherish."

The issue is a complex one, and we don't wish to imply that all hikers or hiking clubs take such a skeptical view of the formal "Wilderness" classification. For example, the Wonalancet Outdoor Club, a very active and informed hiking group in the southern tier of the White Mountains, seems to be strongly in favor of officially designated "Wilderness." Within the AMC, those with a strong conservationist bent argued eloquently for embracing the "Wilderness" concept wholeheartedly, but they were outvoted.

The national organizations whose experience and attitudes have been forged in the great western battles came out strongly for "Wilderness" designation of as much eastern land as possible. The Sierra Club, The Wilderness Society, and national hiking magazines urged their members and subscribers to write their Congressmen demanding "Wilderness" status for all areas under consideration. Their literature portrayed the opposition as motivated mainly by economic interest — the traditional villainous loggers and miners, with a new villain, the snowmobiler, added. In view of the fact that the chief hiking and conservation organizations of the northeast region took a contrary view, not to mention experienced and respected outdoorsmen like former New Hampshire State Parks Director George Hamilton, it may be questioned whether those national organizations are doing their own cause a favor. As GMC and AMC see it, the wilderness experience will *not* be well served by formal "Wilderness" designation.

FOR EXAMPLE

An anecdote involving one of the specific areas under consideration may help to illuminate the problem.

*From *The Living Wilderness,* Oct./Dec., 1977.

One recent September, we decided to go on a long day hike in the White Mountains. Specifically (for those who know the area), we went up the Sabbaday Brook Trail from the Kancamagus Highway to the Tripyramids, crossed over the Sleeper Ridge to Whiteface and Passaconaway and descended via the Oliverian Brook Trail. Since the day was to involve 20 miles and six peaks (four of them "official" 4000-footers), we obviously needed an early start.

Throughout this hike, except for the 2½-mile road walk at the end, we saw *not one* other person, as it was after Labor Day and mid-week. With clear weather, we enjoyed spectacular views, each summit presenting different perspectives.

Now here's the interesting point: The area which we hiked has been designated as one to be considered for "Wilderness" classification as the Sandwich Range. As this book went to press, the Secretary of Agriculture had recommended this area and three others in the White Mountains of New Hampshire for "Wilderness" classification; congressional action was awaited in 1979. One of the chief benefits of such classification is that, in the language of the Wilderness Act, the hiker may have the "opportunities for solitude or a primitive and unconfined type of recreation."

As we have mentioned, experience has shown that designation of a Wilderness Area in New England has at least two results: One is that more hikers are attracted to it, lured by the magic word "wilderness"; the second is that, attempting to carry out the legislative mandate to safeguard "opportunities for solitude," the Forest Service institutes a permit system. Such permits are not required by the act, but they have been regarded as essential to achieving the act's "solitude" objective.

Suppose the Sandwich Range had been designated a Wilderness, what would have happened to our wonderful September hike?

First, we could not have gone on it without first getting a permit. Since a long, strenuous hike requires a dawn start, we could not have obtained a permit on the day we decided to go. We would have had to make a special trip over to the mountains beforehand to obtain our permit, or plan far enough ahead to pick it up some other time when we were over there. This obstacle is perhaps merely an inconvenience, but it does rob one of the flexibility to choose an itinerary on short notice. Many of us have felt that such flexibility and freedom is no small part of the spirit of being in the mountains. In this particular instance, the practical result of Wilderness designation would have been that we could *not* have gone on that particular hike and thus would *not* have experienced the "opportunities for solitude" that the act is supposed to foster.

Second, suppose we had obtained our permit. As has been richly demonstrated in the "Wilderness" areas already classified in New England, many hikers are attracted to them by the aura currently surrounding the term "wilderness." So the chances would have greatly increased that we would *not* have enjoyed "opportunities for solitude," but would have found others out there seeking solitude too. The week before, in a similar long hike in the Crawford Notch area, we ran into several hikers in the Presidential-Dry River "Wilderness." But when we crossed to the other side of the notch, we hiked for hours in solitude. Thus, paradoxically, the legislative guarantee actually seems to reduce the opportunities for solitude.

Third, "Wilderness" classification is supposed to protect good hiking country from the logging companies. From several summits in the Sandwich Range, we could look out over vast stretches of rolling forest land. It was beautiful. If we looked closely we could notice patches of logged land. Since we could also see the cut of the Kancamagus Highway, the fire tower on Mount Osceola, and various other evidences of man's impact, we did not find these logged-over patches especially offensive to the over-all visual panorama of vast forest and beautiful mountains. The fact is that within the White Mountain National Forest, the Forest Service tries to confine the loggers to areas where their work cannot be readily seen from trails or roads. In fact, as pointed out earlier, that 1911 legislation originally set up New England's national forests as a reaction against uncontrolled and offensively obvious logging activities, together with the devastating fires that resulted from careless logging slash. Today the Forest Service compels loggers to screen their activities by leaving intervening patches of unlogged woods.

This is "multiple use" in its best sense. Often conservationists fear that the phrase "multiple use" is merely a euphemism for a lot of logging and a lot of mining. Maybe at certain times and places it has been. But in this particular place on that day, we felt that the hikers' interests were weighted adequately in the balance.

By contrast, a few months earlier we hiked a trail on nearby Carr Mountain over private land. The owner had allowed a logger to cut on that particular land, and it was a terrible mess. The trail repeatedly crossed vast, muddy quagmires left by the loggers. Ugly slash was on every hand. On a recent climb of Cabot, also, the approach through private land had been to the accompaniment of the harsh drone of chain saws.

The point is that when logging goes on within the national forest, the hiker is apt to be protected from its immediate effects. If vast acreage within the forest is classified as "Wilderness," the local loggers will be increasingly driven over to private land. They're not going to cut fewer logs just because we block them out of Forest Service land. The result will very likely be to increase the hiker's exposure to overt, uncontrolled logging right over land traversed by hiking trails.

We have no love for the chain saw and the skidder. We don't like days of freezing rain either, but we've learned that there's nothing we can do to prevent their existence, and it seems unlikely that we or anyone else can prevent the existence of all the unattractive paraphernalia of logging. The question is, Shall it be done on certain Forest Service lands or not? The evidence suggested by our experience in the White Mountains is that logging under the scrutiny of the Forest Service is less offensive than logging on private lands through which hiking trails pass.

But, regardless of whether you buy that point or not, it seems absolutely irrefutable that, had the Sandwich Range been designated a "Wilderness" at the time, we would not have enjoyed our full day of solitude on those mountains.

None of the foregoing is meant to sound as if we're critical of private ownership of recreational lands. Far from it. In fact, one of the weaknesses of the "Wilderness" lobby is their stated or implied position that the only salvation for recreational land lies in federal ownership and "Wilderness" classification.

One leading conservationist of the region, John Cole, an Audubon director and frequent advisor to state and national park managers, has gone the other way and come out *against* further acquisition of public lands and *for* retaining wild lands in private hands wherever that seems to meet conservation objectives well. Writing in the December 1978 *Yankee* magazine, Cole lamented the destructiveness which overuse and misuse wreak on public lands, and went on: "I now argue that the more rare and fragile the natural area in question, the more stubbornly it should be kept in private hands that will protect it. . . . The keys here are protection and preservation. Continued efforts to make more land available to today's public can accomplish neither."

In view of the contributions of private ownership to the conservation of wild lands in this region, some of the ardent champions of the cause would do well to direct their attention to another problem: the preservation of private wild lands in the face of rising property taxes. In a key New York State tax case, state courts have held that The Mohonk Trust is not exempt from local property taxes. This ruling (still being appealed as this book went to press) could have put an intolerable tax burden on that organization and jeopardized its continued ownership and preservation of 5000 acres of mountain ridge in the Hudson Valley. Fortunately, through painstaking and difficult negotiations with the towns involved, restrictive covenants were arranged with The Mohonk Trust, designed to reduce the evaluation of Trust lands and thereby produce a tax level that the organization could pay. But should the precedent stand in New York State, according to one Nature Conservancy official, "It would mean the end of private sector acquisition and maintenance of nature preserves for the public."

ARGUMENTS FOR WILD LANDS

The arguments for maintaining wild lands are too often advanced in purely negative terms—to keep out the loggers, to keep out the snowmobilers, to lock it up for the future. The positive blessings of preserving vast tracts of natural woods and hills are too seldom articulated.

When the Appalachian Mountain Club convened a special Wilderness Task Force, one of its members, George E. Zink, prepared a special memorandum to spell out the *positive* reasons for conserving wild lands. Mr. Zink's six points deserve public attention, and we herewith set them forth:

(1) Museum pieces: "Preserving samples of the New England upland forests as nearly as possible in the primitive condition in which the first settlers found them ..." is one important reason for protecting major tracts of wild country.

(2) Education and therapy: Wilderness can serve as a setting for a unique kind of educational experience, both individually and institutionally. Just a few examples of the latter are the Outward Bound schools found nationwide, National Outdoor Leadership Schools, the AMC's own Youth Opportunities Program, as well as use of the backwoods as a unique outdoor "classroom" by many schools and colleges and even by mental hospitals.

(3) Wildlife habitat: Deep woods provide the essential conditions for animals and birds that like that particular habitat—Canadian lynx, eastern cougar, pileated woodpecker, fisher, bear—as well as for plants that seek deep shade, exposed ledges, acid soils, or thick leaf mold.

(4) Nature knows best: In undisturbed woods, ecological systems can evolve without the interference of man. Argues Zink, "A most important value of wilderness lies in the genetic experimentation which takes place there, continuing unbroken the evolutionary processes."

(5) Science and wilderness: Scientists need natural ecosystems for many of their investigations—from grizzly bears and prairie flora in the west to research on eastern pines and the peregrine falcon in the northeast.

(6) Recreational use of wilderness: Backpackers and hikers, birdwatchers and nature photographers, hunters and fishermen need extensive, unspoiled backcountry for their pursuits. Specifically, they need land in which a high degree of solitude is possible. Mr. Zink quotes James Russell Lowell: "Solitude is as needful to the imagination as society is wholesome for the character."

These are all cogent and positive points as to why land should be set aside. They are excellent reasons why plans for yet another giant shopping center, yet another four-lane interstate, yet another mammoth ski area, or group of condominiums, or second-home development, should be nipped in the bud. They are wonderful arguments for why wild land is so important to our well-being.

With reference back to this chapter's earlier comments on the controversy over official "Wilderness" designation, it may be noted that these six arguments make the case for wild country in general, regardless of whether publicly or privately held, and under any kind of management arrangement. (They do not necessarily argue for "Wilderness" designation under the Wilderness Act of 1964.)

It's also instructive to note that only one or two of the six (#6 and maybe #2) have to do with the narrow self-interest of the recreational hiker. The fundamental value of true wilderness runs deeper than just being a playground for weekenders and vacationers.

As the German conservationist Bernhard Grzimek, who has influenced the increase of national parks in Africa as much as any other man, has said, "People *need* animals." Well, people *need* wild lands too. We need the unfettered backcountry. We need miles and miles of trees and brooks, meadows and mountains where, as John Muir wrote, "The galling harness of civilization drops off, and the wounds heal ere we are aware." And, even if we never go there ourselves, we need to know, as a people, that the wilderness is still there.

CASE STUDY

The Great Gulf Wilderness

*An area of Wilderness is further defined to mean in this act an area
... which ... has outstanding opportunities for solitude or a primitive and unconfined type of recreation. ...*

The Wilderness Act

*During the mid-seventies, a U.S. Forest Service plan was drawn up for the man-
agement of the Great Gulf Wilderness. Without fanfare, the report quietly proposed to discontinue five hiking trails. A schedule was set up and plans developed
for a staged five-year rerouting of hiking traffic, at the end of which time the
five trails in question would have been closed.*

*When word of this plan slowly spread among New England hikers, a rising
chorus of protest began. Greatly to their credit, officials of the White Mountain
National Forest did what bureaucrats are often accused of being unable to do—
they listened. When all the arguments were heard and the tumult and shouting
died away, the plan was changed—all the trails were saved.*

*The controversy illustrated succinctly many of the issues discussed in this
section: preservation versus use, "Wilderness" designation versus maintaining
opportunities for "a primitive and unconfined type of recreation," and an ex-
amination of what backwoods environment we want.*

*We reproduce here what we wrote at the height of the controversy, as one of
our contributions to discussion of these issues. Although this particular fight is
over and the trails are saved, the underlying issues remain critical to future decisions affecting the backwoods environment, not just in New England but
throughout the country.*

For steep and challenging hiking trails, no place in New England can rival New
Hampshire's Great Gulf Wilderness. Not even Maine's Katahdin has so many
strenuous trails in such a setting of magnificent alpine scenery.

But within three years most of these trails may be wiped off the map, the
signs torn down, the trails officially abandoned.

Picture the northeast's highest mountains, the rugged Presidential Range. Now
peer around the gigantic, sprawling northeast shoulder of Mount Washington,

loftiest summit of New England. There you'll find—if you're enterprising enough to hike up 4 miles of rough mountain trail with over 1000 feet of ascent from the nearest road—a high hidden valley enclosed by the four tallest peaks in New England: 5798-foot Adams to the north; 5715-foot Jefferson to the west, with the stupendous ridge called "Jefferson's Knee" jutting into this valley; 5532-foot Mount Clay to the southwest, with its rocky ramparts cutting the skyline; and 6288-foot Washington itself to the south, with its huge northeast shoulder nearly walling in the escape from this valley.

Here, hidden away from all evidence of civilization, is a 3-mile-long wilderness defile known as the Great Gulf.

Through a rich forest of spruce, fir, and birch, punctuated by enormous massy boulders, the west branch of the Peabody River and its lovely tributary brooks drain the great slopes of the mountains. High up on these slopes the trees thin out and eventually dwindle to shrunken, dwarf-like shapes huddling for survival against the arctic force of the Presidentials' famous winds. The fastest wind speed ever recorded by man was on Mount Washington—231 mph on April 12, 1934. On the mountain tops themselves there are no trees, but only tiny, exquisite alpine flowers, like mountain sandwort, *Diapensia,* and Labrador tea.

This is the Great Gulf Wilderness. The *floor* of this valley is about as high as the *top* of such well-known New England mountains as Chocorua, Greylock, and Monadnock. The mountain ridges rise another 2000 feet or more above that. From the floor of the Great Gulf originate eight spectacular hiking trails. For the hiker who loves the feeling of climbing rapidly, with strenuous effort, to reach a lofty summit, these trails are without parallel in the east.

Yet, five of these eight magnificent trails are now doomed to be abandoned, trail signs removed, and all mention taken off official maps.

How could such a deprivation of outstanding wilderness opportunities take place? That question leads to a curious paradox.

A few years ago, devotees of eastern wilderness succeeded in getting the Great Gulf formally designated, by Act of Congress, as the Great Gulf Wilderness. This designation gave the area official "Wilderness" status, federally protected, guaranteeing that no motorized vehicles, commercial operations, or even manmade structures were to be allowed there.

The White Mountain National Forest thereby inherited a difficult job: how to administer this area as an officially designated "Wilderness." The WMNF decided to interpret the Wilderness Act in a very rigid manner, as requiring that people going into the Great Gulf stay in the valley to enjoy the wilderness for its own sake, not as a base from which to climb to the surrounding peaks.

As a result, the WMNF has now set forth a "Management Plan" that schedules abandoning five of the eight trails out of the Great Gulf. Exactly what this abandonment would involve is ambiguous. The trails would be taken off the maps, and all trail signs would be removed, but WMNF Supervisor Paul Weingart has indicated that the adventurous hiker would still be free to use the trails if he wished to, knew where to look, and could stay on them (a problem above tree-line in bad weather, if stone cairns were torn down).

Those who love these historic trails and the adventures they provide are up in arms. The influential Appalachian Mountain Club has expressed their grave concern.

These trails are the priceless legacy of early trail-builders who worked with in-spiration and dedication.

On June 28, 1908, three adventurous backwoodsmen descended from Mount Jefferson over what they described as the "desolate and magnificent" ridge of Jefferson's Knee, dropping "through a charming forest" to the valley floor be-low. Wrote one of them: "We were so impressed with the scenery of this region that we began immediately to plan new trails for the benefit of the public." The Six Husbands and Wamsutta trails—then conceived as one route, down one side and up the other—were the result of "90 long, hard days of labor," involving as many as 33 people. All of the Great Gulf trails were built in the years 1908 to 1910: truly a burst of imaginative mountaincraft unparalleled in New England history. The immediate popularity of the new trails was attested to by the fact that 400 persons registered at a trailside camp during the first year after their completion.

All of this labor of love and the enjoyment it has brought to countless hikers since, is now jeopardized by the plan to summarily abandon these trails.

Consider each of these gems of backcountry travel:

The location of the *Six Husbands Trail* was inspired. It follows one of the steepest, most exposed arêtes of any non-technical hiking trail we know of in the east, with gradually expanding views of Washington, Adams, and the Carter Range. To put a trail up that ridge, called Jefferson's Knee, was an act of creative imagination unprecedented in eastern trail-building. The lower sections actually tunnel their way through boulder caves, at length emerging onto spectacular viewpoints requiring rugged scrambling. A few years ago, before these trails were threatened, one of us who had climbed the Six Husbands Trail for the first time recorded in a journal, "This audacious path . . . is precipitous and very exciting, ascending by caves and ladders fastened to the vertical faces. A tremendous amount of fun, I enjoyed it as much as any trail I've ever climbed."

If you like the headwalls of giant glacial cirques, rather than ridges, the *Madison Gulf Trail* is one of the great headwall trails of the east. Swooping up the ravine between Adams and Madison, it offers scenic views of the rocky heights above, while scrambling through especially lush green moss and undergrowth.

Of all the ways to climb Mount Washington, nothing compares for alpine magnificence with the *Great Gulf Headwall Trail*, with its awesome views of Clay's Ramparts in their most rugged aspect. According to an old guidebook, the distance from Spaulding Lake at the base of the headwall to the rim is "less than 1 mile with a difference of 2040 feet in altitude." That's a steep ascent! In early summer, the middle stretches of this trail pass through a flourishing carpet of golden mountain avens clinging to the steep mountain slopes in all their glory.

If one seeks a commanding view of the Great Gulf Wilderness itself, the *Wamsutta Trail* surely provides perhaps the most distinctive vantage point of all. Not as steep and spectacular as the other three, Wamsutta may give the most beautiful views to the appreciative hiker. It also performs a significant safety function in allowing a way to get down off the alpine gardens to the north in bad weather.

Chandler Brook Trail is not such a precious asset as the other four, but it does offer a useful connection between the lower reaches of Mount Washington's northeast shoulder and the valley floor below.

It is crude irony that trails like these, which appeal so compellingly to the wilderness lover, should be jeopardized by the very legislation that is meant to preserve wilderness! How could this paradox arise?

In undertaking the thankless job of administering the Wilderness Act in the Great Gulf, WMNF management has decided that solitude is vital, and that previous use patterns—of many people camping in the Great Gulf so as to do dayhikes up the spectacular trails to the summits—were inconsistent with the intent of the Act. So, in a "Management Plan" written to implement the Wilderness Act in the Great Gulf, WMNF decreed: "The trail system will be relocated, by design, to discourage the through traffic." Hence, five trails were marked for oblivion, including the marvellous Six Husbands, Madison Gulf, Great Gulf Headwall, Wamsutta, and Chandler Brook.

We sympathize with the difficult job which WMNF confronts in trying to administer "Wilderness" designation in an area which suffers such heavy foot traffic as the Great Gulf. But we and many other hikers that we've talked to totally disagree with the planned trail closings.

WMNF's assumption that Wilderness designation precludes recreational use of the high peaks from the Great Gulf is open to serious challenge. There is nothing in the act that says a Wilderness Area cannot be enjoyed in association with surrounding physical features. There is no congressional limitation, express or implied, on through-hiking, as long as the "Wilderness character" of the area is preserved.

The Wilderness Act clearly states that Wilderness Areas are intended for "use and enjoyment," just as long as such use and enjoyment leaves the areas "unimpaired for future use and enjoyment." Nothing could impair the use and enjoyment of the Great Gulf quite so dismally as removing its fine trails.

The Wilderness Act is quite clear in requiring "opportunities for solitude or a primitive and unconfined type of recreation." Note that's "solitude *or* ...," not "solitude *and*...." Why on earth should WMNF choose to emphasize solitude in an area so heavily trafficked? What the Great Gulf certainly can and does provide, *par excellence,* is "opportunities for ... a primitive and unconfined type of recreation." That is, as long as those wonderful trails are still there to use.

Indeed, the one truly unique resource of the Great Gulf is not to be found in any exceptional flora or fauna along the valley floor, nor any unusual features there, but in the almost unparalleled wilderness hiking opportunities made possible by the Gulf's location right in the heart of the east's highest peaks and most extensive alpine zone. To abandon these trails is to rob the Great Gulf of its most distinctive resource.

As New Hampshire Parks Director George Hamilton has pointed out, the unique attraction of camping there is "the availability of a trail system which allows several loops to be taken on day trips from the floor of the Gulf, enabling you to travel on different trails on several occasions."

The safety value of these trails is one which many people think is being overlooked in this controversy. The Presidentials are always potentially dangerous to hikers caught out above treeline in low visibility, high winds, and cold driving rain. Mount Washington alone has claimed 83 victims through 1976. As author Harry Roberts points out, "Mount Washington is winter—anytime." Hikers unexpectedly trapped above treeline in bad weather need to have opportunities for getting down into the trees, rapidly, without simply bushwhacking down into the puckerbrush. Those in trouble on the side of Jefferson may especially need Six Husbands.

The authors of the Great Gulf Management Plan dismiss the location of these trails as "developed through uncontrolled use by hikers whose primary interest was crossing the area along the shortest route." This derogatory comment does an unintended disservice to the inspired trail-building of an earlier time. Had those who conceived Six Husbands simply wished to get to and from the summit of Jefferson by the most convenient route, there were lots of easier ways to go. Certainly anyone aiming for Washington would not select the Great Gulf Headwall in an "uncontrolled," casual way.

No, these trail-builders knew what they were doing: boldly picking routes of great ruggedness and scenic value. They loved the mountains and built trails from which they and we can fully appreciate their wild grandeur. It's a shame that their daring achievements are so cavalierly dismissed. We have far more admiration for the creative imagination of those trail-builders than for the uninspired routes suggested now as alternatives.

What the early trail-builders did *not* foresee was the heavy use of the late twentieth century and the consequent boot-and-water erosion problem. But that simply means that a management job needs to be done, not that these spectacular trails should cease to exist.

It is only sensible (and surely consistent with the intent of the Wilderness Act) to shape management plans for each Wilderness Area in terms of *that* area's unique values. The Great Gulf's special relationship to the high peaks and alpine zone of the Presidentials is clearly its distinctive quality. To try to confine "use and enjoyment" of the Great Gulf to walking around the valley floor is to destroy its most exceptional wilderness value. To abandon the five trails we've mentioned would be to eliminate some of the finest hiking in the east. Surely this cannot have been the intention of the framers of *wilderness* legislation!

The current management of the WMNF impresses us as being composed of constructive and reasonable people. They have shown on several occasions a willingness to listen to diverse viewpoints and to modify policies when shown strong reasons why they should.

During this spring and summer, the WMNF is conducting a thorough review of all its policies in the Presidentials area. This review provides a good opportunity to reconsider the proposed trail closings.

For this reason, we are guardedly optimistic that these magnificent trails can yet be saved . . . *but* only if WMNF can be honestly convinced that the Wilderness Act will be faithfully served by a plan that provides for these trails' continued existence . . . *and* only if enough people show how much the existence of such rugged hiking opportunities mean to those who love the wilderness.

This column appeared in May 1977 in the pages of New England Outdoors *magazine. Other voices were raised, including the influential one of the Appalachian Mountain Club. Officials of the White Mountain National Forest listened and weighed the arguments—and in late 1978 they issued a revised plan under which all five of the Great Gulf's threatened trails were retained.*

This change was good news to hikers and was greatly appreciated. We applaud the WMNF both for this decision and for the spirit behind it. That kind of willingness to listen to reasonable argument will be invaluable to rational and constructive decision-making as we face other tough choices along the way in working out What Backwoods Environment Do We Want?

13

Silence and Sounds

Heard melodies are sweet,
but those unheard are sweeter . . .

John Keats

MOST PEOPLE think of the attractions of the backcountry in terms of sights: striking mountain vistas, the rolling green carpets of hillsides that flame into orange and red in the fall, lovely waterfalls and cascades, intimate miniatures of moss and fern.

But the *sounds* as well as the sights of the backcountry attract the perceptive visitor. And the principal sound to treasure is that of *silence.*

True silence—not just the avoidance of major distracting noises, but that absolute absence of *any* sound, "the eternal silence of these infinite spaces"—is rare even in the backwoods. The soft, sweet sounds of the natural world, principally wind and water, are very often present, not to mention birds, animals, and those articulate observers and commentators, the trees. We'll talk about these in a moment. But for now reflect for a moment on how rare is true, absolute silence.

The city dweller rarely ever hears the sound of silence. Houses and apartments abound in a diversity of sounds that we normally take for granted and scarcely "hear" with our conscious minds: heating systems stopping and starting, clocks ticking, refrigerators ruminating the way refrigerators do, radiators clucking nervously, air conditioning units muttering and occasionally expostulating, outside street noises of traffic, children, doors closing, dogs barking, airplanes passing overhead, somewhere a radio. Offices are noisier yet, and libraries possibly noisiest of all.

One of the frustrations of modern life is the impossibility of escaping noise. Even that highest creation of the Muses, music, has been debased by being droned into our ears perpetually in offices, stores, supermarkets, airplanes, elevators, everywhere. The quietest places in modern society formerly were the anterooms of dental offices—so quiet you could hear the soft whine of a drill in the next room, remember?—but even here piped-in, innocuous music is now supplied. Few of us command the position of George Bernard Shaw, who was told at a restaurant that the orchestra would play "anything you like—what would you like them to play, Mr. Shaw?" His reply: "Dominoes."

Thirty years ago, C.S. Lewis, devilish author of *The Screwtape Letters,* wrote:

> . . . Noise, the grand dynamism, the audible expression of
> all that is exultant, ruthless, and virile—noise which alone de-
> fends us from silly qualms, despairing scruples, and impossible
> desires. We will make the whole universe a noise in the end. We
> have already made great strides in this direction as regards the
> earth. The melodies and silences of heaven will be shouted
> down in the end.

Getting away from civilization's cacophony is one major reason why people value the backwoods and fly to it as to a sanctuary, "gone far away into the silent land."

Back in 1869, the Reverend William Henry Harrison Murray, writing of a sojourn in the woods of the Adirondacks, observed: "It is the silence of this wilderness that most impressed me." Ever since, people have been seeking that silence in the wild lands away from man's noisy works. We can recall many moments, on still days when the wind was silent, far enough away from any brook, unnoticed for the moment by birds, when we sat perfectly still to hear that rarest of sounds, its absence. It is a void, almost as awesome as being on the rim of some vast, bottomless canyon. Into this immensity of soundlessness, you could drop a whisper and it would seem to float interminably through the abyss. "Speech is of Time, Silence is of Eternity," wrote Carlyle. There is indeed a timelessness, a suspension of events in true silence.

The backpacking boom has brought more people into the woods and hills, and increased the noise level, but the land is large enough to absorb an awful lot of us. You can still find perfect quiet up there on the less travelled ridges, the hidden valleys. You can even get it in the popular, oft-visited places, if you're there at the right time. The President of the Mount Washington Observatory, Alan A. Smith, told us of doing some mapping on Washington in November: "There were a few hikers on top, and some were scattered over the northern peaks—we could see them as we did our triangulation from the summit. Later, however, working our way down the road, there was *nobody*—we could stand and listen to the silence!"

The New York chapter of the Appalachian Mountain Club regularly schedules a unique kind of excursion, known as "silent walks." They are hikes whose itinerary may be like that of any other hike, but during which the group periodically walks for 20 minutes without anyone saying a word. It may sound goofy: a dozen or more people lumping along the trail without speaking to each other. Those who have been along, though, say that once you grow accustomed to it, your eyes open wider to the world around you, you tune in to the wind and water, and to the sounds of the woods, and a sense of oneness both within the group and within the natural world as a whole is felt. We prefer our silence in smaller numbers, but the idea sounds intriguing.

BACKWOODS SOUNDS

Silence, though, is but one of the fascinating sounds of the backwoods. The poet John Keats wrote . . .

> . . . And then there crept
> A little noiseless noise among the leaves,
> Born of the very sigh that silence heaves.

There is the sound of wind, ranging from the sparse rustle of blowing leaves to the shriek of the winter gale above treeline.

There is the sound of water, ranging from the full-throated waterfalls to

> . . . a hidden brook
> In the leafy month of June,
> That to the sleeping woods all night
> Singeth a quiet tune.

> Coleridge

There are the sounds of birds, ranging through dozens of species. Our favorites for the mountain areas and the backwoods are the chickadee's sociable chatter, the clear and haunting whistle of the white-throated sparrow, the intricate trills and grace-notes of the tiny winter wren, and the ominous hoarse croak of the huge raven. In his book, *The Lives of a Cell,* Lewis Thomas writes of birdsong: "Behind the glossaries of warning calls, alarms, mating messages, pronouncements of territory, calls for recruitment, and demands for dispersal, there is redundant, elegant sound that is unaccountable as part of the working day."

Dr. Thomas points out how universal is the need for living things to communicate with sound:

> Almost anything that an animal can employ to make a sound is put to use. Drumming, created by beating the feet, is used by prairie hens, rabbits, and mice; the head is banged by woodpeckers. . . . Fish make sounds by clicking their teeth, blowing air. . . . Animals with loose skeletons rattle them, or, like rattlesnakes, get sounds from externally placed structures. Turtles, alligators, crocodiles, and even snakes make various more or less vocal sounds. . . . Even earthworms make sounds. Toads sing to each other, and their friends sing back in antiphony.

And frogs. They can fill the night air with their chorus. Christopher Morley has observed of his neighboring frogs:

> This pond is a kind of Union League Club for frogs, . . . all night long you can hear them reclining in their arm-chairs of congenial mud and uttering their opinions, which vary very little from generation to generation. Most of these frogs are Republican, we feel sure, but we love them no less.*

Trees, those rooted monarchs of the forest, are not always silent watchers. The wind plays upon them as unseen hands upon a harp. In a cold snap, when the mercury dips below zero, the trees will crack and snap nearly as loudly as a pistol. Squeaking trees, limb rubbing on limb, can be mistaken for a bird or human voice. Woodsman Roger Chase, a man with a twinkle in his eye, is a ranger at Maine's Baxter State Park. A deft man with a jackknife, he carved a "tree squeak" out of cedar—for, certainly, every woods walker has surely seen—or nearly seen—the elusive "tree squeak."

Of course, we hikers and backpackers make sounds too. Not always talking or singing or panting sounds, but walking sounds. Listen to yourself walk. Clothing brushes against itself. Hunters, who try to walk quietly, choose wool, as it is more silent than nylon. Listen to the rub of your nylon parka next time you're hiking—it's really noisy. Feet pounding on the trail or shuffling through the leafy woods of fall, your backpack creaking—it is very hard to walk without a sound.

Not all sounds of nature are welcomed. Two that we could do without, for example, are that penetrating, insistent whine of the mosquito, and the dreadful low dull crack with which a snow slope announces the commencement of a windslab avalanche, with all its destructive fury. These are quibbles, though.

NOISE POLLUTION IN THE BACKCOUNTRY

Looking back at the question that heads this section—What Backwoods Environment Do We Want?—we submit that the sounds of nature, from the perfect silence to the howling tempest, are a vital element of that environment. The sounds, or their absence, are one powerful reason why people go to the backwoods. We therefore feel that it is critically important that:

(1) Individual hikers and campers should so conduct themselves as to minimize noise pollution; and
(2) Backcountry managers should make it a major goal of wild lands management to preserve the integrity of natural sounds and silences.

Back in chapter 6 we mentioned minimizing disruptive noise—whether group voices, transistor radios, or cassettes—as a key step in the new "clean camping" ethic.

*From *Here Are Dogs,* essays collected by Ollie Depew. New York: The Century Co., 1931.

However, keeping offensive noise from polluting the backcountry environment is not always within the power of the individual hiker or backpacker. This is where the land manager has to step in, as steward of silence. Many land managers are sensitive to the problem and have taken firm steps to safeguard the sounds of the backwoods. But often we wonder if enough is being done to reduce noise pollution in the backcountry.

A hiking friend of ours passed a group of youngsters walking in the Franconia Range. His mountain tranquility was shattered long before he saw them, as a transistor radio, blaring the latest hits, announced their coming. He asked, in what he hoped was a gentle tone, but undoubtedly with teeth clenched, "Why do you carry that radio?" The answer was simple: "I just need it."

Has it become impossible for us to live without our manmade sounds? Cushioned by sounds—even noise—as we are in daily life, are we afraid of silence?

No one can disagree that some sounds we hear on woods rambles can have the effect of destroying the idyll of a hike. These are all manmade sounds, and come in the form of motors: the trail bike, the snowmobile, a four-wheel drive vehicle tearing along a beach, the whine of a motorboat, a dune buggy. When these obstacles cross our forest path they leave a torrent of noise in their wake powerful enough to blot out the swiftest of rushing mountain streams. Birds fly away, animals head for cover, plants are crushed, and the hiker is left rooted to the spot trying not to breathe in the fumes of exhaust he sees hanging in the air around him.

Logging methods being what they are these days, the chain saw has now come to add its barbarous racket to the woods. We've noticed that the noise from a well-tuned chain saw has the power to carry over many a mile. Perhaps it gets the award for the second loudest sound in the woods.

Trail crews, a hard-working and diligent group, with a great sympathy for working and living in the woods, have found that many of their jobs go easier with chain saws. Very possibly. But we'd like to report that not all trail crews like to cut themselves off from normal forest sounds. On the Appalachian Trail as it passes through the Great Smoky Mountain National Park, trail crews abandoned power tools in favor of the traditional ax and saw. The Appalachian Mountain Club uses the chain saw as little as possible, as does The Green Mountain Club. We're not overly sympathetic with those who argue that a chain saw is essential to modern trail work. In our Vermont home, we have cooked and heated exclusively with wood for years now, and we use only handsaws and axes to get it in. Trail crews could do the same, as many do.

AIRPLANES AND HELICOPTERS

In wilderness areas throughout the country, overhead aircraft provide a growing menace to the silence of the far-off places.

U.S. Forest Service officials have warned (with sensitivity to wilderness values if not to those of English grammar): "Low-flying aircraft are becoming increasingly frequent and cause much disturbance of the solitude of [wilderness areas]."

In a provocative article in *National Wildlife* magazine, under the title "Off We Go into the Wild Green Yonder," Peter Steinhart documented the impact of low-flying planes on canyon lands in the southwest; condor and falcon refuges in California; and national parks everywhere. Airplanes zoom in close to harass wolves on Isle Royale, bison in the badlands, and moose in Alaska. "There is no place in the world, save perhaps Antarctica, that is free from the sounds of the aircraft engine," concluded Steinhart mournfully.

Only in Minnesota's Boundary Waters Canoe Area has the force of law been brought to bear to prohibit outright all aircraft below 4000 feet. Elsewhere the Federal Aviation Administration applies merely an "Advisory Circular" requesting pilots to stay at least 2000 feet above "noise-sensitive areas," such as parks and forests, including Wilderness Areas.

The FAA concedes that "excessive aircraft noises can result in discomfort, inconvenience, or interfere with the use and enjoyment of property, and can adversely affect wildlife." Since the law has been laid down firmly in the Boundary Waters area, we don't see why it would not be of value elsewhere.

In the northeast, a controversial aspect of this problem is the regular use of helicopters over the backcountry.

Back in 1961, one of the Appalachian Mountain Club's hut boys told Justice William O. Douglas, who was writing a *National Geographic* article on the AMC hut system, that helicopters would never be used in the White Mountain huts. "Not on your life!" he remonstrated. "Then the romance would go out of the huts. Backpacking brings a sense of achievement." Justice Douglas agreed. He praised the backpacking of all hut supplies as bringing "a feeling of fulfillment that makes even sweat and toil a joy."

In the years since 1961, the romance and the sense of achievement have been muted so much that now, at the more inaccessible huts, a large amount of the heavier supplies is airlifted directly in by helicopter. A bloc of time is usually scheduled at the beginning and end of each summer season, in which the bulk of this flying is done. At intervals through the summer months, additional flights may be made to support hut or shelter construction projects. In cases of search and rescue emergencies, the Governor of New Hampshire may and often has authorized the use of helicopters to assist rescuers.

If there ever was a "trade-off" in backcountry management, it's the question of the proper role of the helicopter. Win a little, lose a little ... or, in this case, win a lot of benefits, but at the cost of a lot of disruption.

The benefits which the helicopter has brought to north country recreational management are indisputable. Many cases could be cited in which helicopter rescues have saved life or limb, not to mention sparing rescuers from the brutally hard work of hauling litters for miles over narrow mountain trails. In fire control, the helicopter has been invaluable, both in the east and more especially in the west. In carrying loads to AMC huts, the helicopter has brought in over 400 tons per year for the past eight years, at a cost which has been estimated at about 2 cents per pound, compared with an estimated 7 cents per pound for material packed in on the back. Furthermore, while all that load-carrying may have been romantic to Justice Douglas and his young friend, the old hundred-plus-pound loads exacted a tough toll on hut boys' knees and backs. Helicopter pilot Joe Brigham points out that after eight years of flying loads to the huts, "We have yet to issue a bandaid to anybody." He points out that you used to see knee braces hanging ready on the wall of every hut, but you don't see them any more.

That's the positive side. In addition, the northeastern helicopters have a remarkable safety record, in the light of the hazardous mountain terrain into which they fly. We have nothing but admiration for the skill and courage it takes to fly in and out of high mountain passes in this electrifyingly changeable New England weather. Pilot Brigham, for example, has never made an emergency landing in the backcountry in eight years of flying loads to huts. Another pilot had to crash-land on New Hampshire's Kinsman Ridge once recently ("I ran out of air speed, altitude, and ideas all at once," recalls the pilot), but he walked away unhurt. For our money, flying through those mountain crags falls some-where on the courage scale between capping oil-well fires and filling cavities for irritable Bengal tigers.

The AMC and pilots like Joe Brigham are sensitive to the concerns about too much noise over the New Hampshire woods and hills. Most of the time they make a conscientious effort to minimize the "presence" of the noisy machine. They try to avoid weekends and peak summer periods; try to limit total flying time over the mountains to about 100 hours per year; try to come in at right angles to trails rather than following along them for miles; try to disguise the landing sites near the huts (wind socks are not permanently installed, but only raised on actual flying days, for example).

Sometimes one wonders if they could do better, though. For example, they admit to flying special guests into the huts on occasion to give them the thrill of a dinner up in the mountains without the hardship of walking in. Hikers to whom the challenge of getting there is part of the mountain experience take a dim view of these episodes.

This brings us to the bad news—the other side of the coin. Nothing disrupts a wilderness experience so joltingly as the sudden emergence of a helicopter over the ridge. If trail bikes are thought to be out of place on backwoods trails, a helicopter is many times louder and sprays its noise over a much wider area.

It is not simply noise; it is a more subtle offense. The backcountry recreation-ist is out there to feel pride in reaching remote places on his own two feet, with all the satisfaction he derives from knowing that his physical strength, experi-enced judgment, and determination were essential to his getting there. That pond shore miles from the road, that summit overlooking unbroken forest—it took a lot to get there, and by gosh he did it himself.

Then along comes a helicopter and in an instant the illusion is shattered. No, screams the sound of the helicopter, it wasn't *really* necessary to walk all day to get where you are; I just left the airport down in the valley ten minutes ago. Maybe this offense is more objectionable than the noise.

But the noise is pretty bad. We spent four days in the summer of 1978 in the Great Gulf Wilderness. Throughout one whole day that we were hiking those wilderness trails, the helicopter droned back and forth overhead. On this occasion, it was supporting a mapping project by transporting men and equipment from summit to summit, so that besides the helicopter overhead we had to share each of three summits with a generator roaring away to feed power drilling equipment. As we pointed out earlier, hikers have been asked to make a lot of sacrifices in the interest of preserving wilderness values in "Wilderness Areas": Permits are required, shelters have been removed, trails have been closed. Motorized vehicles are forbidden, yet it would have taken a whole battalion of trail bikes to impose as much noise and distraction on Great Gulf hikers as was accomplished that day by that single helicopter, let alone the generator whirring away on the summits. The FAA's Advisory Circular showed itself a paper tiger that day: The helicopter was frequently less than 2000 feet above the trails of the Wilderness Area. The Appalachian Trail is supposedly off limits to motorized vehicles by Act of Congress, yet the helicopter landed smack on (or right next to) the Trail in at least three places.

In fairness, we should add that the mapping project which was under way is a worthy cause and those responsible for it are sensitive to the need to minimize the use of helicopters and other machines. In fact, they argue that limited helicopter use is the fastest and cleanest way to get this sort of work done. We mean no criticism of the mapping project, those involved in it, or the helicopter pilot. If a topflight map of the Presidentials results, as seems likely, perhaps the few noisy hours will have been worth it. Nevertheless, the fact remains that on that particular day, those seeking a "wilderness experience" in the Great Gulf received a travesty instead.

This is not an isolated occurrence. We've heard and seen helicopters over backcountry hikes in Maine and Vermont as well. Once, in a remote spot in Newfoundland, we climbed an out-of-the-way mountain through some of the toughest bushwhacking we've ever done. The top was a rounded dome of low-growing blueberries and alpine azalea, but the approaches were all either murderous miles of close-growing krumholz (locally called "tuckamoor") or rotten, crumbling cliffs. For all our pains, we took consolation in the possibility that we were the first people ever to reach that summit. When we returned from our long trip to park headquarters, the ranger coolly commented that he had landed on the summit by helicopter once. Shatter one pleasant dream.

Again we emphasize: It's not just the noise, it's the *presence*.

We're tempted to paraphrase George Leigh Malory's famous answer to the question why people climb. Why do we object to the helicopter in the backcountry environment? *Because it's there*.

We suspect that the proper role and limits of the helicopter in the backwoods have not been fully worked out yet. It seems absurd that at present national forest and state park agencies exercise no official restraints on some of the worst sources of offensive noise, such as low-flying aircraft. A White Mountain National Forest official told us: ". . . . a person can land a helicopter above treeline as long as there is no resource damage as a result. In order to control aircraft use, we would have to promulgate a specific regulation and show why such a regulation was necessary." We bring this out only to underline the point that as things currently stand, the managing agencies exercise little control over the loudest single source of noise pollution. Helicopters are legally free to fly over and land just about anywhere in the backcountry.

This is not to deny the useful role of such noisemakers in some contexts. That would be blind—but it is equally blind to ignore their impact on the backcountry experience.

The answer will probably lie in some compromise, perhaps not too distant from present ad hoc arrangements, in which those tasks which the helicopter can do so much more efficiently than any other mechanism will continue to get done by helicopter—but under careful and explicit restraints on itineraries, total flight time, the timing of flights, flights over Wilderness Areas, and what might be called "frivolous" flights for the convenience or pleasure of personal friends. At present, there are very few mandatory controls. If enough hikers have their wilderness experience as rudely shattered as ours was that day in the Great Gulf, however, there may arise a demand for more formal and explicit controls.

Whether from helicopters, chain saws, snowmobiles, or radios—all of which may have *some* legitimate place in the backcountry—there is an imperative need to protect the integrity of the sounds of wildness, including the rarest of all, the sound of silence. These sounds are peculiarly vulnerable—almost more so, if less permanently, than the fragile vegetation on which so much official protection is lavished. Yet little is done to protect them from what Schopenhauer called "the most impertinent of all forms of interruption—noise."

The sounds of the woods are indisputably one of the precious values of wild lands. They are a major element in why people seek remote places. They are part of the answer to that question: *What Backwoods Environment Do We Want?*

14

The High Cost of
Search and Rescue

*Of course there's danger; but a certain amount of danger is
essential to the quality of life. I don't believe in taking foolish
chances; but nothing can be accomplished without taking any
chance at all.*

*I believe the risks I take are justified by the sheer love of the
life I lead. Yes, just being in the air on a flight across the ocean
to Paris, warrants the hazard of an ice field below.*

Charles Lindbergh,
The Spirit of St. Louis

EVERY YEAR some people underestimate the ruggedness of the backcountry
and wind up being hauled out from their mountain idyll on a litter. The lucky
ones are those that live to profit by the experience. Meanwhile the mounting
cost and human effort devoted to mountain rescue is beginning to attract ominous public concern. Let's relate an example.

ONE EXPERIENCE

In 1975, on April Fool's Day—*that* date may be significant—two young hikers
started out to climb in the White Mountains' Presidential Range.

Now there are those who believe that T. S. Eliot may have done some late-
winter climbing in the Presidentials to have come to the conclusion that April is
the cruelest month. It is a time when southern New England is beginning to glow
with spring's first bloom—but the snow and cold still lie thick up on the northern
slopes. Winter lurks in wait for the unwary.

These two young hikers wore summer-weight hiking boots and no snowshoes.
They reached a tiny shelter which the Forest Service maintains for emergency
use only at the high pass between Mounts Adams and Jefferson, the second and
third highest peaks in the northeast. They intended to continue early the next
morning.

In fact, the two were not to leave that shelter for seven long cold days and
nights.

138

Screaming winds, biting cold, and the biggest snowfall of that winter piled into those inhospitable mountains. Soon state officials, Forest Service Rangers, and the experienced personnel of the Appalachian Mountain Club were combing the snow-covered hills, fighting the arctic conditions, trying to locate the missing pair. It was a grueling effort, but unlike many such rescue epics, which all too often arrive too late, this one succeeded in finding and evacuating the stranded hikers with no one seriously hurt.

When the monumental rescue effort was over and all were safely down, people began to think about what had happened. A tremendous number of rescuers had exposed themselves to arduous work and even personal danger. The total cost was estimated as approaching $10,000. AMC's mountain-wise staff alone contributed more than 600 person-hours. The state's Fish and Game Department had tied up many rangers for days. So had the U.S. Forest Service.

People not only began to think; they began to emote. Some of them began to sound off with some highly emotional conclusions:

Many local hunters and fishermen, well aware that hunting and fishing licenses pay the freight for Fish and Game Department work, began to scream about where their money was going.

Newspaper editorials, including one in the influential Manchester *Union Leader,* proposed that hikers and climbers be licensed before being allowed into the hills, the fees going to support search and rescue efforts.

AMC official Robert Proudman in *Appalachia* warned: "If many more rescues like this one develop . . . , someday the hiker may find that laws have been legislated to control his activities and to develop revenue for the inevitable rescues that arise from the pursuit of hiking and mountaineering sports."

Some voices urged an end to all mountain rescues. "It seems to me that the moral obligation of being 'thy brother's keeper' ends at that point where brother knowingly and willingly places himself in the way of danger," cried one letter-to-the-editor writer in *Appalachia*. To such people, the answer to more hikers in distress was simple: Do nothing! Force them to take care of themselves . . . or accept the consequences.

Many people, including climbers themselves, feel that mountain climbing is intended to be an adventurous activity, with genuine risks willingly undertaken. As one climber commented at the time, "Personally, I view the prospect of a guaranteed rescue as robbing climbing of its sense of adventure."

Less than a year after that April Fools' incident, three of us were getting ready to go on a winter climbing venture in the same general area when we stopped for gas at a station near the trail head. We ran into a torrent of outrage expressed by the local proprietor, condemning anyone who went into the hills in winter, and loudly articulating the sportsman's complaint that he didn't want his license fee money used to rescue idiots up there. "Let 'em freeze," he cried.

POSSIBLE REGULATIONS

It looks not unlikely that eventually some of what was predicted in the aftermath of that April adventure may become a reality.

(1) A "hiker's license" for walking in New Hampshire's woods and hills—any time of year—just might become state law one of these years.

(2) Other states may not be long to follow, not just to cover costs relating to rescue but in an effort to generate funds for state activities that serve the hiker.

(3) Rescued victims may find themselves billed for costs of the rescue.

(4) Several people have suggested a federal excise tax on hiking equipment as a way to finance a rescue fund.

New Hampshire is the state in which these proposals have progressed furthest, for understandable reasons. In New England, only Maine has as formidable a mountain and wilderness terrain. New Hampshire's proximity to population centers gives it the dubious blessing of far more visitors. Furthermore, for the past few years, New Hampshire's governor has had a celebrated "no-new-taxes" commitment that made rising rescue costs most uncomfortable. If you're a politician with a commitment to live up to, a license isn't a tax.

So bills are in the legislative hopper—and being taken seriously—that would empower the state to reclaim all rescue costs from the victim. If you get lost in the woods in New Hampshire, be prepared to receive a sizable bill when they bring you out.

. . . Unless, that is, you purchased a proposed new "hiking license." Under one of these bills, hikers could buy a license which would exempt them from being charged for a rescue. It would be a kind of rescue insurance for hikers. If you buy a regular fishing or hunting license you'd already be exempt, because one of the main ideas is to make the nonhunters pay for the time the Fish and Game Department spends on rescues.

Cost to the hiker? For an out-of-stater, $8; for a New Hampshire resident, $6.

You don't have to buy the license. But if you don't, and need to be hauled out of the woods, you'd have to pay a staggering bill. In a recent climbers' publication, *Off Belay* (June 1977), a past President of the national Mountain Rescue Association estimated the cost of a typical mountain rescue at more than $25,000. In a New Hampshire setting it might not run that high, but it would be past the typical hiker's budget for a weekend's mistake.

Much legislative deliberation will be necessary before any such proposal becomes actual law. There are all sorts of practical problems to be resolved, some of which we'll mention in a minute. But make no mistake: The matter is being seriously considered by people with the power to make it come true.

Nor is New Hampshire the only New England state that's thinking along these lines. They're just a bit closer to the point of action in the Granite State.

An official of the Maine Department of Inland Fisheries and Wildlife has complained that "in recent years due to the increased interest in hiking and other outdoor activities, our Warden Service has been called upon much more often in order to search for lost and injured persons." The Department gets a $10,000 biennial appropriation to cover costs of search and rescue; it estimates that actual costs ran $70,000 for the last biennium. "It is quite obvious," points out Deputy Commissioner J. William Peppard, "that the fishermen and hunters of Maine have been providing this service to hikers and other lost persons for many years."

In Vermont, the Department of Forests, Parks, and Recreation feels that additional funds are needed "for all aspects of their hiking programs." Parks Director Rodney A. Barber regards the hiking license as "a viable method of obtaining these funds." Realistically he warns that enforcement and control would be a real problem and enforcement costs could be "so high as to defeat the purpose of the license as a fund raiser." But if the enforcement problem could be resolved, Barber believes that "the 'hiking license' may become a reality."

Even in Massachusetts, where the backcountry is not so formidable as to require extensive search and rescue activities, there has been casual consideration of an annual trail permit for state lands, so that the hiker might help support hiking land in somewhat the same way that recreational vehicle registration goes to support RV programs. Massachusetts Director of Forests and Parks, Gilbert A. Bliss, feels that some such permit "very likely could be implemented at some future time."

Outside of New England, the whole search and rescue matter has come in for much controversy in recent years.

In 1975 there were 49 fatalities in 37 of our national parks. Even though this figure is just one-third the number of people who die on our highways in a single day, the Park Service's solution was to redouble safety efforts. Their campaign included safety folders, ranger talks, warning signs, fencing of open hazards, and spot radio and TV announcements on safety.

In one summer on Alaska's Mount McKinley the National Park Service was involved in 21 rescue missions involving 33 climbers. The bill was high: Taxpayers paid a total of $79,068. As a result many people, climbers as well as nonclimbers, began demanding that climbers pay the cost of their rescue.

In May on Mount Rainier three climbers were rescued at a cost of $2500. The climbers claimed the rescue wasn't needed, but apparently the Park Service disagreed when blizzards turned the mountain into "one big white-out." The question: How to handle the cost of unwanted rescues?

The states of Indiana and Ohio have prohibited all rock climbing on state property. The reason was a single fatality and numerous injuries. Many climbers find it appalling to think that an enlightened state government can restrict individual rights in such an arbitrary manner, but there it is.

CRITICS OF REGULATION

As pressures mount for greater regulations and forcing hikers to pay for rescue costs, however, other voices are being heard that urge caution and warn about tampering with the spirit of the freedom of the hills.

The prestigious American Alpine Club has criticized National Park Service efforts to make parks ultra-safe as "admirable for the urbanized areas of the parks, but is it what we need in the backcountry?"

Backpacker magazine, one spokesman for the pedestrian outdoorsperson, in an editorial suggested, "Let's sign waivers letting the government off the hook for our safety in the backcountry."

Mount Everest climber Willi Unsoeld argues that no one has the obligation to search for "lost" climbers. He contends: "No government agency, especially, has any obligation to save the lives of stupid citizens who take foolhardy risks." Unsoeld is emphatically opposed to the all-for-safety theory of what a climber should undertake.

This philosophy was summed up in its most stirring form by the gallant antarctic explorer Captain Robert Scott, dying alone with his comrades in the frozen wastes, who wrote in his diary: "We took risks, we know we took them. Things have come out against us; therefore we have no cause for complaint."

Some skeptics have asked what would happen if state officials pushed the rescue button for hikers or climbers who felt that they had their situation under control and could get themselves out, as happened on Mount Rainier? Suppose the state and cooperating agencies put in considerable time and cost looking for a party of overdue hikers, but the hikers themselves felt they could have walked out on their own eventually. Would they have to pay?

We were with a party of highly experienced winter climbers on Katahdin one December. One of our people, walking in to our rendezvous point, decided to bivouac overnight along the trail. When he didn't arrive at the rendezvous that night, park officials zoomed out in their snowmobiles looking for him, woke us up to send us on a futile, middle-of-the-night search of the mountain's trails, and alerted all park personnel plus the State Police to be ready for full-scale search operations. The next morning our friend strolled up to our camp, blissfully unaware of all the excitement. Under the New Hampshire proposal he could have been billed for quite a hunk of change.

Another very real practical problem with the proposed hiking license is that hikers who purchase the license may feel that they are thereby guaranteed cost-free rescue services. AMC's spokesman at the House hearings on one bill expressed concern that such a license could lead to more rescues:

> We are rather sure that we will be going up into the hills quite regularly to bring out tired hikers who have realized that rescue service is now available to them for only the cost of their "license." It seems that six or eight dollars is pretty cheap for a helicopter or litter ride out of the mountains anywhere, anytime.

To guard against such abuse, AMC proposed adding a deductible clause under which the rescued party should pay the first $100 of a rescue expense.

Then there is the question of how far-reaching the proposed new program would be. How about the casual stroll in the woods behind your house? What about berry-pickers up on a hillside? Would everyone have to buy a license? What kind of a 1984-like situation might we be headed for when no one can go for a ramble on New England's hills without a license?

Public zeal for safety can be carried too far. We think of America as the land of the free and the home of the brave, yet we go much further than our European cousins in trying to protect the citizen from freely undertaking activities that might be risky. Here in the "free" USA, we require motorcyclists to wear helmets; we put ropes around swimming areas; we install rude buzzers in automobiles to scream at the driver who doesn't don his seatbelt to drive down his own driveway to his own garage.

Yet, when someone's up there in the hills and needs help, people are going to organize rescues. That's sure. All the philosophical reasoning in the world about individual responsibility isn't going to keep the Fish and Game Department, the AMC, the Forest Service Rangers, and countless others from going up there after them. They will go for a wide variety of motives, not all of which are pure altruism or "moral responsibility," but some of them will reflect considerable personal courage and even heroism.

One thing seems clear: It would be a whole lot fairer for the rescued parties to pay the lion's share of rescue costs, rather than the general public or the hunters and fishers. In this light, some kind of legislation may prove inevitable. New England hikers will do well to watch what's happening at their state houses. This is yet another area in which the quality of the hiker's traditional freedom of the hills is headed for some changes.

CASE STUDY

Winter above Treeline

If I ever die, I want to die in Chicago.

Minnie Minoso

THIS IS a tale that almost became a tragedy.

It's about the brutal cruelty of the mountain-gods in wintertime—though on this occasion they chose to spare their helpless victims, perhaps to see if they could profit from the experience.

It's a story worth retelling for the lessons it teaches about winter camping and climbing in New England mountains.

Day after Christmas, 1968. A father and his 16-year-old son started on a trek through New Hampshire's White Mountains by struggling into huge packs and snowshoes, and slowly plodding through a couple of feet of fresh snow up a mountain trail called the Valley Way. Whoever named this trail had his terminology on backwards: The "Valley" Way climbs nearly 4000 vertical feet in less than 4 miles, up into the northern end of the Presidential Range.

Their objective was to traverse the peaks of the Presidentials, and if possible to continue on across other mountain ranges to the west. They never got near those western ranges. The Presidentials taught them several lessons, which we'll try to enumerate as the story goes along.

Father and son got about 3 miles that first day. Besides a late start, their packs were jammed full of enough winter equipment and food to last them ten days, so they weighed over 80 pounds apiece. The fresh, unconsolidated December snow conditions, plus the weight of those packs, meant that at every step the lead man sank in about 2 feet. It was absurdly slow going.

Lesson One: Don't count on moving rapidly in winter. Trail conditions can make ½ mile per hour an exhausting speed. The Appalachian Mountain Club suggests "Guidebook travel times should be doubled in winter." Under some conditions, that advice is not nearly conservative enough.

That night, they camped right on one of the few level spots in the trail and watched the temperature sink to minus 12 degrees. In the morning it was minus 18. But so far they were doing O.K., and soon continued successfully till they emerged above treeline in the Presidential Range in the high col between Mounts Adams and Madison.

Here the full fury of the notorious Presidentials' winter was tuning up. Winds shrieked and howled, buffeting the two climbers at every step. Temperatures below zero in a still valley feel darn cold; these same temperatures on an exposed, wind-raked ridge are of an entirely new order of cold.

A curious feature of the Presidentials in winter is that much of the alpine zone has relatively little snow on the ground. This is due to those ferocious winds, that blow most of it clean off the treeless heights, leaving a frozen terrain of rocks, ice, and very hard-packed snow—with occasional vast snowfields where wind currents permit it to collect, which build up to considerable depth, covering every feature of the mountain and every trace of the trail. Aside from these great snowfields, though, New England's most wintry winter spot paradoxically does not have very deep snow.

Father and son came prepared for this environment. They changed snowshoes for crampons. They pulled windproof nylon pants over their regular wool pants. They donned face masks, around which parka hoods were pulled tight, and "monster mitts" that extended up to their elbows. No flesh must be left to that punishing wind.

Lesson Two: Bring clothing suitable for full-scale arctic conditions. Especially important is adequate headgear (because so much heat loss occurs through the head), genuine winter boots (*not* summer-weight hiking boots), and a good mitten–glove combination.

Our two climbers managed to reach the two nearest summits, Mounts Madison and Adams, by leaving their heavy packs lower down on the ridge and dashing up to the summit and back with just ice ax in hand. The air was crystal clear, and the sky an unbelievably deep blue, so they had no difficulty in finding their packs again each time they came back down from the summits, a fact which they were to recall with grim irony 24 hours later.

That night they reached the col between Mounts Adams and Jefferson, where they huddled into a small emergency shelter which is maintained there by the Forest Service.

In the morning the temperature had risen to 12 degrees above zero. Visibility was socked in and light snow was falling, but the wind wasn't knocking them off their feet any more, so they made the decision to proceed. Their trail was to slab the broad shoulder of Mount Jefferson, then continue toward Mount Washington, largest peak in the northeast.

The decision to move on in those conditions proved to be a dangerous mistake. Visibility was soon no more than 50 feet. Furthermore, it became obvious that they had underestimated how much wind they would be dealing with as they moved out of the col. They had scarcely started when it became evident that a full-blown winter storm was under way.

Climbing out of the col onto the side of Jefferson proved to be hard work under those conditions. Laboring under heavy packs, they became quite warm and shed their wool shirts from under their wind parkas. The father decided that uncovering his pack to stow the shirt inside would risk frostbite to his fingers, so he just tucked the shirt securely under the top flap and resumed the arduous climb.

As they rounded the shoulder of Jefferson, they began to traverse one of those huge snow fields that collect on the Presidentials in winter. This snow field is visible from the highway well into July most years, so its depth in mid-winter is obviously considerable. In fact, it covers almost every cairn or other trace on the trail.

With low visibility, it became difficult for the two climbers to stay on-trail. Then, as they came around out of the lee of the summit, the full fury of the wind slammed into them, blowing a steady torrent of ice crystals into their faces. Progress became painfully slow. To guard against losing their way—which could have been disastrous—the son would go out from the last identified cairn as far as he could and still see it. Then the father would go out from there as far as he could without losing sight of the son, and stand there waiting for some brief lapse in the wind to try to squint forward into the fury of the storm in a forlorn effort to find another cairn. In all that snow, however, only the tops of the tallest cairns showed, and often many minutes passed before they could spot the next one and move on.

To one who has not been up there, it is difficult to convey the full import of a winter storm above treeline. The myriad of unfamiliar sensations include:

(1) Barely being able to stand on your feet, braced always by your ice ax, and moving forward fitfully only between gusts;

(2) The unrelenting din and tumult of the wind, so loud that you must shout virtually into your companion's ear to be heard;

(3) The featureless, enigmatic whiteness created by the unrelieved snow, ice crystals, and cloud which surround you on all sides, up and down;

(4) The sense of every little procedure being enormously difficult and time-consuming (even looking at your watch, for example, involves uncovering that wrist from the monster mitt, parka, and shirt, then painstakingly getting them all snugly back together—it perhaps shouldn't take so long to do, but up there it does).

All of these sensations are exciting enough if you step out into them for a half hour. If you're out in them for several hours, they'll wear you down. If you're out in them all day long and no prospect of escaping them at night save in a tiny tent somehow staked up there, you have to learn to take it as a way of life.

Admiral Byrd, caught in an antarctic blizzard, described it in *Alone* as "extravagantly insensate":

Its vindictiveness cannot be measured on an anemometer sheet. It is more than just wind: It is a solid wall of snow moving at gale force, pounding like surf. The whole malevolent rush is concentrated upon you as upon a personal enemy. In the senseless explosion of sound you are reduced to a crawling thing on the margin of a disintegrating world; you can't see, you can't hear, you can hardly move.

It is this scene which the jealous winter gods of Mount Washington aspire to imitate. Sometimes they do a pretty good job.

Eventually the father and son did get across the snowfield and out onto the southern slopes of Mount Jefferson, where once again they could stumble on blown-clear rocks and ice, where cairns were at least visible from time to time, when the wind-driven ice would permit them to steal a look ahead.

Lesson Three: Never try to move in a full-scale winter storm above treeline. These two should have stayed put in their shelter for a day, as they were to do in an even greater storm later. No one should risk becoming exhausted or lost in a snowfield in the incredible and relentless fury of those White Mountain storms.

When they got to the far side of Jefferson, the cloud cover momentarily lifted, revealing a gentle slope back up to the summit of Jefferson. The two climbers could not resist the lure of the summit. They had already bagged Madison and Adams; they had to grab Jefferson while they had the chance. Dropping their packs, they decided on a quick rush up to the nearly visible summit and back to their packs.

The climb went easily, and they delighted in the freedom of an easy dash uphill without packs and with the wind at their backs. When they landed on the summit and congratulated each other, the Mountain King stopped smiling and frowned.

The clouds came down again, the wind picked up. Father and son suddenly realized that they could not see more than a few feet; that they had lost all sense of which direction they had come up from, or which direction to descend; that the wind-driven snow had completely obliterated all trace of their tracks in a matter of minutes; that each rocky outcropping on the mountain looked like all the others; and—the crushing blow—that the father's compass, which he always carried handy in his wool shirt pocket, was right there: in the wool shirt which he had so carefully tucked in the pack that now lay down there on the trail somewhere below them.

How can you be lost when you know just where you are (in this case, the very summit of Jefferson at 5715 feet, in a howling, screaming, swirling thicket of fog and driven ice crystals)? For several minutes the two tried to remain calm and move about the summit slowly, trying vainly to get some sense of which way anything lay. Discussion is difficult when to make yourself heard you must stand right up against the other person's ear and bellow at the top of your lungs.

At length, they agreed on their best guess as the way down and resolutely plodded ahead. After an eternity, repeatedly suppressing fears that they might be going in the wrong direction, they were overjoyed to see the sight of one of the cairns of the trail that they had been on before. But when they arrived there they were soon able to figure out that they were back now on the north side of the mountain—which meant that in their careful calculations as to which way to descend from the summit, they had been precisely 180 degrees off course!

Now they had once again to face the risks and difficulties of crossing that same snowfield. Their tracks were, of course, long since wiped out in the wind-driven snow. Now, furthermore, the wind had considerably increased, the snow lay deeper (covering more of the cairns), and they were much, much more tired after all the buffeting they had already taken at the hands of the storm. They did manage somehow to swim or sink or wade or creep or flounder across the snowfield. Finally, out of the implacably swirling cloud and snow, they once again saw ahead of them on the trail their packs, now all encrusted with snow and ice.

Lesson Four: Never go anywhere without a compass. It is hard to imagine getting turned around 180 degrees on a familiar summit, but it happened in this case and it can happen again. Once you lose that all-important sense of the direction of things, that alpine world up there suddenly appears featureless and inscrutable—and totally hostile. Without a compass, you're dead lost, body and soul.

Lesson Five: Don't count on following your own footprints. The wind can blow them to oblivion in a minute or two. The hole left by an ice ax lasts somewhat longer, so look for these rather than your crampon tracks—but nothing lasts long in a serious Presidentials' gale.

Lesson Six: Never separate yourself from the equipment you require for survival. These two reckless but lucky adventurers eventually found their packs again before being overcome by fatigue, darkness, or just plain inability to find their way in the storm. Without their packs—and spare clothes, sleeping bags, tent, stove, food—they would surely have perished in the open. With their packs, their chances of at least surviving anywhere were considerably improved.

All of these exhausting perambulations left both father and son very tired and consumed a considerable part of the available daylight hours. It soon became clear to them that they had neither strength nor daylight left in which to go on to climb the enormous summit cone of Washington—over 1000 feet of elevation—on which the fury of the wind would certainly increase.

Lesson Seven: Remember that early winter days have the fewest daylight hours. As Yogi Berra said, it's the time of year when it gets late early. This fact should be kept in mind in all winter trip-planning.

The prospect now confronted them of trying to set up a camp in which they could survive a night immobilized in this awesome storm. Having come this far, they were now many miles of formidable mountain terrain from any trail that led down out of the alpine zone to a nearby road. The only trail near them was the Sphinx Trail, which led sharply down into a vast wilderness area known as the Great Gulf, through which they would have to lug themselves and their enormous packs for many miles, in several feet of unbroken, unconsolidated snow, the depth of which must have considerably increased during this storm. That course could probably not be done in one day, and in any case would mean a total defeat to their plans, and perhaps two hard days of dispirited plodding through the woods to safety.

So they felt themselves strongly committed to sticking out the storm. Perhaps it would die down during that night and the morning. (Mountaineers tend to be ridiculously optimistic when all nature is screaming evil tidings at them.) They noticed at least that the temperature felt warmer, and mistakenly took that to be an encouraging factor.

Dropping a bit below the crest of the ridge, they carefully selected a spot in the lee of some large rock outcroppings, and laboriously levelled a site for the tent. As they got it up, they noticed that the snow had changed texture—in fact, it was more like a sleet or freezing rain. The temperature had indeed climbed, but that meant trouble, not relief.

They managed to get set up inside the tent just before darkness. Then the wind shifted. That night proved even more frightening than the day out there on the snowfield. The wind repeatedly swelled into great buffeting blows, at which the helpless inmates of the tent would grab its A-frame poles, trying to hold it together against the force of the tempest, wondering how long the fabric would hold up against this punishment. Fortunately it did last through the night, but just barely.

In between the worst gusts of the storm, the father spent a full hour methodically scraping the encrusted ice and snow off his wool shirt, which had sat exposed on the outside of his pack during the day. He correctly reasoned that it would be vital to survival, since down garments lose their value as they get wet, and thus the time spent cleaning the ice off his shirt was a good investment. But the price of lost sleep was a stiff one to pay.

Lesson Eight: Always take the time to pack essential items properly. In this case the price was only lost sleep. In other cases failure to stash an item inside your pack can result in its becoming so soaked as to be useless for the rest of the trip—or at the worst it can be torn off the pack unnoticed, and turn up missing when it's needed.

Early the next morning, the wind finally wore down the battered tent. Shortly after daylight, a brief but unmistakable ripping sound announced that the outer fly had given way. Within seconds, it was reduced to tattered shreds flopping noisily at the downwind end. Father and son knew that it was an unnecessary question to ask how long the main fabric of the tent might hold out.

Lesson Nine: In setting up a tent, never assume that the current wind direction will necessarily hold constant. As a matter of fact, it is tempting to make the generalization that no tent made can stand up to the fury of a Presidentials' storm at its worst. You're better off not putting your confidence in any above-treeline shelter if you have no easy escape route. Snow caves or igloos offer a better chance for survival, but they are very time-consuming to erect, can get you very wet in the process, and cost daylight hours that can probably better be spent getting to some less exposed spot, preferably below treeline.

Somehow father and son got their tent dismantled and set off desperately to get down out of the wind. The Sphinx Trail proved extremely steep and difficult to negotiate with their gigantic packs. Between the time it took them to pack up, the difficulty of descent, and the formidably deep, soft snow they encountered down in the woods, they made very few miles that day, stopping for the night at one of the shelters that have since been removed from the Great Gulf Wilderness. By nightfall, the storm had abated. It stopped sleeting—but this only brought a new danger. All of their clothes had become wet, and now the temperature again began to drop.

Lesson Ten: In winter, neither wind nor cold are as deadly an enemy as warmth and rain—followed by cold. When a winter storm turns warm and drops rain, that's the time to look out for your life. You'd better be prepared to get out of the mountains fast, especially if your clothes and other essential equipment have been getting wet. A sudden drop in temperature after a freezing rain can catch you with your defenses down.

As it was, this father and son spent their worst night yet shivering in down sleeping bags that had lost most of their insulating warmth from the soaking they had received. Both wore all of their clothes, but those big fluffy down jackets that had felt so warm a few days earlier now clung damp and clammy.

Lesson Eleven: Many layers of wool are worth the finest down gear when wetness is a potential problem. It's a mountaineers' cliche that wool is "warm even when wet." Most experienced climbers place little reliance on those big down parkas you see in the ads. Some newer fabrics are being developed that may eventually prove mountain-worthy. Meanwhile, a series of wool sweaters, shirts, and underwear are far more reliable when the chips are down.

Somehow they shivered through that night. The whole next day was spent in a dreary plod through bottomless soft snow, laboring under huge packs, oppressed additionally by the sense of having been totally defeated by the casual fury of what was only a typical period of bad weather in the Presidentials.

The foolish pair didn't know when to give up. After spending a morning in a laundromat, repeatedly dropping dimes in the driers till their sleeping bags and clothes were fluffy again, they set off at noon the very next day to climb directly up Mount Washington, this time using the 8-mile summer auto road for their route of ascent.

Along that road, where it rises above treeline, there are, at half-mile intervals, a series of boxes for the emergency refuge of the summit weather observers on their trips up and down. Each one is roughly a cube, 7 feet each way on the inside, with one double door for access and one double window for light. They are, needless to say, extremely well secured to the mountainside.

Our intrepid pair reached one of these boxes at 5500 feet on the afternoon of December 31. They did not leave again until January 3.

What happened was another storm, this one seemingly designed to make the earlier one look like a faint breeze. For three nights and two days it was unthinkable to move on that mountain. The summit weather observatory recorded winds of over 100 mph for 23 straight hours at one point, with peak gusts well over 150. The temperature dropped to minus 26 on January 1 and ranged between minus 11 and minus 18 on January 2, warming up to a mild minus 3 on January 3.

Inside the box, father and son were far better off than in the previous storm, having learned to stay put. When they started their stove for a meal, the temperature even got above zero (though never above 10). They lived inside their down sleeping bags.

Their biggest problem, besides boredom, was getting snow to melt for water. Any loose snow had long since been blown off into the next county. To get snow, one of the two would get dressed in full climbing regalia, including face mask, monster mitts, and crampons. Then the other would open the doors, the first would hop out and wrestle the outer door closed, while the second slammed the inner one shut. Ice ax in hand, the person outside would creep up the slope to where a cornice of hard-packed snow had accumulated nearby. There he would spread open a stuff sack, holding it open with one knee and one hand. Then he would strike the cornice repeatedly with his ice ax. At each blow, chunks of snow would dislodge and immediately be picked up and shot off by the wind—but some of them might land in the stuff sack. This process would be repeated until enough of the precious snow had accumulated in the bag to satisfy their water requirements for the day. Then the weary and frozen climber would creep back to the box, knock hard on the door and jump inside. The next half-hour would be devoted to assiduously sweeping snow off sleeping bags and everything else, since opening the doors for even those split seconds resulted in filling the box with a thin coating of spindrift over everything. It was, of course, vital not to allow the snow to stay on the sleeping bags where it might melt into and soak the down.

Boredom was combatted principally by some reading matter brought along in anticipation of the prospect of being pinned down like this. The son made out all right with some dime-store mystery stories. The father had made the mistake of bringing Dostoevsky's *Notes from the Underground* and a poetical translation of *The Iliad*. Such heavy stuff had absolutely no appeal in those surroundings and went unread.

Lesson Twelve: Sex and violence are the only reading matter able to command attention at 5500 feet in a howling tempest.   Can the culture.

They also ripped out the last 52 pages of a small memo pad and made an impromptu deck of cards. In the ensuing poker games each used his precious lunch and snack items for chips. This resulted in a deadly serious game: When you are staking your last best candy bar on three nines, you've got to be sure they're winners! Even a small hard candy must have the support of a pair of face cards at the least.

On January 3, with the wind easing off to something in the general neighborhood of 50 mph, they managed to leave their box and struggle to the summit and back, later descending back down the road, much subdued and humbled by their vacation in the mountains.

These two were lucky. They survived all their mistakes and inexperience. Others have been less fortunate.

Lesson Thirteen: Never trifle with winter in the mountains.   If you decide to undertake this special madness called winter climbing, prepare yourself well. Read up about it, get the correct equipment, but most important of all, hook up with someone who has experience in that unique world. Start slowly, with day trips only at first, then plenty of overnight experience below treeline, where you can learn to deal with the cold without the additional devastating problem of wind.

It's not just that the wind *feels* stronger and colder in winter. It *is* stronger. The average wind speed on Mount Washington in July is 24.7 mph; in January it's 43.8. From 1948 to 1975, the fastest wind recorded during July averaged 80.7 mph; during January it was 124.9.

Another way of putting it is that your chances of encountering winds of 50 mph during the summer months are very remote—on the order of 2 percent probability. But during the peak winter season, the probability is that you'll get 50 mph winds about one day in three.

Everybody knows where a 50 mph wind takes you on those famous "wind chill" charts.

To repeat, the wisest procedure is to learn directly from more experienced climbing partners. Clubs like the Appalachian Mountain Club in the White Mountains, the Green Mountain Club in Vermont, and the Adirondack Mountain Club in New York State have organized programs for helping novices gain experience under counsel from those who have been through it all.

Above all, try to avoid the mistakes we've outlined above, which that foolish father and son encountered many years ago.

You can profit from mistakes, as they did. The son in our story went on to become an outstanding mountain climber, with "first ascents" in the Canadian Rockies and Alaska, including the East Ridge of Mount Huntington and the South Face of Mount Hunter, both climbs of exceptional difficulty. The father went on to many more years of pleasurable winter climbing in the hills of New England, and wound up co-authoring this book with his wife, Laura Waterman.

PART IV

The Spirit of Wildness

What Are We Trying to Preserve?

WE HAVE TALKED about what individual hikers and backpackers are doing to help preserve the backwoods environment. We have explored some of the complex decisions facing managers of wild lands. We haven't suggested many simple answers, but we hope we've shed some light on the questions that we all should be asking ourselves.

In this final section, we come back to certain underlying values which we, as two hikers who love the woods and hills in which we walk, feel should not be forgotten. In these remaining chapters we are addressing ourselves to the fundamental issues: What is it, in the last analysis, that we go to the backwoods to seek? What are the rare qualities that define an outdoors experience? *What, really, are we trying to preserve?*

To preserve the mountains themselves, first of all. To preserve the green woods, the pure waters, the quiet valleys, the windswept ridges . . . the moss on the boulder . . . the raven on the cloud . . . the frost feathers on the summit cairn . . . the varicolored rocks beneath the clear pool . . . the star flower at the trail's edge. . . .

The physical environment is the *sine qua non* of the backcountry experience. Much of this book has spoken of measures needed to preserve it, and many others have written far more eloquently in its defense—from Bryant and Muir to Colin Fletcher. Safe-guarding the vegetation, soils, and watersheds of the backcountry already commands the urgent attention of the managers of wild lands. Eternal vigilance is the price of its preservation.

As we've said in many ways heretofore, however, there's a lot more at stake. If all we wanted to do was preserve the land, the obvious solution would be to lock it up and throw away the key. What the game is all about is preserving a right relationship of people to the land.

Hikers have a strong root attachment to something which the Seattle Mountaineers immortalized in the subtitle of their widely read book: *Mountaineering:*

The Freedom of the Hills. Freedom, at least as defined by an absence of restraint, is one attraction of the backwoods. It's why people go out there.

Yet, with growing numbers of people and their terrible impact on the resource, freedom has to be limited to a degree. *What* degree is the critical question. As climber Royal Robbins says in *Basic Rockcraft:* "A simple equation exists between freedom and numbers: The more people, the less freedom."

Part of the answer lies in that age-old implication of freedom: responsibility. The sensitive hiker and backpacker of today has come a long way toward this obligation, as we've tried to show earlier in this book. Obviously, we yet have a ways to go.

Where individual responsibility can't do the job well enough or soon enough, land managers can be strongly tempted to impose flat regulations. Many times there is no escaping this necessity. On the other hand, as the Appalachian Mountain Club's Backcountry Management Task Force pointed out:

> Regulations are one of the least desirable techniques for controlling backcountry use because by restricting the user's freedom, they themselves have a negative impact on the quality of the recreational experience. Before imposing regulations, managers should try other approaches such as information and education programs. . . .
> Regulations are not justified simply to make the manager's job easier or to protect the user from himself.

The issue is broader, though, than one of freedom and responsibility for the resource. Apart from and deeper than both the policies of managers and the practices of hikers is the spirit of the hills. We have used the term, "the spirit of wildness." Maintaining that spirit—more than just preserving trees and flowers, informed freedom and sensible rules—is one of the toughest jobs for all of us. It is also critical to preserving the underlying reason why we go to the hills.

As Rene Dubos expressed it in *So Human an Animal:*

> . . . human beings need primeval nature to re-establish contact now and then with their biological origins; a sense of continuity with the past and with the rest of creation is probably essential to the long-range sanity of the human species.

When we use the phrase "the spirit of wildness," we refer to a wide spectrum of loosely connected elements of the backcountry experience: to solitude, to difficulty and challenge, to that indefinable but intensely real feeling that grips the hiker buffeted by wind on the rocky heights, or held in fascination by the silence and greenness of deep woods. It is this spirit of wildness which civilization or man's tailor-made imitations of nature can never replace. It is irreplaceable, and to many it is essential to life's spirit. Frederic Harrison once put it (in James Ramsey Ullman's *High Conquest*):

Our present world is a world of remarkable civilization, but it is not very natural and not very happy. We need yet some snatches of the life of youth ... to draw sometimes great draughts of simplicity and beauty. We need sometimes that poetry should not be droned into our ears but flashed into our senses. And man, with all his knowledge and his pride, needs sometimes to know nothing and to feel nothing, but that he is a marvellous atom in a marvellous world.

15

Solitude Amid the Multitude

To climb the trackless mountain all unseen . . .
Alone o'er steep and foaming falls to lean;
This is not solitude, 'tis but to hold
Converse with Nature's chorus and view her stores
*   unroll'd.*

Byron

MOUNTAIN solitude; is it lost and gone forever?

Many hikers deplore the loss of solitude, especially when they've just shouldered their way through the crowds on the summits of, say, New Hampshire's Mount Washington or Chocorua on a summer weekend, or arrived late at a popular campground to find all available tent sites taken. We've joined in many a trailside conversation with old-timers who speak of long-gone days camping alone at once-secluded spots where they now find 40 people crowded in regularly on weekend nights.

The feeling of solitude is vital to enjoyment of the mountain experience. Most people go to the hills to get away from city crowds, to drink deep draughts of nature's cool wildness. Sitting alone on an alpine summit, with rolling forested ridges dropping away on all sides, no sign of man in any direction, is a unique and priceless aspect of wilderness.

After a typical summer's trip in the popular White Mountains of New Hampshire or Maine's Baxter Park or Vermont's Mount Mansfield area, many are inclined to pronounce obituaries for solitude in New England.

We disagree completely. We'd like to show in this chapter that mountain solitude *is* available anywhere in New England, or in any other mountain area, any time of year—*if you really want it*.

The point is of more than academic interest. Some of the authorities in charge of wilderness areas are using the lack-of-solitude misconception as a basis for considering regulations which would deprive hikers of that other precious ingredient of the wilderness experience: the freedom of the hills. If some of these plans go through, you won't be able to hike when and where you want because of complex and stifling rules—imposed in the name of solitude.

For example, the White Mountain National Forest's official planning documents call for placing limits on forest use in order to afford a "recreation experience level" which includes a "high degree of opportunity for isolation." Already a permit must be obtained if you want to go into designated "Wilderness Areas."

The Appalachian Mountain Club's planning documents also cite a "modicum of solitude" as justification for limiting access to the backcountry.

Some managers have even proposed making certain trails one way only, like city streets. The rationale is that if everybody's going up Trail A and down Trail B, they'll see each other less frequently.

Now, we think most hikers are willing to give up some of their freedoms if they are persuaded that restrictions are necessary to preserve the experience of solitude. But our point here is that solitude assuredly *is* available; therefore, restrictions on freedom are *not* justified on these grounds. Moreover, the sense of freedom is equally essential to a rewarding wilderness experience.

To be sure, if you *like* crowds in your "wilderness experience," you can find them. If you've been having any difficulty, we present herewith a list of ten places in New England where you can "get away from it all" in a thoroughly sociable way—the backwoods equivalent of "tourist traps":

(1) Mount Washington	*(6)* Vermont's Long Trail
(2) Mount Chocorua	*(7)* Mount Mansfield
(3) Allagash River	*(8)* Mount Monadnock
(4) Appalachian Trail	*(9)* The Franconia Ridge
(5) Mount Katahdin	*(10)* Tuckerman's Ravine

There now: Are all of the crowd-lovers headed for those ten pleasure-spots? Now then, for the rest of you, here are four cases that illustrate why we say solitude is still available.

Case One: On July 4, 1976, the most crowded holiday of the summer season and the Bicentennial year to boot, we went to the most popular mountain area in the northeast, maybe the whole country: New Hampshire's Presidential Range. We were camped just below treeline. We got up on July 4 and strolled up the popular Randolph Path to the summit of Mount Jefferson, third highest in the Presidentials; this climb took an hour and a half, during which we saw not one other climber. We sat on the summit for a half-hour, with nobody else anywhere in sight; then we meandered slowly down the long ridge known as Jefferson's Knee, studying alpine flowers, many of which were in bloom. We descended the spectacular Six Husbands Trail, which some people rate as the finest hiking trail in the northeast, into the Great Gulf Wilderness. There, after *four hours* of hiking we came across the first other people we had seen that day.

Mountain solitude? You bet! Plenty of it, right there on the Presidentials on a splendid July 4. How come? Simple! We got up at 5:00 A.M. and were on the trail at 5:30. This may well be the most beautiful time of day in the mountains, but apparently very few people care to get up that early. Sunrises can be even prettier than sunsets—and lonelier. You can count on solitude during those magic hours on any mountain, any time of year. Later on that same July 4, we counted 117 other hikers on a 3-mile stretch of trail. But from 5:30 to 9:30 A.M., we didn't see a soul.

Oh well, you say, but nobody wants to go to the trouble of getting up *that* early. Our response is that it's a matter of values. If you *really* want solitude, you don't mind getting up early. Nobody *has* to, but don't tell us that solitude isn't available just because most people like to sleep late.

Case Two: Three of us left the famous Lakes of the Clouds area on Mount Washington one day at the decadent hour of 9:30 A.M. At these Lakes, at 5000 feet, the Appalachian Mountain Club maintains a hut that's normally packed with guests, but on this day there were no guests and no hut crew within miles; just us three. We climbed Mount Washington and sat on the summit in bright sun, eating lunch, and seeing not one other person. We then traversed over Mount Clay to Mount Jefferson, without seeing a solitary soul. On our return to the Lakes, we passed two other people, the only people we saw during that entire day.

Mountain solitude? You bet! Right there on Mount Washington, all day, in spectacularly fine weather. How come? Simple! The date was March 14. Quite properly, very few people venture above treeline in the dead of winter. The weather can be atrocious. The combination of intense cold, high winds, and low visibility can kill—in a matter of minutes—if you're not fully equipped with winter climbing gear, experienced at dealing with such conditions, and sensible enough to hole up when the weather turns bad. On the day before and the day after our beautiful day on Washington and Jefferson, above-treeline travel was unthinkable. We just burrowed into our down sleeping bags and sat it out until the good day came. All three of us had extensive experience in being browbeaten by White Mountain weather at its worst. This was no place for a novice at winter climbing.

But, apart from the specialized world of winter climbing, we don't all have to climb Mount Washington in mid-summer or on Labor Day weekend. The fall is a superb season for hiking. And the fact remains that anyone who *really* values mountain solitude can find it in abundance if he is willing to learn what it takes to travel in winter among the high peaks.

Case Three: On three successive days in mid-July we climbed three of the loveliest mountains we've come across in New England, passing but one other party low down on one of the three and not seeing anyone else otherwise. We hiked the standard trails on these mountains and didn't get off to any early-morning starts.

Mountain solitude? You bet! We had the summits and trails all to ourselves. How come? Simple! These three mountains were off in obscure corners of Maine where the hiking crowd doesn't realize yet that there are some great places to go.

We're not mentioning the names of these three peaks, because we don't want to set them up as targets for everyone who reads this book, but there are plenty of such places—marvellous hiking trails which no one much uses.

You can find your own secret places. Just get a map or two and start exploring. But tell it not in Gath, publish it not in the streets of Askalon.

Case Four: On a popular summer weekend, we descended from a camp high in the Presidentials, leaving our camp at about 9:30 A.M. and reaching the road some time after noon. This was not early in the morning, but in broad daylight. It was not the dead of winter, but a popular summer weekend.

Mountain solitude? You bet! Didn't pass a single hiker during the entire trip out. How come? Simple! We descended a little-known and little-used trail, not one of the standard trade routes that everybody seems to congregate on. This trail is right in the popular Presidential Range, is on every map of the region, and there are plainly visible signs at junctions with other trails and at the road head. But it just happens to be one that very few people choose to travel. As a result, it's a narrow, twisting trail over lovely moss-covered boulders and logs through lush growth of ferns and dark, quiet stands of spruce. By contrast, most of the popular trails have been beaten into muddy, eroded yards-wide tracks.

Nothing prevents anyone from using this trail (whose name we're not mentioning, you notice). It's just that most of the time, on the popular mountains, 90 percent of the foot traffic goes up and down two or three well-known trails. Most people apparently *want* to travel the familiar routes where they'll meet everyone else. The hills are full of out-of-the-way trails where you can find beauty, quiet, and solitude any time.

This leads us to an observation that we wish backwoods managers would note carefully: Most "wilderness" recreationists apparently don't *really* want to be alone. Sure, they want to get away from the city and they seek some reasonable degree of solitude, if solitude can be said to have degrees. But they don't *really* want to be completely alone out there, as evidenced by the fact that so few people avail themselves of the ample opportunities for 100 percent solitude to be found in the early hours, or on little-used trails, in out-of-the-way mountain ranges, in bad weather (if you learn to like all-day rains, that's a great time to enjoy popular mountains by yourself), or in seasons of the year that others shun.

Of course, if you just abandon trails and take up the arcane art of bushwhacking with map and compass, you can get away from people even in the most popular ranges. You may tear your trousers in the puckerbrush, your pace may slow to a quite-literal crawl, and you may even get thoroughly lost from time to time, but it all depends on what you're looking for in the mountains. On one splendid July 4, three of us climbed New Hampshire's Franconia Ridge. A steady stream of crowds walked the trails that day, but we chose to leave the trail, follow up a close-grown stream bed, clamber up long slabs of steep open rock, pass briefly over the crest of the ridge (momentarily amidst the crowds there), then plunge down a long dirt-and-scree slide on the other side, and out through trailless woods. Except on the ridgeline trail and at the very beginning and end of the trip, also on trail, we passed no one—*on July 4!*

How many times do you see popular tenting areas overflowing with people, all camping within a couple of acres, when vast stretches of woods on either side go unoccupied? People must prefer the social experience of talking with other campers, comparing tents, and perhaps engaging in a bit of one-upmanship about their equipment or their experience.

In one of the east's most popular rock-climbing areas, there are miles of rock-climbing cliffs; yet virtually every climber can be found at one of two relatively short sections of cliff, where the routes are familiar and well documented in the local guidebook. Lots of climbers *talk* about going to climb on the many other available cliffs, but almost no one ever does.

One summer at a roadside campground near Moosehead Lake in Maine, we found about a dozen campsites in a large open field, plus three secluded spots off in a little woods by themselves. When we arrived, we found all but one or two of the field sites occupied, cheek-by-jowl—but none of the three secluded spots (until we took one).

If this is true—that people like a little company with their "wilderness"—then the implications for backcountry management are interesting. Surely there is far less need to infringe on everyone's freedom in the name of preserving an experience of solitude.

For example, we'd take a dim view of declaring certain trails one-way-only so that hikers don't encounter as many other hikers, when it's perfectly possible to walk those trails for hours without seeing anyone else—from 5 to 8 A.M., for example; or to hike on other trails that the multitudes voluntarily seem to avoid.

We chafe at the idea of requiring permits to enter wild areas, to the extent that preserving a "wilderness experience" is given as one of the reasons for requiring such permits. In the first place, we question whether campers really want to be alone when they all flock to the same mountains, via the same trails, stopping at the same campsites. In the second place, anyone who *does* value the experience of solitude can get it, as we do, by the methods we've been indicating. But permit systems arbitrarily clamp down on where and when you can travel. When all the permits have been handed out, you can't go into the area.

What an irony: Under a permit system, you can be prevented from getting mountain solitude in certain areas by the very rules designed to promote that solitude! As Phil Levin wrote in *Appalachia* magazine: "It would be ironic if we saved wilderness from the exploiters only to lose it to the managers and the masses. It could happen."

We don't mean to imply that overcrowding is not a problem in the northeast woods. It certainly is, and results in terrific problems of trail erosion and soil compaction at popular camping areas. Whether permit systems are justified to reduce the impact of sheer numbers is another question; we're simply saying that permits and other restrictions on freedom are *not* justified in the name of solitude.

Solitude is of the essence of wilderness. If we lose the opportunity to be alone in remote places we can never get it back. We're for maintaining opportunities for solitude at almost any cost—but it's not yet time to destroy the freedom of the wilds on these grounds.

16

In Defense of Difficulty

No result is easy which is worth having.

O. W. Holmes

A FEW YEARS ago, an Italian party used helicopters to help them climb Mount Everest. The mountaineering world was aghast. What was the object? Why not just build a gondola to the top? Of course the flying machines couldn't land climbers on the summit of the world's highest mountain, but the helicopters did eliminate some of the risk and challenge. And risk and challenge is why climbers go to the mountains.

Challenge, at least—and for some, risk—is at the heart of American backpacking and hiking, from New England to the Sierra.

Why is the backpacker spending the night out there in the woods instead of at a modern motel? Why do we labor under 40 or 50 pounds over mile after mile of rough trail or bushwhack? Set up a flimsy tent or hammock in the pouring rain? Slap at mosquitoes and no-see-um's all day and night? Sleep in a soggy sleeping bag instead of between clean sheets? Try to cook a meal on uneven, muddy terrain, over either a tiny portable one-burner stove or a wood fire that alternates between being a smoke-belching inferno and almost out?

A verdict of insanity is tempting, but since many backwoodsmen show few other symptoms of mental distress during their regular work-a-day lives, one must conclude that they rationally choose to inflict these miseries on themselves. Why?

One could answer: Because the rewards of being in the woods outweigh all its inconveniences. We're more inclined to say, however, that the hardships are part of the *reason* why people go to the backcountry. The backwoods camper is *seeking out* difficulty. He is voluntarily thrusting himself into situations of challenge. He is, in his pedestrian way, seeking what Antoine de Saint-Exupèry, the great French aviator and author, conceived of as "that new vision of the world won through hardship."

Thomas Hobbes described "the privilege of absurdity" as that "to which no living creature is subject but man only." Backpackers sometimes seem to go further than necessary to prove Mr. Hobbes' point.

So why are some park and wild lands managers trying to make the backpacker's life too easy? We say, keep life difficult in the backcountry—that's why people go there.

Let's consider a couple of examples:

Crossing swollen mountain streams can provide some of the more hair-raising interludes along the trail. We recall with relish many a precarious crossing— teetering on narrow tree trunks over raging torrents of swift water, or hopping from boulder to moss-slippery boulder, occasionally dropping a boot (or more) into the icy waters. Great memories of exciting moments. Sometimes terrifying. Sometimes hilarious. Always memorable.

But there are sober, serious bridge builders at work in the backcountry who'd like to exorcise such moments from the backpacker's experience. These over- eager engineers will slap a huge log bridge, complete with cement foundations on both sides, over any flowing water too wide to jump. Instead of experiencing an interesting challenge, the hiker just puts his head down and plods over a tailored bridge-way. The mentality that regards such offenses as trail "improvements" can only be achieved by cross-breeding a beaver with a desk-bound colonel from the Army Corps of Engineers.

We should take lessons from our western hiking brethren. Out west difficult river crossings are accepted as part of the game. In Alaska they can be really wild. Sometimes you even have to improvise a raft.

Yet land managers all over the northeast seem bent on eliminating the dif- ficult stream crossing from our backcountry experience. Recent bridges over the Dry River near Mount Washington, on the Cascade Brook Trail in New Hampshire's Franconia Notch, or over a minuscule stream draining Katahdin near the Abol Campground in Baxter State Park are all illustrations of the bridge-builder mentality run riot, to the detriment of the hiker's experience.

This kind of thinking would have offered Michelangelo a can of spray paint to do the Sistine Chapel. Surely it would have made the job easier and safer. Wasn't that the point—just to get the ceiling painted?

Another challenge of the backcountry is the steep little rock "step" on a moun- tainside. When you have to scramble a bit, crawl up with hands as well as feet, maybe stop a moment to figure out how to negotiate a near-vertical 15 feet— that's the sort of challenge that makes a steep trail memorable.

Ah, but let us help you, sir (or madam), says the overeager trail crew. Out come the chain saws, axes, even jackhammers. On the steep South Ridge of Mount Willey, in New Hampshire's Crawford Notch, where once we enjoyed scrambling up challenging little rock moves, we now confront massive wooden ladders with hand railings. Worse still, a few miles away on the Fishin' Jimmy Trail (one of the most moderate of the many trails in Franconia Notch), some oversolicitous trail-"improvers" actually blasted steps in the rock to make it easier, in places setting square wooden steps into the rock itself. What a desecra- tion! If we want to climb stairs, we'll go to the Empire State Building. Who goes to Franconia Notch to climb stairs?

The AMC's Backcountry Management Task Force put it well:

> Risk is implicit in all backcountry recreation. It is naturally present and is a desirable feature of the backcountry. While the manager should work to educate users about the risks involved in backcountry use, it is not his responsibility to eliminate those risks.

Again, on the steep Wildcat Ridge Trail in the Carter Range across from Mount Washington, overzealous trail crews have taken a big L-shaped slice out of a boulder that we recollect had made for exciting scrambling. We asked the managers responsible for this degradation, how many people had died there. "None," was the response. "Was there ever an accident here?" we asked. They looked down in silence. We observed that our impression was that where a bit of steep scrambling was involved, people tended to be very careful. Not only that, but those little challenging rock steps are the very things they remember most vividly about their trip in the mountains. They're what lend zest and adventure to their experience. You're doing them no favor by making it easy. Some managers misread the hikers' temper, we believe. They think we want it all Easter and no Ash Wednesday.

In truth, we hikers are not guiltless in this regard. We recently went on an adventurous bushwhacking trip into a remote valley, where there are no trails or any evidence of man, rarely visited by anyone. It's in New England (we'd rather not say just where, to protect its pristine character), but we might as well have been in the remotest forest of Siberia—we thought. As we plunged through the untouched woods, feeling that sense of awe and inspiration which only true wilderness brings, we came upon bits of shiny red tape tied to trees at 100-foot intervals! What a sudden end to our idyllic sense of wilderness! Vandalism in our loveliest stretches of natural wild country!

Those bits of shiny red tape were probably strung up in that remote watershed by hikers planning a winter trip. It's often considerably harder to find your way in winter, so climbers who plan an ambitious outing in January will often scout it out in September. A temptation is to mark the route by hanging tape on trees every 100 feet or so.

That's fine for the *convenience of the hiker*, at least those who are involved in that trip. But we wonder whether those individuals ever considered how their action might destroy the spirit of wildness for the next party.

In our view this marking of trails is a lamentable procedure for several reasons—it eliminates the challenge of staying on trail, which is one of the great adventures of winter climbing; it constitutes an inescapable reminder that others have been or will be there, thus destroying the illusion of solitude; and it is, to put it bluntly, a form of litter.

Incidentally, in the places we have seen these tapes, the safety argument is absolutely irrelevant. These are trails or routes where anyone who got lost could simply follow his own snowshoe tracks back; none of them are sufficiently exposed to blow over so fast that you couldn't follow them back. It's not at all like wandering above treeline, where safety is a factor.

We believe in a maximum of freedom in the mountains, but only up to the point that one person's actions do not adversely affect another person's experience. Those who rag trails are destroying the most important attribute of adventure and the feeling of remoteness which others seek. Furthermore, in our opinion they're doing themselves no real service by eliminating the challenge.

Henry Aaron could have hit more homers had he stayed in the Little League all his life; his achievement is great only because he did it against the finest pitchers of his generation. The response to challenge is what made it all worthwhile. So too in the backcountry.

The late Hubert Humphrey once made a comment about life that applies with special force to this subject: "If anything's easy, it's not likely to be worthwhile."

Warren Doyle, an athletic young enthusiast who has set a speed record for hiking the 262-mile Long Trail in Vermont (nine days), may scarcely be a typical backpacker, but it may be instructive to note his comment on why he undertook his feat. Doyle was quoted as alienated by society's "striving for comfort, safety, plushness and such." He told *Rutland Herald* reporter Steve Baumann: "I've known failure and success in my hikes. When I succeeded, I knew it wasn't by luck. When I failed, I couldn't blame someone else."*

This is a proposition on which all lovers of the outdoor world ought to be able to agree. Hikers, hunters, birdwatchers, technical rock climbers, anglers, skiers, canoeists—all these and many more turn to the outdoors to find challenge, not ease . . . uncertainty, not security . . . "preferring hard liberty before the easy yoke of servile pomp."

Since different uses of the backcountry sometimes seem to conflict, we like to point out areas like this where we're all agreed.

Hunters? No hunter worth the name seeks an easy prey, with guaranteed success on the first day. Wildlife writer Frank Woolner has stated: "We would quit if the game were easy. . . . We respect our quarry, and we know that we will be humiliated in the field."

Respect—humility—that's what we're trying to talk about. We've climbed a lot of mountains, but we still have enormous respect for what these little New England hills can throw at you; yes, and plenty of humility about our own ability to get in trouble if we're not careful how we climb. If you can do it blindfolded, why bother? When they start providing graded paths and railings, we'll go somewhere else.

Birdwatchers? One of the most difficult things to do outdoors is to identify what species of warbler is flitting around in a grove of evergreens 50 yards away. There is no short-cut to finding out either; you have to invest hundreds of hours in the field, patiently stalking, listening, peering through binoculars at those perpetual-motion creatures no bigger than a small mouse but far more elusive. Like hunters, anglers, and mountain climbers, the avid birder is up before dawn to get out to where he needs to be when the winged mysteries start playing their games of hide-and-seek. But oh, the rewards! If you've ever been standing next

*Quoted from *The Long Trail News,* GMC, November, 1978.

to someone who finally spotted their first blackburnian warbler on their own, you'll know a happy person.

Nor do the birdwatchers want it made easy. It's no accident that when you're recording birds on your "life list," you can't count caged-up birds from a zoo or private aviary. You've got to earn each one the hard way.

Anglers? From what we hear, the followers of Walton are happiest when the pickings are leanest. Bringing in some wily trout or bass that's eluded you all summer in some dark private pool seems to be the angler's prized moment. If the fish hooked onto the first cast, he'd earn less respect—and yield far less satisfaction.

Canoeists? If the object was simply to get from here to there by boat, you wouldn't hear people talk about white water. Once again, the idea is to challenge your skills, intelligence, coolness under pressure. Challenge is what it's all about.

Back before World War II, an earlier Waterman (Guy's father) used to take six weeks each summer to canoe the Allagash. It took a couple of days then to drive from our house in Connecticut to Maine's Moosehead Lake, and once back in the lake region there was literally no way to get back to civilization fast or even to communicate with it. When those canoes shoved off into that network of backwoods lakes above the Allagash headwaters, they were committing the half-dozen occupants to their own resources for six weeks, during which they would not see more than one or two other parties. The modern Allagash runner rips down the river in a week or ten days, elbowing other parties for the better camp-sites, greeting others who land on the lakes in seaplanes, never far away from communication with the outside world in the event of emergency. Could anyone suppose that the satisfaction derived from those two divergent experiences is equal?

We have a rare and precious "resource" in the backcountry and it isn't defined by just the physical resources of trees, wildlife, streams, or even mountains. What we have to defend is the opportunity for people to get on one-to-one terms with the natural world, to experience the full challenge of the backcountry—not some phony or illusory sense fostered by well-groomed trails, bridges over every stream, and instant rescue available if you stub your toe.

Katahdin is not just Central Park 400 miles removed.

Not all the blame lies on the manager's doorstep. We hikers and backpackers tend to foster too much tameness within ourselves. Managers may simply be reading their clientele's wishes too well. Writer–backpacker Harvey Manning deplores in *Backpacker* magazine the lack of adventure in the contemporary hiking public, who "shun a vacation on Mount Obscurity in favor of Big Deal Spire, throng Many People Camp and avoid the lonesome heart of the Godforgotten Wilderness."

The decline of adventure in the outdoors reminds us of so many forces in modern life that seek to eliminate all discomforts and difficulties. Ad writers sell electrical appliances as servants that "eliminate household drudgery." No one is supposed to wash dishes or clothes personally any more; just press a button and go watch television. We're not even supposed to brush our teeth by hand any more. Our reading habits have been steered gently away from the elegant but demanding prose style of Edward Gibbon or Sir Walter Scott to the easily digested spoon-fed *Reader's Digest* condensations.

But what remains in a life from which difficulty and work are omitted? "Too much rest itself becomes a pain," says Homer in the *Odyssey*.

All too evident today are thousands of affluent but nervous people, seeking some sort of synthetic physical challenge. In every outdoor activity that once demanded well-earned skills and genuine honest-to-God risk, you can now buy a guided weekend of imitation thrills on a guaranteed no-risk basis. Go rock-climbing, scuba-diving, sky-diving, with some certified "expert," making sure that you only *appear* to be really risking danger. Your professional guide will guarantee to get you safely back to your desk on Monday morning.

In one recent year on Mount McKinley, 155 climbers put together their own parties to attempt to reach the summit. Another 98 climbers signed up with professional guides to be led up. Somehow we suspect that the experience of the former was more complete and more satisfying.

Not so long ago there were corners of the globe which only the most courageous and adventurous explorers had ever seen—the arctic and antarctic snows, the remote and hidden passes and peaks of the high Himalayas, the savage wasteland of the Patagonian ice cap, to name just a few. Within the memory of living man there were literal blank spots on the map, where no one had ever been. What a treat to the imagination—what a challenge to the most resourceful of adventurers!

Today Mountain Travel and a dozen other paid professional organizations will take you to any of these places, for a fee. No experience needed. The porters will carry your tent, sahib, and cook all meals. All you do is bring lots of color film and a pair of dark glasses—and enough other fancy gear to give everyone the illusion that you're really roughing it.

Philip Levin, writing in *Appalachia* magazine, warned about this development:

> . . . we have developed an impatience with constraints, including the constraint of unattainability. We have developed the technology to break the latter constraint, without once pausing to consider the invaluable role that the unattainable and its pursuit by visionary individuals have played in the civilization of the west.

Maybe that's a bit heavy, but the underlying thought is one we'll buy.

A few winters ago, the Appalachian Mountain Club opened two of their eight high-country huts in the wintertime, stationing a caretaker at each one. At that point, a number of winter backpackers and climbers began to fear that the AMC would ultimately open all of its high huts, thereby making it relatively easy and safe to travel in winter over high country that now affords tremendous challenge and risk to the adventurous.

Much to its credit, the AMC decided not to open up the remote winter hills in this way. The club has confined its winter facilities to the two relatively accessible huts. We applaud that decision.

In this push-button age, humanity needs recourse to difficulty. We need to encounter nature in ways that fully impress on us its enormous power, and set our own efforts in perspective—feeble compared with nature's, but heroic compared with what we were tempted to shrink into.

While there is still difficulty, there is still opportunity to test what a person's made of. The hunter and fisherman know this. The birdwatcher knows it. All lovers of the outdoors tend to respond to the zest of challenge.

Conservationist Bradley Snyder has written:

> It is a common observation of life that an experience that requires little yields little. . . . The best things, fortunately, are quite demanding. . . . The real benefit of the "wilderness experience," for example, lies not in *being* in the wilderness but in taking the *initiative* in your life and getting there on your own. People do not need fresh air and sunshine half so much as they need a sense of being in command of their own minds and bodies, of planning something difficult and then doing it.

These days people want high adventure with low risk and lower personal hardship. No such thing! Joseph Wood Krutch put it most succinctly: "No cross, no crown."

We side with the sentiments expressed so well by mountain climber Gene Prater in his book, *Snowshoeing*. We commend these thoughts to the attention of all who care for maintaining the spirit of wildness in the woods and hills from New England to the Sierra and beyond:

> There is a feeling of personal insignificance standing on a high point with ridge after ridge extending to the horizon. . . . Man's efforts at creativity simply cannot compare with the natural scene. You may feel a deeper appreciation for the power of natural forces, not just the violence of storm and avalanche, but also the quiet Being who must have clad a thousand hills in forest, and added snow each winter to nourish the rivers and give the land a rest.
>
> We are strangers in an alien land; man doesn't belong in the winter wilderness. The mountain landscape speaks visually through its beauty and the silence of calm days of eternity, in contrast to people who are short-lived visitors. The roar of the storm does not dim the grandeur, but emphasizes that man must tread gently and with the utmost care. A gust of wind-blown snow and man and his snowshoe trail are gone. . . .

Index

Other STONE WALL PRESS Books
for Hikers:

MOVIN' OUT: Equipment & Technique for Hikers by Harry Roberts. 160 pages, 6" X 9", index, paperback $4.95.

Harry Roberts, ed. of *Wilderness Camping,* has written what the *International Backpackers Assn.* calls "an excellent, down-to-earth book on backpacking information." This updated edition includes solid advice on boots, clothing, packs, and sleeping bags, as well as techniques for staying warm, eating well, and learning to be at home in a natural environment. Illustrated.

MOVIN' ON: Equipment & Techniques for Winter Hikers. 135 pages, 6" X 9", illustrated, paperback $4.95.

Harry Roberts' companion volume ". . . sets down a lot of good, common-sense advice and he does it in an engaging, unpresumptuous style." Furthermore, "Roberts' wilderness techniques work. They work well." (*Mountain Gazette.*) "This is a superb book, even if you are just thinking about maybe going winter camping." (*Backpacker.*)

INTRODUCING YOUR KIDS TO THE OUTDOORS by Joan Dorsey. 128 pages, 6" X 9", photographs, paperback $4.95.

Beginning with a carefully planned day hike, and proceeding to extended trips, canoeing, bicycling, and ski touring, Dorsey presents straight-forward advice about outdoor trips with the kids along. "Attitude is as important to the author as equipment, and she talks about her own rewarding wilderness experiences and all the reasons why children should get outdoors." (*Adventure Travel Newsletter.*)

ENJOYING THE ACTIVE LIFE AFTER FIFTY by Ralph Hopp. 192 pages, 6 1/8" X 9 1/4", photographs, paperback $5.95.

Those who are resigning themselves to an indoor life can find new worlds of fun and fitness with 20 activities detailed here. Photographs provide inspiration as well as techniques that make these pastimes safer, more enjoyable, and easier.

WILD PRESERVES, Illustrated Recipes for over 100 Natural Jams & Jellies by Joe Freitus. 192 pages, illustrated, paperback $4.95.

The most comprehensive book yet published on preserving wild fruit. 48 clear illustrations are provided for easy identification, followed by over 100 recipes for jams, jellies, pickles, preserves, conserves, butter, and even wine. Well-known wild fruit such as blueberries and blackberries are covered, and the adventurous epicurean will delight in such delicacies as Irish Moss Jelly, Carrion Flower Spice Jelly, and False Solomon's Seal Jam.

160 EDIBLE PLANTS, Commonly Found in the United States and Canada by Joe Freitus. 96 pages, 160 line drawings, paperback $3.50.

This field guide carefully identifies the 160 most commonly found edible wild plants throughout the U.S.A. and Canada. Each plant is listed in alphabetical order for easy reference and is accompanied by a line drawing. Besides a thorough description of each plant, the author further identifies each plant as to habitat, range, edible properties, and preparation. This is an excellent survival booklet as well as a handy reference to supplemental foods.

SELECTED REGIONAL TITLES

THE NORTHEASTERN OUTDOORS: A Field & Travel Guide by Steve Berman. 272 pages, over 200 photos, maps, and illustrations, Kivarbound $7.95.

A very practical yet exciting introduction to our regional outdoors. The first section contains a wealth of fascinating factual information about our natural world complete with vivid photographs and illustrations. The second section is a practical travel guide for more than 100 nature trips throughout the Northeast—complete with maps, concise directions, entertaining narrative and occasional photographs.

EXPLORING NEW ENGLAND SHORES, A Beachcomber's Handbook by John Waters. 208 pages, fully illustrated, clothbound $7.95.

In a concise, lucid fashion, John Waters carefully explores every aspect of the New England shore—how the coastline was formed and changes, the various types of beaches, their inhabitants, and rewards to be found by the beachcomber.

*   *   *

Ask for these books at your bookstore or outfitter. They may be ordered through our distributor—

The Stephen Greene Press
Box 1000, Brattleboro, Vermont 05301